HOW SPACES BECOME PLACES

T0373147

How Spaces Become Places

Place Makers Tell Their Stories

Edited by John F. Forester

With a foreword by Randolph Hester

NEW VILLAGE PRESS • NEW YORK

Published in the United States by New Village Press
bookorders@newvillagepress.net
www.newvillagepress.org
New Village Press is a public-benefit, nonprofit publisher
Distributed by NYU Press

Publication Date: October 2021
First Edition

Library of Congress Cataloging-in-Publication Data
Names: Forester, John, 1948– editor.
Title: How spaces become places : place makers tell their stories / edited by John F. Forester.
Description: First edition. | New York : New Village Press, 2021. | Includes bibliographical references and index. | Summary: "A diverse set of place makers describe how they transformed contested or empty "spaces" into vibrant and functional "places." Spanning four countries and ten U.S. locales, these projects range from building affordable housing, to community building in the aftermath of racial violence, to the integration of the arts in community development. By recounting how they built trust, diagnosed local problems, and convened stakeholders to invent solutions, place makers offer pragmatic, instructive strategies to employ in other communities"—Provided by publisher.
Identifiers: LCCN 2021006279 | ISBN 9781613321423 (paperback) | ISBN 9781613321430 (hardcover) | ISBN 9781613321447 (ebook) | ISBN 9781613321454
Subjects: LCSH: City planning. | Urban policy. | Urban renewal. | Place attachment
Classification: LCC HT166 .H678 2021 | DDC 307.1/216—dc23
LC record available at https://lccn.loc.gov/2021006279

For my students,
searching for possibilities,
sources of surprise and insight

CONTENTS

As if I needed to be reminded of the singular importance of John Forester's How Spaces Become Places: Place Makers Tell Their Stories,
the events of January 6, 2021, delivered a final notice. As we watched the
mob attack the US Capitol, I searched for ways to contextualize the mad-
ness for my eleven-year-old grandson, whose schoolwork had been
undermined by the breaking news. The context and the lesson were
stark: democracy is fragile and vulnerable, and freedom without individual responsibility is short-lived. Unless each of us takes responsibility
for the democracy to which we aspire, unless we practice it every day
and contribute to its well-being with tithes and personal offerings, its
demise is all but assured. But democracy also requires places where it
can thrive, where grievances can be aired and addressed respectfully,
where common purposes can be discovered, and where justice can be
given an opportunity to bend itself toward the arc of the moral universe.

For nearly half a century, John Forester has aggressively listened to
people who take seriously their responsibility to enact participatory democracy in their daily lives and the work they do. He listens between the
lines, hearing what is said and what is not said, posing the essential question at the appropriate moment, helping people tell their own stories of
building place as a way of building democracy. He seeks to get the truth,
the whole truth, and nothing but the truth. He builds theory from the
bottom up, from the chronicles of everyday practices of planners, activists, actionists, and decision makers. Their stories and his interpretations
provide unique insights that improve collaborative planning, policy making, conflict resolution, and distribution of public resources.

In How Spaces Become Places, Forester focuses expressly on the details of how vibrant democratic places are shaped, with stories told by
designers and activists themselves and conclusions carefully considered
by Forester himself. The result would make Alexis de Tocqueville (Democracy in America), Richard Scarry (What Do People Do All Day?),

and Lawrence Halprin (Taking Part: A Workshop Approach to Collective Creativity) each nod with appreciation. Here there is comparative meta-analysis at the level of participatory democracy that only Forester can provide, nitty-gritty details of everyday city making that only the makers themselves can describe, and insights into the creative process of place making that only such a collaborative undertaking can reveal. Then bridges can sing, spiders can anchor us in their webs, toy tractors can cultivate the arts, and stained glass can celebrate many religions.

Here are themes familiar to democratic designers: the eternal importance of working face to face, listening to people and to the place itself, learning from and teaching others, sharing expertise, rightly understanding self-interest, spatializing values, sketching what people say, and prioritizing both process and product. The stories that Forester shares explain how creativity arises from conflicts, how difference, imagination, and ownership transform inert space into meaningful places that enrich our lives.

Ultimately, great places are about meaning evoked through the senses. And these stories detail how planners and community members develop civic vocabularies of physical qualities about space that enable meaningful settings. Each story establishes a shared spatial literacy as a foundation for making places. This is not design-speak but rather thoughtful discussions about the materiality of place. Should we bulk up the mass? How tall is too tall? How short is too short, how wide too wide, how brown too brown? What about Mission-style affordable housing for progressive nostalgia? How many fires are necessary along the river to command the space? Can a place accommodate twenty-thousand people as elegantly as 150? Does a two-meter square make a garden? Does a sound check for a concert work the same in community planning? Can warring religions rally around a single symbol of light? The practitioners whose stories fill these pages confront these questions and more. Their answers are expressed in their crafting of meaningful places, built of sense, memory, and emotion to express the best of community values.

Here, also, are painfully honest admissions, seldom told by designers, of spatialized racial hatred, enemies within communities, and cultural stigmas that must be purged, truthful messages about the fine lines that democratic designers must draw for themselves. We know that showing disrespect, often expressed by professionals who intimidate residents with their expertise, is fatal in community planning. But these stories indicate that acquiescence without questioning community members' opinions is just as disrespectful as an expert's arrogance. A fine line indeed. What do you do if residents want low riders parked in single-family houses but you value density and car-free places? Do you pursue your activist preference or the community's need? How far do you go into unspoken and forbidden territories that are crippling community fulfilment? Such questions confront all of us who shape cities and in turn shape democracy. Forester and the contributors to this striking book are masters at answering our questions by modelling thoughtful and thought-provoking avenues we ourselves can pursue.

Yes, democracy is fragile. Mob violence disheartens us. Prejudice, injustice, and hatred challenge our optimism. But these stories shine brightly, illuminating what freedom and responsibility can produce. Forester shows us ways through seemingly irreconcilable differences to a more fulfilling democracy where those who were voiceless now speak and are heard, where wrongs are righted, and where community places enrich our lives.

—Randolph Hester

Professor Emeritus of Landscape Architecture and Environmental Planning, College of Environmental Design, University of California, Berkeley.

Hurdle Mills, January, 2021

EDITOR'S PREFACE

For years, I have had a simple agenda: to learn from the practices of planners, mediators, and place makers. My students and I had a strategy: we would explore central problems by gathering grounded and detailed practice stories, which we would get from people who had dealt for years with the issues we wanted to learn about, such as housing affordability, immigration, climate change, conflict resolution, and coalition building.

We believed that experienced, deeply engaged people could do something more than work on these important issues: they could describe and reconstruct their efforts as practical, even instructive, stories. Whatever subject our curiosity in urban studies might focus on, we tried to find people who had been up to their eyeballs in that field for years so that we might learn from them. But this involved more than wishful thinking. It demanded a particular strategy of interviewing to ask about place makers' lines of action instead of asking about their theories. The results have led my students to produce and analyze many hundreds of profiles of practitioners.

My research, too, has led to such results—striking profiles of Italian, Dutch, and Israeli planners and design professionals and analyses of participatory, deliberative mediation practices and Katrina responses among them (De Leo and Forester 2018; Forester, Fischler, and Shmueli 2001; Laws and Forester 2015). Although I am neither an architect nor a geographer, I have studied the engaged practices of planners and designers, organizers and mediators, for several decades. The interviews in this book have grown from years of curiosity about the engaged complexity—the day-to-day work—of place makers on the ground.

But there was a problem. Because of competing book projects, this book marked an unintended personal record: the longest time to publication from the initial glimmer of the idea. My earlier books all had their delays. Editors fell ill or changed jobs, or they had lost coworkers and manuscripts were piling up on their desks (so they explained)—mine, of course, near the bottom. Editors promised letters about next steps while months went by with little progress toward publication. I tried, with mixed success, not to take these delays personally.

But now, having broken my previous record of ten years or so, I have no editors to blame. After spending a sabbatical year interviewing street-level democrats in Amsterdam in 2008–09, I returned to Cornell with an embarrassment of unpublished riches. I vividly recall saying, in some frustration, to my partner, Anne Kilgore, an accomplished book designer, that after years of work, I seemed to be 80 percent of the way toward publication on four parallel projects, but I had nothing to show for any of it. Anne said, with one of those looks you don't forget, "Well, pick one, and send it to a publisher already!"

This book was one of those four, years before I knew that a next sabbatical in Rome six years later would lead to a fifth. So for whatever compelling reasons—obligations to co-authors and co-editors and more—this book has followed good company. Fifteen years of interviews with planners and mediators led first to *Dealing with Differences: Dramas of Mediating Public Disputes* (Oxford University Press, 2009) and then to what I have always called my best teaching materials, the practice stories in *Planning in the Face of Conflict: The Surprising Possibilities of Facilitative Leadership* (American Planning Association Press, 2013). My collaboration with Ken Reardon in *Rebuilding Community after Katrina: Transformative Education in the New Orleans Planning Initiative* (Temple University Press, 2015), a project centered on participants' accounts of Hurricane Katrina, became the publishing story from hell, arriving ten years after the storm. Work with sabbatical hosts led to *Conflict, Improvisation, Governance: Street Level Practices for Urban Democracy* (Routledge, 2016, with David Laws) and then to *Reimagining Planning: How Italian Urban Planners Are Changing Planning Practices* (INU Edizioni, 2018, with Daniela De Leo). Only then, with the image of Dutch and Italian planners in mind, was I able to add several stunning interviews to this collection to show how spaces become places through the imaginative, creative, and collaborative work of skillful planners and designers, neighborhood activists, and community leaders. This mea culpa is, of course, a clumsy apology to this book's contributors. Academic publishing can move glacially at times, and these related books were, in fact, also in the queue, but these delays, in the end, have helped make this a better book.

If our place-maker contributors are astonished to find their accounts finally in print after all this time and concerned about their relevance, they need not worry; their stories stand the test of time. They are engaged, revealing, moving, funny, eye opening, surprising, constructive, instructive. My students—critical graduate students in city and regional planning and sharp undergraduates in urban and regional studies—and I have learned from them with every reading. I am confident that many more readers and students in the fields of urban studies, planning and geography, landscape architecture, and in the design professions more generally will also find themselves enriched by these practice stories, in debt to these contributing practitioners.

If the practice stories in *Planning in the Face of Conflict* have been my best teaching materials, this book now provides serious competition: less narrowly focused on resolving public disputes, more focused on the broader but no less engaged work of transforming spaces into vibrant places. As my afterword, written in the summer of 2020, argues, these practitioners' accounts are now more important than ever in the midst of the COVID-19 pandemic and the abiding forms of racism and white supremacy so keenly highlighted by the Black Lives Matter movement.

The passing of time has also meant that I have been indebted to more colleagues and, especially, to more students than I would have ever imagined. For heroic efforts helping me organize this book very early on, thanks go first to Eric VanderMaas. Eric transformed a disparate set of student profiles, eventually to be complemented by several of my own, into a plausibly coherent book. Many thanks for transcription, bibliographic, and editorial assistance also go to Samuel Coons, Nicholas Cowan, Daniel Forester, Emily Hackerson, Andy Love, Hannah Plummer, Noah Schumer, Nancy Sprehn, Mathew Styer, Malia Teske, and Roana Tirado. They all had work to do, I am thankful to acknowledge, only because of the initiative and gifted interviewing and analysis of Cornellians Khairul Anwar, Ellie Bomstein, Christopher Donohoe, Agnes Ladjevardi, Stephen Miller, Kerry Quinn, Sarah Pressprich, Jeremy Siegfried, Joanna Winter, and Jessica Yoon; these were Cornell students who taught all those who came to know them. For comments, tips, and encouragement along the way, thanks also go not only to my partner, Anne Kilgore, but crucially to critical and helpful colleagues: Patsy Healey, Charles Hoch, Paula Horrigan, Richard Kiely, Lynne Manzo, George McKibbon, Thomas Oles, Scott Peters, Jennifer Rowe, Robert Shibley, and Leela Viswanathan. Lynne Elizabeth gave crucial advice for publication in the time of the pandemic and Black Lives Matter resurgence. All their help notwithstanding, I am responsible for the mistakes and gaps in this volume, as it must fail to do justice to such a broad and challenging topic.

Most importantly, I am also grateful for, and perpetually moved and inspired by, the contributions of these ever practical and imaginative place makers. In what follows, their practice leads theory; our strategy has been to show rather than to promise. In every chapter, our contributors provide details of their work, their struggles, their responses to challenges, their accomplishments with others. For their generosity with their interviewers, for their care to refine these accounts, and for their commitments to crafting transformative places in our communities, my thanks go to Laurence Baudelet-Stelmacher, James Brodick, John Davis, Barnaby Evans, Michael Hughes, Mark Lakeman, Michael Pyatok, Doug Rice, Wendy Sarkissian, Father Phil Sumner, Karen Umemoto, Malik Yakini, and Al Zelinka.

Introduction

Place Making, Not Plan Making—Learning from What Takes Place

They transform intersections. They rebuild community. They create urban gardens and provide affordable housing in diverse neighborhoods. These place makers have experiences and strategies, discoveries and wisdom that will surprise us. As their work "takes place," they transform ordinary, taken-for-granted spaces into places that matter, and in doing so, they reanimate the social and political geographies in which we live.

As they work with others on the ground, they can make places of wonder and conviviality, of respect, dignity, and belonging, places of social justice, community, and safety. In a world wrestling with the dangers of the COVID-19 pandemic and the white supremacy made so vivid by the Black Lives Matter movement, these place makers' practices are more important than ever. But how do they do what they do?

This book answers this question in three distinctive ways. First, we examine the strategies of place makers informed and shaped by diverse backgrounds and disciplinary trainings. We consider the richly varied contributions of organizers, artists, planners, mediators, and clergy, as well as those of urban designers and landscape architects (Hester 2010; Schneekloth and Shibley 1995; Steinitz 2012).

Second, these chapters focus on the engaged practices of making places, to complement and to extend in a more practical way our traditional analyses of spaces and places themselves (Gavin 2016; Gehl 2010; Healey 2010; Lefebvre 1991; Staeheli 2003). This distinction matters. The creative, critical, and pragmatic work of place making can no more be reduced to the analysis of place by itself than can the practices of cooking be reduced to the analysis of diet or cuisine, farming or agriculture. Yes, meat and vegetables matter, but to truly understand cooking, we must understand its skillful process. So while spaces and places matter, this book is about the careful work of actually *making* places.

Third, we enter this creative world in a welcoming and narratively based way—through the grounded and detailed, instructive, and even inspiring practice stories of accomplished place makers' work as told in their own words (Forester 1999; Peters, Alter, and Shaffer 2018). We learn from these practitioners how they cultivated not only trust but imagination, not only the relationships but the support and coalitions that enabled them practically and creatively, as the makers of places, to improvise their work.

In Rochester, New York, for example, when Doug Rice faced resistance from the city's traffic engineers, what did he do instead of giving up and going home? When Father Phil Sumner faced deeply divided ethnic enclaves in the English city of Oldham, near Manchester, how did he handle that? When Laurence Baudelet faced the bewilderment of professional landscape architects suggesting that community gardens in Paris were surely going to be disasters, what did she do to develop an innovative, novel program? Their responses and the responses of others—as ordinary as they are extraordinary—provide us not with how-to-do-it guides but rather with a sense of how we got it done, showing us through their engaged accounts details of obstacles and accomplishments and of their useful responses and lessons learned. These practice stories convey the voice and the concerns, the imagination and the strategies, and the emotions and insights of key actors who show us place making as it can evolve from early inspiration to legislative funding, from initial goals to building and implementation.[1]

We will read in these chapters of house painters who organized and developed local arts centers, lapsed architects who allied with neighbors to transform city intersections, and socially engaged young professionals who partnered to create multiracial community justice centers. These are all community members who have joined forces with other community members in caring about the places where they lived. Their work, though often ingenious, did not require that they be geniuses or heroes. We see the challenges they faced and the skills and strategies they used to overcome them. Their stories leave us not awed and starstruck—as if thinking, "We could never do that!"—but inspired and encouraged, open to creating our own new possibilities of place making. Reading the practice stories that follow, we are less likely to be stymied and much more likely to be curious, wondering, "What if *we* did something like that?" or "Why not?" or "What if we pulled some people together?"

These chapters, then, present cases of instructive practices, with insight and working theory emerging as place makers and activists, neighbors and community leaders reflect back on what they have done. These are grounded accounts of engaged place making. In plain language, they can speak to diverse readers, free of professional or academic jargon and double-talk.[2]

Ordinary cases with serious challenges, surprises, and consequences come first. In urban Oregon, intersections became meeting places for community building, not just spaces through which cars sped toward remote destinations. In Minnesota, highway engineers faced a challenge they had never before imagined: the new bridge "has to be beautiful, or you're never going to get through this gauntlet of twenty-eight stakeholders. They'll never let you build it!" In Providence, Rhode Island, fires on the river after sunset transformed a quiet promenade into a busy festival ground and an economic development boon. In Red Hook, Brooklyn, a new community justice center renewed confidence, ownership, and citizenship among underserved local residents struggling to resist gang and drug cultures. In Detroit, local food-justice advocates merged community organizing and empowerment with lessons about outsiders' good intentions that seemed well meaning yet blind to the history of local race relations and white supremacy that shaped everyday life (Schein 2006).[3]

In all these places, expertise is diversely held. Readers can appreciate a central irony of place-making expertise: design professionals, no matter how brilliant aesthetically, seem unable to make great places without the ordinary, everyday users of those spaces whose interactions there actually make those places great, not just in a designer's intention alone but in deeds, in ongoing, grounded, specific fact. Place makers without place users risk being aspiring conductors without orchestras, band leaders without bands.

Place makers, we shall see, work neither solo nor in silos. A river festival with fires on the water might be an interesting idea, but without families and couples attracted there by the installation, it is not a transformation of Providence. An ARTWalk without walkers, without pedestrians, in Rochester remains an empty sidewalk with signage, not an attraction channeling citizens to galleries and museums. Community gardens without community caretakers, without the public joys of community members preparing and tending the soil with eager witnesses on hand to see new shoots breaking the ground, remain landscape designers' good wishes.

Rethinking Place Making

If place makers cannot really work in silos, they must collaborate, deliberate, and make decisions with others. So the professional roles of planner, landscape architect, and architect are neither really nor ideally positions of autonomous, master designers. To have influence and be responsive to complex settings, they must be connected to, and even ultimately accountable to, place users (Bishop 2015; Hester 2010; Hou 2010). This much might seem obvious, but it represents both a political leveling and a small intellectual revolution in the world of place making.

In intellectual terms, this means that place is a temporal, living concept; a "place" is not a static, once-and-for-all container of hopes but a malleable and vulnerable site of ongoing uses, interactions, and inevitably moral performances, a space where morally significant actions matter, where actions take place. So in Portland, Oregon, not only do cars not speed through intersections, but neighbors reclaim intersections to mark their domains, to meet one another, to share resources and one another's company, to build community together as they reshape their streets. In Detroit and Paris, too, urban agriculture gardens grow not only vegetables for consumption but also citizenship and organizing skills for local community development.

As a result, the character and lived realities of places depend on designers and users, experts and community members alike. The work of place making, it turns out, includes the designers' drawing boards as well as the city council's chambers, the spaces of neighborhood meetings, the streets and parks of our towns and cities. Place making designers can anticipate working with diverse users and diverse materials; they can create form and cultivate use, shaping inert substance and creative, evolving processes. Place makers, we shall see, can respond to naysayers with information, expertise, support, and partnerships. In the editor's afterword that follows the contributors' stories, the political and social significance of these practices in a time of global pandemic, in a history scarred by white supremacy (Blight 2018), will become the central focus.

Transforming Spaces into Places

When we move across a space, we can move across time, too—this is where I met that crazy guy, heard John Coltrane on the radio for the first time, had that wonderful dinner, decided to move to New York. Doing things in space, we make locations into places of memory—we create a history of place—as we remember or recognize performances: this is where we broke up, this is where Kate was born, that's where my parents came from.[4] J. E. Wideman (1985) once observed that repetition dignified certain rituals; so too can our repeated actions, for better or worse, dignify spaces, as those spaces become places with special character— places of worship and community building as in Oldham, or places of entertainment and festivity as in Providence, or places of growth and development as in Brooklyn or Paris or Detroit (Hester 2010).[5]

Consider a few examples. When James Brodick worked to create a community justice center in Red Hook, Brooklyn, he had few rules to follow. He was not just organizing social services or putting on athletic events for youth in the summer. His context was daunting, if not intimidating. The community need—and the distrust he faced—had grown from earlier events in Red Hook, not least among which was a drug-related murder of a popular community leader. By addressing both that need and that distrust, Brodick worked slowly to build new relationships with neighbors and his AmeriCorps staff, and as he did so, he helped change community members' actual experiences of neighborhood together in that place. Now they had a center serving them in deed, not just in theory.

When Brodick organized sporting events for youth—to take a deceptively simple example—he not only re-created a baseball league; he also enabled the Red Hook youth to reclaim their ball fields, their recreation areas. These young residents could now enact an everyday claim to the land and the spaces that became once again their sites to play, their places for glory and loss, their places to swing and miss or knock in a winning run in a time and place they might always remember. Brodick was not just facilitating recreation, getting kids off the streets. He and his staff improvised and negotiated to turn an empty space into an arena for community drama, for the experience of not just teamwork but the lived forms—the lived aesthetics—of a beautiful catch, a botched throw, a tag made or missed, all vividly taking place—taking place in these deeds—in our memories in a space transformed into a particular, now community-recognized place: a ballfield, a place marked out to allow and enable and host a summer baseball league.

This involves far more than talk, far more than just conversation or discussion, for it organizes words and hopes and encouragement. Such place making as community organizing does much more than use some technical expertise to solve a problem; it involves coaching and practice, encouragement and deliberation, along with technique and kindness, skill and errors (Forester 2020; Hoch 2016).

James Brodick's organizing of the community justice center and the youth leagues was hardly his work alone; it was both improvised and interactive, and it involved a deliberate and creative negotiation that enabled play, community building, and discovery. Here were negotiations oriented toward both recreation and the re-creation of community. Always responsive to context, Brodick's place making had to take the form of improvising. He was creating places without a score to follow—a community center, ballfields, and more—places with legal and athletic drama, with festivity, beauty, and solidarity, with memory and evolving identities and senses of self, not least of all senses of social justice and safety.[6]

When Doug Rice found himself negotiating with the transportation engineers and staff in Rochester, he was not simply "doing the best he could" with respect to the streets in question and the neighbors' conflicting claims about what needed to be done there. To say that he had to negotiate or mediate to deal with differing priorities, values, and interests tells us little more than that he had to deal with others to resolve their practical differences of wants and needs and priorities. Rice listened not only to neighbors' various wishes but also to the arguments of the city's experts concerning the technical capacities of the street system underfoot.[7] Together, they had a deliberative dance to do, one that could easily have gone wrong, one informed by ongoing studies, by checking traffic counts, by making local experts accountable to local residents.

Rice knew that the neighbors cared about safety, human scale, and pedestrian amenities. Their negotiations would change existing spaces of speeding traffic into safer places for pedestrians to walk without taking the risks they had faced earlier. Improvising in this way, Rice and his colleagues did not oppose expertise; they opposed instead the autonomy of expertise divorced from community concerns. Their working conversations, their practical deliberations, would transform the same spaces into new places in which the sidewalk one walked on now became an ARTWalk, no longer merely a strip of concrete bordering traffic but a material link to the world of nearby museums, art institutes, and galleries. They followed no written rules that told them what to do, but they worked with what was at hand: the resources of the museums, the streets, the expertise of the city, and the concerns and worries and hopes of the neighbors (Coons 2020; Latour 1992).

If Rice and his colleagues felt the constraints of the street grid and its rules, of the materials and norms of the traffic system in Rochester, they also negotiated creatively to use what they found at hand to make it into, and to market it as, an ARTWalk in innovative and attractive ways. But how did they do that?

If the meaning of any material object—for example, a sidewalk, a "side walk"—always depends on its context, then changing that sidewalk's context—by slowing the traffic, perhaps—can change the sidewalk's lived meaning. That was just the point; being there on that sidewalk, after Rice's initiatives, was now to be consciously linked to the Rochester art institutions, to be on the way to this museum or that gallery, to be nearby, to be enriched by that surrounding of art history and resources—not simply to be at this spot on a piece of concrete at this geographic point on earth.

To anyone with children, the negotiation about the speed limits of traffic, the encompassing rules of the land-use game, can become an effort not just to regulate space abstractly but to create safer places for our children to walk, to live safely, or to risk being struck by a car. So here, meeting, deliberating, and negotiating with the city experts about traffic flow involved politics and values, status and trust and regulations. And all that takes place not in an abstract exercise of spatial planning but in the concretized, life-or-death shaping of place making and remaking.

What does this mean for spatial planning? These place-making practitioners are particularly concerned, as we shall see, not so much with making beautifully rendered plans but with changing existing spaces into new places. They are trying to create not only new material forms of spaces but also new possibilities of living together and inhabiting the places they live, whether this means converting an empty lot into a community garden, slowing traffic so children in neighborhoods are less at risk, transforming a patch of dirt into a baseball field, or transforming a river through the center of town into a summer festival's sound and light show. These place makers, curiously enough, did not let anyone's formal plans displace their actions or become ends in themselves; plans and designs expressed preparatory hopes, means not ends (Hoch, Nollert, and Grams 2018; Hopkins 2001). These place makers acknowledged cultural precedent not as all-controlling last words but as first words calling for creative responses—along the way to creating new arts centers, community-controlled gardens, collaboratively designed bridges, community workshops confronting racism on the streets, and affordable housing design.

Place Making Is Improvised: Interweaving Value, Expertise, and Action

The creative and improvised work of place making is almost always interactive, building on the past's legacies of both materials at hand (Beauregard and Lieto 2016; Latour 1992) and of actions, what has taken place here before. These place makers' work exemplifies not top-down planning but deliberative improvising, designing in a way that is collaborative and inquisitive, even constructively dialogic, built through many meetings, many cups of tea, and slow organizing, as much as through brilliant sketching on drawing boards or computer screens.

We will see that experts matter, of course, because they bring knowledge and technique. And we will see that city residents matter, too—if not always initially—to define the problems that need to be solved in the first place. City residents can wrestle with possibilities that the experts can shape and inform, reject or recommend, but the residents are often the ones who will identify the facts that matter, the problems that press, the debacles to clean up, the waste of space and place to remedy and repair.

But what about more controversial cases? Listen to architect-planner Michael Pyatok as he addresses the distrust or skepticism that place makers and designers often face as they work with community members who are not completely sold on the designer's intentions—in this case, developing and building affordable housing:

> By engaging those who might resist the introduction of lower-income folks into their community in the design process, we get a read on what's important to them as neighbors to help shape the site plan and the units and the appearances so that it fits in from the viewpoint of the neighbors; so not only are *we* getting information from *them*, but *they're* also getting information from *us*. Little by little, they begin to learn about who is going to be there. They learn to realize that they can trust us, that we really are listening to them, that the design really is responding to their concerns, and they see from week to week as they work with the modeling kits that in fact, what they've requested has been incorporated into the design as it emerges.

Pyatok tells us about much more than simple listening here. Learning matters, and learning means changes of mind, seeing new issues, seeing new opportunities, debunking past fears, developing a new realism with more satisfaction. Trust matters not simply as a good intention but as social and political infrastructure; trust is built, not presumed, earned not assumed. Not only does Pyatok's site plan change, but so does the recognition of what matters to the neighbors, so does the shape of the units, their appearance, "so that it fits in from the viewpoint of the neighbors." Legitimacy and consent are at stake here along with design qualities—because the designers want to see their designs built, used, maintained, and improved, not reflecting good intentions alone.

Place making as a practice not only shapes material arrangements in space, then, but also transforms the social and even political relationships that will ultimately enable and sustain those new places over time. All this matters more than ever in the time of public-health threats like the COVID-19 pandemic and the pressing resurgence of the Black Lives Matter movement. Without building and sustaining social relationships of cooperation and trust, place makers will always be on the defensive, responding too feebly to suspicions they hardly understand. Without political relationships of consent and support, place makers' good ideas may be nonstarters, and even if blaming opponents might feel good, it won't get projects built or places improved. Pyatok argues that good design can include political vision, achieving a form of public recognition of new possibilities, literally a re-cognition: "We feel that through good design, we can change public attitudes about affordable housing and about the people who live in it. So good design, high-quality design, is really a form of politics."

But Pyatok shows us more. He is designing and planning housing, yes. He is building trust, yes. He is building political support, yes. But he is doing more than that, even if he is less explicit or abstract about it. Like a fine woodworker, he has a feel for the material at hand, and in the case of place making, he needs a feel for space, for place, for materials, for timing, and for the people involved; all deserve his respect, and he warns that showing disrespect will be costly, if not fatal. All these deserve his attention, and he knows that if he ignores timing, a design can be great but too late. All these represent relationships with clients, regulators, opponents, and others whose support can be fluid and can matter a good deal over time. That means that for many if not all the place-focused practitioners in this book, a choice between process and outcome, or process and substance, would be seen as a false one. A concern for process that neglects outcome will be blind; a concern for outcome that neglects process threatens to be merely wishful or magical thinking.

Once we appreciate place making as creative and responsive to context, as interactive, improvised, and deliberative with others, we see that place makers do not tear apart, abstract, or segregate problems of knowing from problems of doing. They can rarely allocate a year to research, then another to action. They learn by and in doing, and so they are continually exploring, not just alone but with others, together asking, "What if we tried *this*?" What if we tried this at the Portland intersection, in the Brooklyn community center, in community gardens in Detroit or Paris, along Rochester's boulevards? Questions of what should be done and how, questions of values and ethics, are tightly and integrally woven with questions of how much we still need to know and learn and with questions of research and science, as the COVID-19 pandemic showed so poignantly.[8]

Combining big-picture thinking and pragmatism in the cases that follow, these place makers also link imagination and practical judgment, connecting the image of what Red Hook could be to the everyday steps that are necessary to take now. In Oregon and in Paris, we shall see, these planners and designers and activists are worried both about small, tactical steps that will achieve outcomes and about systemic effects and influences (Grose 2017; Lydon and Garcia 2015; Rydin 2011). They know they cannot act alone, that they must act with others. They know that they cannot ignore the city as the context of what they do, and yet they know, too, that if they worry about the big-picture context only, as if it were a given and static once-and-for-all project, they would risk paralysis, risk being so overwhelmed with future complexity that nothing would ever take place, nothing would change (Forester 2018). Just as the Black Lives Matter movement called attention to policing and schools as well as to the ingrained habits and presumptions of white supremacy, so too do these place makers' stories focus on both place and context, on gardens and intersections and streets and housing no more than on the relationships of power and exclusion and voice that thwart or enable any creative place making at all (Agyeman 2020; Blight 2018; Purcell 2014).

As Pyatok's example suggests, even if these place makers have no simple rules to follow, they cannot do whatever they want; they are not free from constraints. To improvise well, they must appreciate the contexts at hand to see just what they might work with—support from neighbors, resistance from bureaucrats, and so on. They must use whatever available knowledge and expertise they can that is relevant to the problems and opportunities at hand. But just as obviously, they cannot stop there. They must try to act, making proposals here, testing options there. They have three paths to explore: one about what matters, a second about what is known or can be learned, and a third about what they can do *now* (Forester 2018). Diagnosing the context, what is important at hand, practically and institutionally, in Portland or Rochester or Detroit or Oldham or Paris, always matters. Leveraging expertise from others will always matter, too. But just as importantly, these practitioners will show us, questions of action must be central: practical proposals for this design or that one, for this layout or these speed limits or these festivals or activities. Improvising in context-responsive ways in place making shares an elemental structure with improvisation in planning (Forester, Verloo, Laws 2021).

Place makers will have to wrestle with three persistent questions or problems as they try to act well: what is important, what is known or unknown, and what can be done with others now. We might summarize these three problems as the challenges of appreciating what matters in context, accessing and leveraging expertise, and building coalitions for spatial action. This triplet of problems appears in any given case in planning not just once but over time, and so asking these questions over time becomes practically a triple helix of ongoing practical concerns with what is important, with established and evolving expertise, and with joint action (Laws and Forester 2015).

Working with what matters, what is known, and what is doable shows us how place makers—without having clear prescriptive rules to follow—can both act well and improvise skillfully as they work to come up with creative and efficient—even inclusive and democratic—solutions to complex problems (Forester, Verloo, and Laws 2021). Most importantly, though, this triplet of concerns warns us of three potential failures of place making: solving the wrong problems, acting without necessary knowledge and expertise, and studying problems to death without acting on them spatially.[9]

The Roots of This Book, and Practice-Focused Oral History Methods

The following chapters emerged from the practice stories of creative place makers who generously agreed to share their experiences—rather than their theories—in practice-focused interviews.[10] These were not your normal interviews. They focused not on what practicing place makers thought about but on what they acted on, not on examining their opinions or ideas but on evoking their engaged experiences, not on examining their grand visions but on learning the details of how their projects unfolded. These conversations have produced a broad but grounded and rich collection of practice-focused oral histories rendering vivid and instructive practice stories.[11]

These practice stories teach us as readers through their detail—even through their messiness—about the complexities and opportunities of this work. These place makers imagined better spaces, and they knew that if they were to have a prayer of realizing those better spaces, they had to build support, to anticipate and respond to conflicting interests, to think about design challenges, at times, as actual negotiations—not to compromise felt values but to create actual value, not to undermine design integrity but to improve design quality (Forester 2009). Their accounts are surprising and instructive, moving and encouraging.

In our concluding chapters, particularly in the editor's afterword, we will argue that the twin crises of the COVID-19 pandemic and persistent police brutality, against which the Black Lives Matter movement has stood so potently and emblematically, have made the lessons of these place makers more important than ever. In the conclusion, we will revisit the significance of place makers not working in silos, alone, but in variously negotiated, more or less cooperative arrangements with others. Place making efforts can teach us not only about physical places and spaces themselves, but about the requirements of actually creating places of respect and reciprocity, safety and dignity, justice, compassion, and wonder.

PART ONE

Design, Collaboration, and Ownership

Introduction to Part One

In part 1, we see that place making happens not only on sketch pads, computer screens, and newly drawn maps but through designers' work with users who become codesigners along the way. We see design taking not only graphic but also democratic forms in local workshops, for example, or in design charettes. We see design imagination not hidden away but shared by neighbors and business owners. We see place-making design appearing not magically as a rabbit from the magician's hat but evolving over time, always informed as conversation leads to new ideas that lead to further conversations and more refined design possibilities.

All this can happen, we will see, in the design of affordable housing in urban contexts, in the land-use and environmental planning along a coastline, and in neighborhood or historic-preservation planning. Designers must learn about contexts to get relevant ideas, and that learning involves looking and seeing, asking questions and listening, offering suggestions and sketches and probes, and much more.

But all this work with others requires that designers and place makers meet and talk with—and listen carefully to—public officials, community residents, environmental activists, and transportation, engineering, and legal experts. Of course, that's not always easy to do. Among people who care deeply about where they live, differences of goals and interests will arise, as will hopes and fears, and arguments and public disputes will follow (Manzo and Perkins 2006; Susskind and Cruikshank 1987). Place makers cannot hide from the work of "dealing with differences" but must heartily engage in the everyday dispute resolution that any successful collaboration requires.

Place makers often celebrate public participation, in contrast to more formal top-down planning. But this leads to new problems. Participation means surfacing and engaging popular differences, and engaging differences means thinking smartly about negotiation, which can call for the skills of adept managers or mediators along the way. Throughout the place-making examples in this volume, we see differences engaged to produce not the rosy harmonies of ideal consensus but the realistic practicalities of what we can call working agreements. Our examples range from reaching practical agreements about the desirability and meaning of "mixed-use development" to nationally prominent cases of resolving historic preservation and transportation disputes.

The cases in part 1 present working examples, not recipes. Taken together, these cases sketch a repertoire of community-based design exercises that allow the future users of a space to transform it into a different place. Whether in charettes or neighborhood meetings, through storefront displays or mediated negotiations, neighbors and residents, officials and local leaders can experiment, brainstorm, play, think about priorities, and invent options together (Schneekloth and Shibley 1995). Here we see place makers finding creative ways forward even as public authorities might differ among themselves or be undecided about what and where to build, what and where not to build, and how they want to improve the community spaces in which they live.

Working with others means that place makers can be both teachers and learners, and local residents can come to appreciate that sense of humility. These design professionals and planners know that even as they have expertise and skills to offer, they need to learn and listen carefully to even begin to imagine what might be possible to do, to build, to enjoy, to cultivate in *this* unique place (Zelinka and Harden 2005). Their listening allows them to be—and to be seen as being—respectful and responsive, not to be taken as arrogant outsiders who already have their solutions even if they don't yet know what problems they're actually solving (Vazquez 2012).

In these chapters, we see not just that place making can involve a wide range of skillful processes—convening design exercises, building trust and relationships though community organizing, integrating planning with local journalism and other forms of local accountability, and mediating contentious relationships between diverse advocates—but *how* they do so. How do they bring to working agreements the transportation proponents who want a new bridge, the historic preservationists who want to keep the old one, and the well-organized residents who do not trust the engineers to design a bridge that would be aesthetically or historically or politically acceptable?

The place-making cases that follow present the work of skill, not the work of genius, not the work of heroes, but the work of real exemplars, people whose good work offers us working examples of physically sensible, culturally sensitive, and politically successful place making (Kresge Foundation 2019). In part 1, we see many of the central elements of place-making work set out. We begin with Michael Pyatok's robust account that introduces us to issues of culture and timing, politics and expertise, community skepticism and buy-in. Al Zelinka's case then shifts from a project focus to a larger, small-city scale; he interweaves issues of planning process and local politics as he tackled questions of land-use and urban design on the Oregon coast. Mark Lakeman complements these introductory essays by de-centering the place-making design process; in a neighborhood in the southeast quadrant of Portland, Oregon, it was not design firms but neighborhood residents who mobilized to reclaim their neighborhoods' places and spaces. Michael Hughes then adds cultural and organizational conflict—and an insider's view of a mediator's role—to the design and place-making list of relevant concerns. In his striking account, we see a democratized design process that celebrates diverse voices even as it relies essentially on engineering expertise to produce a beautiful and functional new bridge over the St. Croix River.

1

Affordable Housing, Ethnicity, and the Construction of Place

Michael Pyatok's Practice Story

Editor's Preface

Michael Pyatok seems to be equally at home as a teacher in an architectural studio and as a designer working in systematically participatory ways to build affordable housing for low-income communities of color. Working with residents, he creates places from spaces in ways guided by goals of equity as well as aesthetics, goals of functionality as well as form.

This story interweaves issues of culture and politics, finance and real estate, and community building and learning. Pyatok shows that in a world of diverse cultures, classes, ethnicities, and politics, good design is both an inherently political product and a concretely expressive form of political vision.

High-Quality Design Is Really a Form of Politics

Before talking specifically about any one project, I would like to explain, in general, why we get involved with engaging the community. I see two fundamental reasons. Because we're primarily trying to house folks who are of lower income, we're working either in neighborhoods whose incomes are similar to the incomes of the people whom we're housing or in neighborhoods where they're different, where the incomes of the people we're housing are lower than those of the neighborhood. These are two very different kinds of situations.

If we're working in a neighborhood where the incomes are similar, then the purpose of engaging the community is really political—that is, to get as many people from the community involved as we can. They're usually proactive, they're usually in favor of the project to begin with, because they want to see either dilapidated, run-down, vacant housing eliminated and replaced by actively occupied housing and affordable housing, or a vacant, weed-infested, and garbage-strewn lot eliminated from the neighborhood by having new housing on it.

The lower-income neighborhoods would want to see it happen, and we and our nonprofit client would then want to use the community process as a means to help educate the community on how the real estate development system works—how you go about getting approvals, how you deal with the planning commission, or the city council, or with others in positions at those levels, or at least how to deal with the bureaucratic stumbling blocks that could throw a monkey wrench into the process.

If we can have mobilized a hundred people from the neighborhood who participated directly, hands-on, in the design and who really have a sense of authorship, they will be motivated to come out to the city council and the city planning commission hearings to argue in favor of moving the project forward or funding the project. That's because often at city council, the decisions are not only made to approve the project, but also to provide the funding.

These type of projects can be started from the community or by a nonprofit developer who comes into the community. More often than not, it's the nonprofit that may have entered that community; the nonprofit might be from the same town, or it might be from a different town. But there are local, community-based organizations that want to see a property developed, and they can invite a nonprofit to collaborate with them to make sure that it happens. That could be anything from a church group to simply a community-based activist organization that's trying to resuscitate or reinvigorate investment in their community because it's experienced a long-term decline due to redlining and other factors. Those are some of the different ways that a project can actually get started.

When we are working in a lower-income neighborhood and the idea is to mobilize the community around the project, it's to build a political force that will argue on behalf of the project. It's also, on a cultural level, assisting us in really understanding what the values of that community are and in what ways they can affect the organization and design of that new development. We're trying to get a kind of cultural relevance—social and cultural relevance—to the design by having that kind of hands-on focus group. So there are both political and social/cultural reasons why we would want to engage the broader community around a particular project if it's in a low-income neighborhood.

We primarily focus on the work of the nonprofit sector. So we could be working in lower-income communities, or we could be working in middle-income communities trying to do low-income housing. About seventy-five percent of our work is for the non-profit sector. Of the other twenty-five percent, about half is for universities doing student housing, and the other half is for private developers doing market-rate housing. But even the market-rate housing, for the most part, involves developers who are trying to hit the low end of the market without government subsidy, so they're trying to do first-time homeowner housing, for example.

The second category of community involvement would be in neighborhoods that are of higher income that might potentially—or have already indicated that they would be willing to— resist the introduction of lower-income folks into their community. Then we want to engage that neighborhood to get them on board, to educate them as to who's going to be living there, and then, also, to the quality of housing that will emerge if they get involved, and that they have nothing to fear—their property values will not drop, the schools are not going to get inundated with troublesome children, etc. We try to get them to understand that the folks moving into their community are going to be hard-working people who just happen to earn lower incomes for the hard work that they do. We're trying to dispel myths and to get them on our side.

Now, those can be a bit more contentious, because we're dealing with trying to help a community go through a major cultural shift, ideological shift, or attitudinal shift from what they may have felt for a long time about what they think is "public housing." Even though what we're doing is being developed by private nonprofit corporations, they don't understand the difference, and they think somebody's bringing in public housing. So they have misconceptions about who's bringing it, but they also have misconceptions about the history of public housing and a lot of misconceptions about who the people are who are going to be living in it and what their needs are.

So by engaging them in the design process, we get a read on what's important to them as neighbors, to help shape the site plan and the units and the appearances so that it fits in from the viewpoint of the neighbors; so not only are *we* getting information from *them*, but *they're* also getting information from *us*. Little by little, they begin to learn about who is going to be there. They learn to realize that they can trust us, that we really are listening to them, that our design really is responding to their concerns. They see, from week to week as they work with the modeling kits, that in fact what they've requested has been incorporated into the design as it emerges. So we're gaining support from people who could potentially be opponents at a city planning commission hearing or a city council hearing. So, again, we're doing it for political reasons as well as for cultural and social reasons.

It's hard to just talk about one type of project and not the other, as a comparison. In one project, we were doing low-income senior housing, and one would assume that no one would ever object to having seniors brought into their community. But there was a very solid middle-class white community that objected.

By the way, in both instances that I'll describe here, we held the meetings in a church facility. The reason for that was because in that kind of a physical setting—because that physical setting also has its social and symbolic meaning—people are a bit more well-behaved. If they dislike an idea, dislike the people who are presenting that idea, they're going to be a bit more courteous to each other, a bit more civil, and at least hear each other out before they raise their concerns. Sometimes, their concerns can be made to feel a bit shallow and small in the implied sense of purpose of the religion within whose house we happen to be sitting to discuss the assignment. I think every religion in the world says that those who have should be helping those who have not; that's a principle somewhere in every major institutionalized religion. So that understanding is there on the surface, and then people in the audience who like the idea of the project, if necessary can call upon it in such a meeting, and it would have more meaning because we're sitting in the house of that religion. This is the reason that we like to hold meetings in a faith-based setting, even though that particular church may have nothing to do with the actual development; they're not part of the development team.

So in that first instance I'm describing, a project that was for senior housing, some elements of the neighborhood were fairly outspoken, and the fifty or sixty people who showed up at the first meeting were very contentious, and they said that they did not want this in their neighborhood. We said, "Well, it's really only for seniors, low-income seniors," and the response of some of them was, "Yeah, but those seniors have children, and the children are going to come and visit." We said, "Well, those children are probably in their forties," and then they said, "That doesn't matter; They may have had a life of crime."

So these guys were stereotyping low-income seniors, and the race word was not used, but it was always implied, as if the majority of the residents of the housing were probably going to be African American. This was a lily-white neighborhood. This project was located just on the border between Oakland and San Leandro, and it was in San Leandro. Quite frankly, I think, the resident mix was half and half in that development—half white and half Black. In any case, that was the response of some of the concerned neighbors.

I responded to them by pointing out that [the new residents'] children were going to be in their forties and that it was presumptuous on their part to think that just because they're low-income, their kids live a life of crime. Then somebody else said, "Yeah, but you know, people of those incomes will frequently have problems with the parents, and the grandparents are actually raising the kids, and before you know it, that senior housing is going to be filled with a lot of young kids that the seniors are expected to then raise." To that we can respond by saying, "Well, this is being funded by HUD [US Department of Housing and Urban Development], and they're not allowed to have anybody living in with them. Grandchildren cannot live with them. They can be visited for up to one week, but they cannot establish residence in the building with the seniors."

We got over those hurdles, but what really won them over was our method of engaging people, which is to build a model of the neighborhood; then the site itself is removable from that model. We try to get a minimum of fifty or sixty people engaged, and that allows us to create four to six design teams. Each of those design teams has a basic model of the site, and then they receive a kit of parts that includes all of the units that have to go on the site, plus the parking requirements and any open-space uses.

With that design kit of parts, each of those five or six teams begins to assemble a solution in the first workshop. They spend about an hour doing that, and then for the second hour, each of them elects a spokesperson who presents to all the others, explaining the pros and cons of their solutions. After that, I facilitate a plenary session that discusses each of the solutions, and I try to get consensus as to which were the best ideas from each, which were the worst, and what is the general direction that we should pursue in the next modeling session, which might occur two weeks from that point.

So they began to work toward a consensus, some shared agreement in the design, and all that we were hearing from them we would try to incorporate into the kit of parts for the next time around. There might be setback requirements, for example, that they demanded to match the neighborhood. There might be certain height restrictions that they wanted to see maintained as the housing approached the street edges and the adjacent properties.

We bulked up the mass, and this came out of their models. They bulked up the mass along the main street, and then they lowered it to two stories along the two residential side streets and along the rear of the project with space for parking so there could be no buildings adjacent to the neighbor's property line fence.

Then, when it came to appearances, we gave it character that was much like some of the cherished buildings in the area, which were sort of mission-style architecture. And they just loved it by the end. They understood that they could trust us; they saw that we were listening to everything they said and that we were incorporating what they'd said into the design—so much so that we won them over by the end, and when the project had to appear before the city council for approval, they spoke on its behalf in seeking the parking variances that we were requesting. We actually ended up gaining not only their non-resistance, but also their approval and support. The city had required 1.25 cars per unit; we were allowed one car per unit—sixty units, sixty cars. We got full approvals from the city council that evening, and the project's already built. So that's an example of how this process can work in a relatively higher-income neighborhood.

A second example of a community-based project took place in a low-income Latino neighborhood in East Oakland, a neighborhood that functioned as a little village because it's cut off to the west by a highway, to its east by railroad tracks, and to the north by industry. As a neighborhood, it had its own church and its own school nearby, within walking distance, and some industry. There was actually a job space in the community. They were very upset because one of the industrial parcels that had been cleared of its buildings was about to be sold off to a trucking company. The trucking company was just going to use it as a storage yard.

There had been a factory there on the site, whether or not it employed people directly from that neighborhood I'm not clear. But it had been cleared, and the people were very upset that a truck storage yard would bring danger and pollution into their neighborhood—and no jobs. Their sense of danger was that all these semitrailer trucks would be driving through their small streets to get to that storage yard, with pollution coming from the diesel trucks. But then their third concern was that truck storage is a terrible underutilization of inner-city land—they're not even going to get jobs out of it; maybe one night watchman. So they came to me and asked, "How can we stop this project?"

I said, "Well, you're going to have to get the zoning changed." So for the next year and a half, they organized and held their meetings in the local church. There was an umbrella organization in Oakland called Oakland Community Organizations [OCO], and this neighborhood was a member of that organization.

A lot of faith-based neighborhood groups are members of that larger organization, and one of the OCO community organizers lived in that neighborhood, so they were ripe for being well organized to help change the zoning, which they did succeed in doing. During that process, I linked them up to a nonprofit housing development corporation that swooped in, bought half that parcel as soon as the zoning was changed, and then with them organized the community to hold a series of workshops. We had about five or six that designed the site, designed the units, designed the appearance of the units. That project went on and was built, and now it's occupied.

They had wanted a first-time homeowner development; at that point, I think it was seventy-five percent of the median income that was the average income in the development. They wanted first-time home buyers because a lot of the folks in that neighborhood, in that it was really like a village, had relatives and friends who they wanted to have the opportunity to grow their families and stay with them in the neighborhood. I think the ownership rate was about sixty-five percent. There was about thirty-five percent absentee ownership, and there were renters who would have loved to stay in the neighborhood and own their own homes.

In fact, they had designed the homes to be expandable; they had extra volume in the attic, and the stair went up into the attic so that they could add two more bedrooms and a bathroom in the attic. Many of them just had carports, but they were designed so the carports could convert to garages with one bedroom above the garage so that they could eventually have a five-bedroom house. They could grow in place.

They had live/work opportunities as well as the expansion potential. They also had some with bedrooms on the ground floor with handicapped-accessible bathrooms so that the grandparents could live as part of the extended family. All of these were ingredients that came out of the community workshops and the focus groups, and they were highly motivated because they succeeded in fighting off the trucking company. They were highly motivated, too, because it was getting designed to their needs as Latino Catholic families that, they knew, were going to grow. And the priest of the local parish was happy because he was going to get fifty-three more families in his parish. So we had unanimous support for the project when we went before the city planning staff and the city council.

Working with different cultural groups, sometimes we've had to have several different interpreters with headsets so that people who didn't speak any English could participate in the meetings through their interpreters. There was a group in Fresno, California, that we worked with, a neighborhood that had well over a hundred people involved, and we had Hispanic, English-speaking, and Hmong people—so the Hmong folks had their interpreter as well.

There was another neighborhood group we worked for in Seattle, where there were four different Southeast Asian groups, each one having its own language. So we had to have a series of workshops separate from each other, because it was hard to hold all four at the same time. Then, as we began to reach a consensus on the ingredients, we were able to bring all four together. But at the early stages, we kept them within their own language groups to make life easier. It wasn't a difficult thing to achieve consensus—shared agreements—because they were already active in the organization that was working with Southeast Asian immigrants. So while they spoke different languages, they shared one thing in common: they were all newcomers to the United States, and they came from different Southeast Asian countries. While historically they may have considered themselves to be different from each other when they were local to their region, now they all had something very much in common. They were all foreigners in a new land; that in itself created a bond. They all had the same needs as immigrants to a new country—trying to understand how to get things done, how the place works, struggling with holding onto their traditions as their kids get absorbed into the American culture. Before they knew it, as different as their origins may have been, they now had a hell of a lot in common. So it was not that big a deal.

To some extent, I know what I'm going to be facing going into projects with different cultural groups, though you never quite feel completely knowledgeable, and there are always surprises of some kind. For example, I remember one Latino group that we worked with in San Jose, California. They were developing about forty units of housing plus a childcare center and a special social-service center for women and children. That particular group, both men and women, went through that community-planning process, and they went through a number of different site-planning options.

In the Latino culture in California, there is a tremendous need for the automobile, and there's a certain amount of what we might call "identification" with the car by the Latino men. During that whole exercise of looking at all the different ways by which the housing could be put on the site, along with the parking, they actually ended up with a solution that did not have a car in every house, which is the way that the process had begun.

There were five teams, and in one of the teams, the men dominated and insisted that their cars were their pride and joy. A number of [the cars] were low-riders, and they wanted the car in the house so that they could hear its heartbeat at night. As they looked at the other options that emerged, they saw some schemes where the cars were all pulled out to one side and people left their car in a secured parking area but then walked into the site; the entire site was housing and open space free of automobiles, which allowed for a much more relaxed way of life for the kids when they played and for the families to have their vegetable gardens. It just opened their eyes that there were other ways of organizing the land than to have the typical approach of a car in every house.

That was a surprise to us—that they would, in the end, choose to take that route. And when we brought it to the city planning staff before bringing it to the city planning commission, the planning staff and staff of the city's housing department, who was going to subsidize the project, both balked at the idea and said, "There's no way that Hispanics are going to live with clustered parking and not have their car in their house. It's just not the way they live."

So we said, "Well, that's the only model they've ever been shown, and in fact, we went through a series of community workshops—or focus groups, if you will, of potential buyers—and this is the plan; this is the approach that they took. And it was very clear to them—it was made very clear to them—that some of the families would have to walk as much as 150 feet from their car to their house. That's only about three-quarters of a small block, really only half a block. That's not a big deal, and they all agreed it was not a big deal given what they were going to gain in the site planning by taking that approach."

So both Housing and Planning were skeptical of it, but nonetheless, they had to accept it, because we had all these slides and images of the workshops, and we had representatives from the neighborhood show up and say, "Yeah, this is the preferred way that we would like to see our site organized."

That was a big surprise to us—that the guys would accept that. I remember distinctly in one of the meetings when one of the leaders of the young guys, with tattoos and all, was standing next to his wife, who was pregnant, expecting their first child; he was the one to first say, "You know, I originally wanted the car in the house, but now when I see what can be done here for our kids, I think that I would prefer this alternative model." That swayed the other guys into taking his position.

I can't think of any cases where the city council or planning commission has blocked what the residents wanted, and it's primarily because in this day and age, any elected official knows that you don't mess with your constituents when they prefer something over something else. You go with what the people want, otherwise you're going to find yourself in deep trouble.

I have not seen that kind of resistance to what people say they would want from the design process. If people have spoken, they say, "Yeah," unless you're engaged in a situation where a private developer has different interests and is trying to discredit what the community is saying. Then politicians will side with whoever is politically more powerful in their eyes, and sometimes, those who have money are listened to more than others, and so private developers will rule the day.

I saw that happen in a situation where we were hired by the private developer because they knew we were good at working with the community. We soon found out that the private developer was really not that sympathetic to what the community wanted to do. Fortunately, we brought the developer to a certain stage of the approval process, and we weren't needed any longer, and we didn't have to stick around to watch the subsequent mayhem unfold as the developer had to face the wrath of the community.

The developer had tried to proceed without the recommendations of the community because the community was trying to limit density in a certain area. I think there was a certain amount of selfishness on their part, but on the other hand, there was some wisdom behind their concerns regarding traffic and drainage that were overblown but that were still real concerns.

We had recommended—the developer had wanted—something like seven hundred units in that location. In private meetings after our major workshops and our talks with groups of the citizens, we understood that if the developer had really proposed more like four hundred units, [the citizens] could have lived with that; they would have been less fearful of the impacts. But seven hundred, they thought, was off the chart. I brought that information back to the developer. I said, "You know, you can save yourself two to three years of agony here by just accepting something more in the four hundred to four hundred fifty range, and you're going to diffuse a lot of this anger."

They refused to do that, and it became apparent why. I hadn't realized this, but these guys were going to be the developers of the land; they were not going to be the builders of the housing. They were trying to maximize the number of units on the site because they were the land developers. They were going to get all the planning approvals and entitlements, and then sell it off to people who would build it. Their interest was to get as many units as possible approved, because that would increase the value of the land and their land sale—the purchase price of their land. They were not about to really collaborate with the community, whereas if they truly were the people who were going to build the housing, they, like anybody who is in the business of building, would be interested in moving as quickly as possible and making accommodations to find a way to negotiate and compromise. Well, these guys weren't about to do that.

In that particular case dealing with conflict between the community's wishes and my professional recommendations, I called up the developer and said, "You know, if you did this and this, you'd be home-free," and they said to me, "No, that's not in our interests. We don't want to do that." I then said, "Well, you know what, guys? You hired the wrong architects." Because we really do believe that we should represent the interests of the community as well as the developer, that both have to be listened to in order to find a middle ground. Then the guy panicked over the phone because he knew it would be a disaster, public-relations wise, for the architects to pull out because we felt they were not abiding by what the community was seeking, in their best interests. They came back to us and said, "Look, this is our strategy here. We want, for now anyway, to understand what this community is willing to tolerate." They said to me, "We know that you believe it's best for Oakland that as many people as possible get to live in the city to increase the population and the density and the mix of folks and the tax base, etc. etc." They were playing upon my values; they knew what I tend to believe.

I said, "That's fine, and you're right, and I'm willing to stick it out here to see how much of an addition can be achieved," because they said to me, "We know that you know, in your heart of hearts, these are higher-income people who are just being selfish about their neighborhood and that they're just trying to keep people out. Now that they have something, they want to limit it to themselves only." They knew that I would get taken by that argument, because in fact, it *was* an upper-income neighborhood behaving in the usual way of resisting change.

They were playing upon what they knew my politics were by saying, "Look, you can get more people to live in Oakland here, and you know that some of these concerns by this neighborhood are just rich people being selfish." I said, "Well, that's true to some extent, but on the other hand, there is always something legitimate about people's fears, and you have to get to the bottom of it." They said, "We agree with you, but it needs more time to play itself out. Help us get to the bottom of it." So I said, "OK, we'll hang in there."

So we did take it through the point of achieving the status of going into the environmental review process, and at that point, we completed our portion of the work, and they began to negotiate with some Southern California builders who would come in and buy the land and the right to develop it. We were no longer needed.

At the point we decided to stay on the project, we tried to learn what the community members' fears were, and we tried to show them that what was being proposed was not going to create the traffic impacts or the level of drainage problems that they were all trying to scare up as an impediment to development in that area. What kept us going and made us feel that we were making an important contribution, that we should continue to move forward, was that this development was occurring in what was a gray-field site because of its use for the previous hundred years. That site had become a gigantic scar on the hills of the city, and this development would heal that scar and allow for the revegetation of a good deal of that hillside. Maybe eighty percent of it was going to be revegetated, repopulated with life, both flora and fauna, with only twenty percent for development.

To restore the appearance—because you can see that scar for miles around when you drive around the flatlands of the city—we were helping to get that remedied. We felt that in the long run, this was a good thing to be doing. We felt we were, in the long run, on the right side of the fence and that this was an example of a community group that just needed to have a little more education about what the consequences would be of this development—the housing development would pay for the restoration of the hillside.

I was pleased with the outcome of our work, and it's now well under construction. It took a couple of years to get through the battle of the environmental process. Again, we were no longer needed during that portion of it, so I didn't have to face those continuing arguments. But now, a huge scar on the hill is gradually getting grown in, and the lower portion of the site, which was on the more shallow slope, is now getting occupied—I think, in the end, with four hundred seventy-five units, the number of units, roughly, that I had originally recommended they should go with. But they lost a couple of years in the process of getting to that; that's what seemed so silly to me. But the developer didn't mind. They weren't in that much of a hurry.

When it comes to designing housing for lower-income folks, it's political by its very nature, in that what you're attempting to do is change public opinion about the very people who live in the housing and the level of density that needs to exist—not just to achieve affordability, but to make our cities more sustainable. As I said earlier, there are a lot of misconceptions about who lives in publicly assisted housing and why. We feel that through good design, we can change public attitudes about affordable housing and about the people who live in it. Good design—high-quality design—is really a form of advocacy politics.

When you think about it, every building is playing this game of conveying a message. The purpose of an art museum, for example, is to create the impression that there's something highly mystifying and awesome that is contained within the bowels of this building. In fact, most of it is owned by rich people whose investment value is increasing with every day that the art hangs there on the wall. So they have to make museums that have this kind of mystifying, almost religious quality about them. Some museums are designed that way, as are government buildings. For highly symbolic government buildings—for legislative bodies or those that have to deal with the public forum—they try harder to elevate them above the norm.

For publicly assisted housing, everything that we're designing has to be a landmark in the WPA [Works Progress Administration] fashion; what we're doing here is showing how public investment needs to be above the norm. People have to turn their heads and look at this thing and say, years from now, "Wow, people live in that historic landmark, and people live around it," so that thirty or forty years from now, when it will need renovation, the neighbors and residents will want to preserve it and renovate it and not tear it down and throw it away. In that sense, all publicly assisted housing is a political design task.

Now, it's political in other ways, too, because you have to also convince the immediate players and gatekeepers who could stop it; through good design, you have to get it past those first hurdles. But it also has to pass the test of history over the next subsequent decades as something that is lovingly cherished, and the people it serves are seen as deserving a respectable place in society. Publicly assisted housing is too often shortchanged with nasty budgets or with people who took it on as an assignment and either didn't take it seriously enough or saw it as an arena in which they could engage in some strange, avant garde experiments that only broke the mold from the past and ended up stigmatizing the residents in some kind of oddly configured building type.

* * *

I see now that over the years, community participation has become much more the norm. I mean that a lot of developers recognize that it's just a given—you've got to do it in some form or another. They like to believe that it's possible to do it as a co-optive process just to silence the community or to win them over—that's their mission, often—and we try to avoid getting involved with those circumstances. But it's certainly something that's here to stay.

There's one that we did last summer in Hawai'i, on the island of Kauai. A private developer there was planning to do a fairly high-end development—a resort development, including second-home development—and the county required that in addition to the fifteen hundred high-end units, they also develop some affordable housing for the workforce who make the wealthy island function properly. This particular developer does very, very good work at the high end. You know, surprisingly, there's a lot of junk that gets done for the high end, and those people don't even know that they're buying junk.

There are developers that do extraordinarily good work. They take seriously what they feel these folks at these income levels should have and deserve for the buck that they're spending—they preserve and enhance the local natural environment so people and wildlife comfortably coexist, within a regionally appropriate architecture that works with the local climate and material resources.

So when this high-end developer was asked to do affordable housing for lower-income households, they turned to me and said, "You know, we've never done this before, and we want to make sure we do as good a job for this income level as we do for the high-income level, and so we're hiring you to help us do that." I said, "Well, the best way to achieve that is to go directly to the people who you think you're going to be providing housing for and create focus groups and solicit their opinions."

They're trying to provide housing for people whose incomes are as low as fifty percent of the median income all the way up to one hundred fifty percent of the median, because people even at one hundred and fifty percent of the median in Kauai can't afford to own a home.

So they worked with us to organize the whole process, making certain that participants spanned the spectrum of jobs in the tourist industry— from restaurant workers, hotel workers, and sales clerks to hotel middle management. And they absolutely loved it—everything that we did to solicit all the opinions from probably about fifty or sixty folks on the island, using modeling kits to design homes and site layouts. Then, we and they went ahead to refine the design thinking about all that had been said in those workshops. So even at the high end, there's recognition that if you're going to incorporate housing for low-income folks in the same community as people with high incomes, you'd better do it right. You'd better get it right, or you're actually going to hurt the other folks whom you're trying to please and hurt your profit margins.

So good design—high-quality design—is really a form of politics.

2

Engaging Communities with Expertise and Accountability

Al Zelinka's Practice Story

Editor's Preface

Al Zelinka applied to a request for planning proposals and won the contract. He and his staff would have to fly from Southern California to work with four towns on the Oregon coast—four towns that had fired the first planning team that they had hired. Bringing expertise from outside hadn't worked so well the first time, and Zelinka thought his team could do better.

In what they called an immersive and responsive community-engaged process, they partnered with the press, rented a centrally located storefront to display plans and proposals for comments and refinement, and collaborated with local Oregonians to blend planning expertise with local concerns and priorities as they integrated land-use and environmental planning with community building and public education. Here is Zelinka's account of key aspects of their place-making work.

Community Building in Place—Analysis, Design, and Collaboration

One of our projects happened right in the beginning of the year 2000, in Lincoln City, Oregon, and we worked with their urban renewal agency. This city comprises six historic villages that came together in the mid-sixties and incorporated into one big city so they could develop infrastructure together. The project was to prepare a community-based redevelopment plan for the village of Taft, the oldest of all the villages in Lincoln City. It was the first time in the city's history that they had a planning process conducted.

I think something like seven or nine other firms from the western United States had submitted proposals. An interesting aspect of the project was that every team was required to work with Dan Burden, from Walkable Communities. We were required to have him on our team, as was every other team. He's dedicated the last ten to fifteen years of his life—in two hundred twenty communities a year—getting them acclimated to traffic-calming and making streets more pedestrian friendly throughout the United States. He's worked in every state in the country.

Here's how we got involved. We subscribe to a marketing service that tracks requests for proposals from all over the country. We received a lead that Lincoln City was looking for proposals for a redevelopment plan. So I, the project manager, flew up there and met with the director of the Lincoln City Urban Renewal Agency. He showed me around, and we talked and spent the day together. I got a good sense for what he wanted, what the community wanted. I talked to merchants, I talked to property owners while I was there, and after that, I talked to other city officials, just to get a sense of what this project entailed. I was there just for a day, a quick flight up there in the morning. I did the interviews, took the tour, and then flew home that night. We prepared a proposal to undertake the project.

We won the job. We were selected largely because I went up there, I hit it off with the redevelopment director, and our approach was very, very community based. Probably half the budget was spent on community involvement. The other firms would have had a couple of public workshops, but they would design it and see if the community liked it.

Our proposal was organized, more or less, into three distinct phases. This is a structure we generally use for all our projects. The first phase was understanding the place and the politics and the economics—all the dimensions of the project—as well as having some additional community involvement to get an understanding of community values, challenges, assets, and so forth. That was about a two-and-a-half-month part of the process.

The next phase was developing the vision. That was, essentially, what it did. Based on our understanding and the community's understanding of the project, where did they want to go? This second phase was about a month-and-a-half-long process.

The last phase was preparing the redevelopment plans and the implementation program in the last two months. The total six-month process was incredibly intense.

Keep in mind that I'm in Southern California; we were flying up and down quite a lot. We assembled a significant team. We had about four or five specialists, including Dan Burden; we had a landscape architect, an economic developer, another specialist, a local engineer, and a local artist.

To start, we collected all the documentation that we possibly could from the city, and we reviewed it. Then we went up there for a seven-day period where we met with all the state, federal, and county agencies that had an influence on this project and with whom we needed to build partnerships.

The village of Taft sits on the Siletz Bay and on the Pacific Ocean. It's on the state highway. There are wetlands involved. There were many layers of government involved, which we looked at as an opportunity for partnership and funding. In some cases, there were specific representatives who were assigned to the city. In other cases, it was a larger district that they represented or were assigned to. We very much took seriously the fact of building partnerships and of talking to them as people, not as members of a big bureaucracy.

What we did was to set up one-on-one meetings with them or group meetings. We went onto *their* turf and learned from them what was on their minds about existing issues and challenges in Lincoln City. We built a fantastic rapport, and we kept everything upbeat and maintained the understanding that they were a valuable asset—that *their* role was paramount to the success of the project. Through the process, they became hooked into the project and felt that individually, they mattered.

We dedicated an incredible amount of time on the front end, building relationships with people in organizations and then people in the community. With the community, we did a lot of one-on-one interviews, walks around the town, workshops, bicycle rides—we did all kinds of stuff. We had between ten and fifteen different events that occurred every single day for a week. It was incredibly intense.

For this project, we coined a process that we called "community immersion," and we use it to this day. Essentially, we just immersed ourselves and our entire team. We demonstrated to the city that we were absolutely invested in their future. We would go there and eat dinner with community members, and we'd stay in the local hotels. I mean, we were *there*, and we were investing every ounce of energy for a week in their community. We had a lot of workshops, a lot of walking tours, all focused on, "Help us understand this place and you as people and what you want and don't want. This is all about *you*. It's not about what we want, but about what *you* want."

The other thing that happened, prior to our being hired, was that the Lincoln City community, which was rather conservative and independent minded, had run out of town a progressive Portland-based new-urbanist firm, one that had gotten a grant from the state to prepare a mixed-use development code for the city. The firm came in with a mixed-use zone for the village of Taft, and the community became unglued. I wasn't there, but they told me that the firm was effectively asked to leave by the city council. The community spoke so much against it because the community was not involved. One of the big issues on the front end of this for us was the idea that we heard, "We don't want mixed-use," and we just listened to them. But on the first tour, a walking tour, they kept pointing out a few of the buildings, and one of the buildings—Kenny's IGA grocery store—was beloved because there was a grocery store on the ground floor and there were apartments upstairs.

"Well, you understand that *that's* mixed use?"

"Oh, *that's* mixed-use? Well, we like *that*."

It was just a basic fact, it seemed, that the other consultant didn't take the time to understand. So in the end, the mixed-use zoning district and standards prepared through our process was something that they adopted unanimously right from the get-go. There was no controversy about it.

Taft was not a racially diverse village. I would say that at that time, it was ninety-plus percent Caucasian, but I would also say that it was definitely *economically* diverse. There were a lot of low-income community members in this village. The most common type of housing was, and still is, mobile homes or very small cottages left over from the days when fishing and timber were the big industries. So ethnically, it was not diverse, but economically, it certainly was.

A lot of effort went into making sure that every single step of the process was in the community. The community members involved ranged from retired ladies, to the young couple with two little kids who had just opened a bed-and-breakfast and were trying to keep it in business, to the old-timer business owner of the hardware store, to residents of the mobile-home park, to real estate agents—just a real range of people, and it truly was a reflection of their community; these were not just those property owners who had the most to gain. It included members of Veterans of Foreign Wars and members of the local merchants' association, the local business association. It was truly a representation of the community.

One unique thing we did in the first phase was to open a storefront information center. We suggested that this was something we could do because we thought, "Even when we're gone, we need to have a presence. This is such an important first-time effort for this community, we can't let this process feel like it stops when we're gone. We have to keep it alive even when we're not there." And we did it in the nature of a community base—we did it through volunteering.

There were a number of vacant storefronts in this village. We worked it out with the property owner to allow us to set up shop in one of these storefronts, and for the entire six months, we staffed it with community volunteers. The kids would go there after school and get tutoring. During the daytime, we had a professional sign, an A-frame sandwich board, along the sidewalk.

As soon as we had a draft of anything done, it would go up in that storefront. Routinely, all throughout the day, people were coming in there to see what was new. It was open several days a week, sometimes twelve hours a day. A lot of senior citizens volunteered their time.

Another of the major stakeholders that we got involved with was the local media, the newspapers in particular. We tapped them not to publicize our events, but rather so we could say, "Tell us. Because you've been in this community, you've talked to everyone, you know what's going on, we want you to be consultants, resources to us." So we befriended the newspaper people and built relationships with them, so much so that they ended up preparing a project website—and this was in 2000, so the internet was relatively new. They stocked it and maintained it. We would send them material, and they would upload it. It was a fantastic partnership that was built there. Because we involved them as informants and community members, they also became the greatest assets to the project. They never gave a bit of bad press; they were factual. The radio station operated in the same way. We'd call in regularly, send them faxes, give them updates to be regularly reported on the radio—all to let the community know that things were happening.

Our client, the redevelopment director, was new to this ballgame of planning. He caught the fever very quickly, and he became a very enthusiastic cheerleader throughout. He's very well connected throughout the state, so he would go regularly to the governor's office, to the department of transportation—all over the place, publicizing and preaching the goodness of the unfolding of the process.

Let's fast-forward to the visioning process. We got all the baseline stuff together, and we started out the process with, "This is what we know to be true and what we learned in the first month and a half. This is an opportunity now, to engage you in a multitude of different exercises for envisioning what you want."

We did everything from doing an intergenerational logo contest, to coming up with a logo for the village, to doing youth visioning sessions, to senior-citizen visioning sessions. One thing we did that was really cool with the community happened because they didn't want to be told what to do with respect to the design of their buildings. When we did these walks, though, they certainly told us about buildings that they thought were ugly and the spaces that they *didn't* want. So we assigned the communities to a task over a month. We gave them all the disposable cameras they wanted so that they could go around Lincoln City and other parts of coastal Oregon and take photographs of those buildings that they liked, those attributes that they would like to see replicated in Taft. Then we came back together in a workshop setting, and we essentially picked the images that they liked most. We organized them, and then we had one of our urban designers render some line drawings of elements of those pictures. We put together a design-guidelines poster. The poster was adopted by resolution as policy—but not as "Thou shall." It was just "Thou should" type language.

The community loved it because it was a poster; it wasn't this big, voluminous set of design guidelines; it was just a single poster about the basics that their buildings should include. So today, when you go up to the village of Taft, you can definitely look at that poster and at all the rehabs that have been done. They all follow that poster.

At the end, together with the entire community and all those various stakeholder agencies, we held a two-day-long design charette. It was about a five-day process in total. At the end of that five-day process, an actual vision graphic, a design, and a policy vision were formulated. It was then presented back to the community, and the community critiqued it.

We took that information home with us back to our offices. We worked with city staff to refine it, to bring it back in a more polished form for the city council, for the community, and for the planning commission—all for us to present to them and to engage them in an exercise to critique it.

So there were feedback loops to the community. They were never surprised by anything, and they always understood the basis of every element of the vision plan. So once we went through the process, the community reviewed it, the planning commission reviewed it, and the council reviewed it.

At the end of the day, the vision was unanimously adopted by the city council, and the community unanimously approved it. There were a lot of hard decisions they had to make, things like installing a median in the middle of the highway and cutting off cross-highway access points to their businesses because they wanted to create a more pedestrian environment. But they did the hard things because they were so engaged and understood the issues. They made the tough decisions they had to make to get the results they wanted.

Once the council approved the direction of the vision plan, we moved into the third phase to actually prepare the redevelopment plan and the implementation plan, both in very detailed ways. Our economic consultant also put a very detailed economic development implementation plan together.

The redevelopment plan was not an ordinary plan. The entire plan broke the vision down into projects and programs. Each project and program had the most detailed action steps necessary to achieve that project or program and to identify who, what, when, where, why, how, and how much. It identified who needed to lead the project or program, the action steps, who needed to be on the team, when it needed to be done, how much it would cost, and what resources there were to help do it. We spent an inordinate amount of time—literally, a month—with almost full-time staffing preparing this implementation plan.

For every project or program in the plan, we provided the contact information of other communities who had been there and done it before, so that they could serve as a resource. Some we had worked with before; some were communities that we had read about; some were merely those who had simple solutions.

We reviewed every excuse possible for the community to not implement this. Taft has amazing beachheads, and one of the things that was very important to the community was that there was a contingent of physically challenged individuals who said, "You know, we can't enjoy the beach." So we did some internet research on those communities that have those beach wheelchairs, the ones with the big tires. After a couple of minutes of Google searching, we found a community that had those beach chairs to check out. So we identified those communities and actually provided pictures, and we identified the manufacturers of the beach wheelchairs. Something as small as that was really important to the community, and we didn't want to lose it.

We always turn our visions into vision posters so they can be used both for marketing purposes and for people to hang up in their classrooms or in their offices or in their storefront windows to keep these ideas alive. They're very attractive. One of the things that the redevelopment director did was to shrink the vision posters down small enough that they could be rolled up in wine bottles. He put a little bit of sand in the wine bottles and a cork on them, and I think he sent out something like five hundred of them out around the state of Oregon to developers, to key government officials, to all sorts of people who could help him implement. I forget what the note said, but it was something like, "Look at what we're doing at the beach. Come put your feet in the sand for yourself. Come help us implement." And he got a huge turnout.

To this day, this is still the best plan we've ever put together. Before the plan was even unveiled, probably twelve property owners in Taft had already started implementing. They understood the vision so well that they started redoing their buildings. They had banners out on their buildings saying, "We Support Taft Urban Renewal."

They had T-shirts made; they had jackets made. It was crazy. It was a fever. People *knew* they could do it, and they had faith and confidence.

We had money already secured for the entire highway segment re-make before the plan was even unveiled. Because of the partnerships, the bay walk was already lined up to go through permitting through the state—the Department of Fish and Wildlife and the Army Corps of Engineers—before the plan even came off the shelf. People just understood and felt so engaged that things were being implemented even before the plan was issued.

We were done by the summer of 2000, and it was adopted in the fall of 2000. Well, they had adopted the plan but needed to make refinements for the zoning; that was adopted in September or October. At this point, it's been seven years since, and all but one or two of the major implementation items have been implemented. They have just gone gangbusters.

Taft went from being this really economically depressed community to one that still has the mix of incomes and residents. Again, Lincoln City as a whole was about sixty-five hundred people, and Taft represented seven or eight hundred people. But it still has the economic mix of residents. It's gentrified a little bit, but the mobile-home parks are still there, the little cottages that lower-income people lived in are still there—they're still living in them. There certainly has been some gentrification, I can't deny that, but the last I heard, there were twenty new businesses, about seventy new jobs; and there's something like twenty-five or thirty million dollars of reinvestment in public infrastructure that has occurred—and public infrastructure yields private reinvestment. Just incredible success.

Planning was a big part of it, but it was really about extracting and engaging—engaging the community and extracting from them what they want and don't want, informing and educating them on different options, and then letting *them* select. Then, we could provide professional guidance and recommendations. It was about building partnerships; it was about constantly marketing a good project—being positive about it. At the end of the day, it worked.

And now, the urban renewal director is a major hero in the state of Oregon; he's the go-to guy right now. Everyone thinks he walks on water, which he does. He was hired away at the end of that project by the big city of Medford in southern Oregon; they paid him much more than he made in Lincoln City. He stayed there for three years, then he came back home, and he's now the urban renewal director there in Lincoln City again. But now, the guy's a huge hero. We've worked with him now on one, two, three—we're getting ready to do a fourth redevelopment plan. All the subsequent plans have been very different from this first one.

These different projects are all still in Lincoln City but are different in design and different in process, largely because the needs are so different. The village of Taft was really hurting; it was in this incredibly perfect, picturesque, environmentally sensitive spot. It really demanded a community-based approach. A lot of the other districts are auto oriented, or they're solely bedroom residential communities, so they're just very different.

In another village, it's nothing but a vacation-home district, so the owners of the homes are totally disengaged. So Taft was really the hallmark of all the redevelopment projects that they've been undertaking. The other communities are changing, but not to the degree that Taft did. I think Taft, even in my career, was certainly one of four or five projects that I've been involved in that have really had a renaissance-like change.

Getting communities on board is increasingly difficult. In the late nineties, early 2000s, it didn't seem like it was as hard. More recently, especially out here in California, it's because of the extreme commuting, the extreme costs of housing, the pressures put on families. People just don't have the time or aren't taking the time to participate in community-based efforts. They're much more interested in doing a quick internet survey or quick telephone survey than they are able to invest the time, energy, and effort that the folks up in Lincoln City did.

We're going through a process right now, the consulting firm, to figure out what to do, because community-based planning is a hallmark of what we do. We're trying to figure out how we can get the richness of community input, recognizing the lifestyle challenges that our residents have in these communities. That's the challenge of our day.

It's interesting, I would say, that up until maybe even a few months ago, it seemed that social equity was an issue that was pushed *way* down the line. But now, the whole global-warming issue is really raising the triple-bottom-line issue. Social equity is coming up on the radar, and politicians and clients are recognizing that they are going to need to integrate social equity into their policies and plan making. So it's a really exciting time for us, because that's what it's all about for us.

Most of the time, we would pursue social-equity policies or planning ideas in a non-explicit way. We would work with our clients to implement different things that address social equity issues.

We just got a call on Thursday from a small town in the Central Valley of California, a really conservative farming area. The planning director said, "You know, I want you guys to come in and evaluate all that we do so that we can most effectively be recognized as a city that's committed to sustainability." I specifically said, "Triple bottom line with environment, social equity, and economic justice, and economic balance?" He said, "Absolutely. You're right."

Many cities do use it as a marketing tool. They're trying to position themselves economically as a sustainability community. But you know, even if that's the case, as long as the net effect is that social equity results—or greater levels of attention to social-equity issues result—I don't care.

Our firm is part of an engineering company. With this push for sustainability, we very much influence their corporate culture. Now it's an eleven-hundred-person company. About eighty percent of the business that our company does is in land development, and it's in sprawl and subdivisions. We in the Urban Design Studio don't get involved with any of that; we try to pretend that that doesn't even happen. We set up the features and do redevelopment in urban areas. We've been working very hard over the last ten years to get a company position to start refocusing its land development and engineering services on the built environment.

We had a stockholders meeting about a month ago, and there were various developers who were speaking to us who basically said, "Folks, the days of suburban greenfield land development are coming to an end. It's all going to be redevelopment and reuse. You better get with the bandwagon, or you're going to be left behind."

So finally, the message that we've been saying for a long time is up on the radar screens. We've been developing more and more credibility, and definitely now we are influencing the corporate culture.

* * *

I've got a pretty good design background from Cornell and from my undergraduate studies, but I've found that it's my people skills—my ability to come up with ideas, my ability to connect the dots, whatever those dots may be or really are—that has allowed me to become a leader in our group and in the profession. I understand design, and I understand planning. But it's about getting people aligned and showing them the way—but actually, it's letting them show themselves the way.

One resource that I would recommend is NeighborWorks America. I think it's the best organization in the United States for bringing together public and private nonprofit sectors. I teach community economic development and neighborhood revitalization for them. They really get it. I've also received training from NeighborWorks America, and I would recommend their programs.

I'm also a certified main street manager. After I had enough downtown revitalization experience under my belt, I went through the National Trust for Historic Preservation's National Main Street Center. I went through their rigorous training and testing to become a certified main street manager. That was really, really beneficial.

But one of the easy things that I had some training in early on, and that I just refreshed recently, was graphic facilitation, and just how to graphically record people's comments during workshops and meetings. It's visually rich, and they understand how the pieces of what they're saying fit together. A good example is the Grove Consultants International, who are really the founders of graphics facilitation.

I know some folks in DC who used to work for the Grove, but now they're independent consultants. They provide training all the time. But that's one skill that has made a huge return on investment in terms of letting community members understand what they're saying and the implications of what they're saying. Being able to graphically record what they're saying on big pieces of wallpapers and then showing them *how* what they're saying connects with what other people are saying is very, very effective.

* * *

After Cornell, my wife—my girlfriend at the time—who is also a Cornell grad, and I went to San Francisco. We both worked for consulting firms. Then, after two and a half years, I took off and became a VISTA volunteer in Alaska and worked with native rural Alaskans.

I didn't work explicitly as a planner; it was largely geared to recognizing that the forty million acres of native Alaskan land was largely not managed by native Alaskans. So my job was to get apprenticeship opportunities for high school native youth in resource positions, with the thought being that if they enjoyed that, then we would raise some money to give them scholarships, to get degrees, and then they would go back to their homelands and manage their tribal lands. It was a very meaningful VISTA experience.

After that, I wanted to work for a city. I went down to Phoenix; I worked for the Phoenix city planning office for a few years, and I did all kinds of interesting things in the central area of Phoenix. I realized how badly most city governments deal with inner-city issues. From there, my wife and I decided we were not going to do this long-distance thing, and we hooked up back in Southern California, where we could be closer to her family and my family.

3

"Absolutely Not. That's Public Space, So Nobody Can Use It"

Mark Lakeman's Practice Story

Editor's Preface

Mark Lakeman asks us to take a fresh look at the spaces we've been accustomed to seeing every day. If plazas and piazzas are really meeting places—quite literally intersections of flows of people coming and going—then shouldn't we see the intersections all around us as potential plazas, potential piazzas and meeting places? Lakeman's work in Portland, Oregon, wove together this reimagining of space and place with community building and conviviality.

Mark Lakeman worked with neighbors and local residents to reclaim their streets, street corners, and at times even intersections, sometimes painting them, sometimes adorning them with street furniture. His efforts involved design and aesthetics no more or less than community development and organizing, engaging public authorities and citizen constituencies to see their own spaces as potentially new places. Lakeman brought an earlier design training to suggest that urban design was too important to leave entirely to the narrower conventions of planners, architects, and other professional designers.

Designing Again in a Totally Different Way

Both of my parents are architects and planners, and they both had East Coast, Ivy League–type educations. So I was indoctrinated into the elite culture of design practice. It's important to mention that at the beginning, because I'm *not* doing that anymore, by choice.

With that kind of background, there's a very strong emphasis on what things look like, and there's a high level of awareness that architecture is relevant to culture and cultural development. But there's a really underdeveloped awareness about how it might relate to things like cultural development connected to social justice or democracy when you're building. There's a very limited understanding, generally, about how to engage people in a creative process in a way that leads to successful projects.

There's just such a strong aesthetic bias in architecture and planning that a lot of people aren't attracted to working with communities, because theoretically, it doesn't lead to anything very exciting or interesting. So I had to move through that kind of bias at the start of my education.

Early Design Thinking and the Roots of City Repair

I studied architecture at the University of Oregon, a good local school with the virtue of being pretty balanced. It's got a really strong ecological-design aspect as well as design theory; it's just got a broad spectrum.

I did work in large corporate offices for several years, and I was there long enough to confirm the things I had been told by my parents about the compromises of the profession. When you're chasing notoriety or when you're trying to become published, you don't end up taking risks or even taking initiative; mostly, you're just taking work that developers bring you. The reason I'm going on about that is because I had to abandon that; I had to walk away from conventional practice in order to strike out on my own and figure out how I wanted to do things.

Fortunately for me, something really outrageous happened one day at the end of my employment with a certain office. It was a disclosure by one of our clients that they had been routinely and brazenly covering up toxic-waste situations—paying off inspectors—and they were just kind of laughing that they were doing this. It was during a meeting, and there were a lot of people, and the vice president of the biggest construction company in the state was joking about how they pay off inspectors, and I decided I would quit that day and walk away.

I ended up traveling for something like seven years, going from one culture to the next. I went back to school, in a way. I wanted to look at settlement patterns and cultural development and how that relates to place and the spatial expression of culture. So I went from one place to the next, trying to peel back the layers of time, until I ended up living with a group of pre-industrial people. I just wanted to see, when people aren't colonized or dominated by an ideology, how they behave with each other in terms of creating a sense of home, and then how they draw boundaries between themselves. What I learned eventually was quite enough to bring back to the modern context and start experimenting. That's what City Repair came from—bringing those patterns back into the modern city that is so removed from a lot of patterns of basic human nature.

People don't like to draw lines between each other, and yet that's what the city is all about. What I've seen over and over in different cultures is that they're not interested in treating the world as if it's for sale, and yet that's driving modern American life. So the idea of City Repair was to question things: What is democracy? What are the potential benefits of participation? Does it really matter what something looks like, or does it matter more that someone has a sense of ownership of it? Then there were all these ecological questions, too: What, fundamentally, is the most sustainable way of creating things? What is the basis of a sustainable economy? So I got great answers to those questions and so many more. When I came back to Portland in 1995, I was ready to start designing again, but in a totally different way.

When I came back, I realized that the neighborhood that I had lived in all my life was never created by the neighbors themselves. That neighborhood was Sellwood, but it's true of virtually every American neighborhood, especially everything west of the East Coast. For example, take the Portland suburb of Gresham. It was created by developers and to some extent by politicians. In Gresham, there's not one single housing tract where any group of neighbors ever said, "How about if we lay out the pathways or the roadways like this? How about if we orient our public spaces so we can look at Mount Hood?" There was never *ever* a dialogue like that.

So when I came back from traveling and visiting all these indigenous societies, I knew that there were gathering places in the lands of my own ancestors and everyone else's ancestors for millennia, and that in Sellwood, where I had lived all of my life, there weren't. There wasn't even a park that a kid could get to in my part of the neighborhood without crossing a busy street. But I grew up thinking development was normal and that was just the way the world works.

But when I came back, I realized, "Oh my God! There are meeting houses, there are public squares that are all missing." As I walk through my own neighborhood, there's nowhere to sit. Yet in the villages I visited, there were places everywhere for people to come together and get to know each other.

City Repair began with a series of interventions—to do something where you wouldn't expect it. I was involved in those; I didn't really care to wait around and get permission anymore from authorities.

The first thing we built was a teahouse, and it was built in a pretty typical American neighborhood in southeast Portland, where I had lived since about 1974. It was a community gathering place. It was, in a way, modeled after the rainforest people whom I had visited, who were actually Mayan. It was a bit like a Mayan meeting house, a bit like a British teahouse; all these different places I had visited I pieced together into one kind of architecture. I knew that it would work to bring people together because I had come to realize that type of space was missing. It's just simply missing. If neighbors had a month and a half, or even less, of actually having time on their hands, one of the first things they would do is start to build a cultural landscape that reflects their needs.

Fundamentally, we have this idea of freedom of assembly, but in American neighborhoods, typically, there is nowhere to assemble. If you do want to meet, you'd have to believe in Christianity or something in order to gather at a church. There aren't places, like on the East Coast, where there are many small towns on the Eastern Seaboard that still have village halls and places like that. So the idea of freedom of assembly is that you need a place to assemble, and it's not just something that's written in the Constitution; you need it because it's your nature to have it.

So I built a teahouse, and it brought together thousands of people. All across the city of Portland, but especially in the Sellwood neighborhood, all these people came together, and they started to realize all of these issues having to do with place, most fundamentally that there aren't these kinds of gathering places that are creative and open, that you can access without having to buy something, as you must just to have a seat in a restaurant—just a place that you can identify with, that any kid can go to and know that they'll find a friend or a grandmother there.

Share-It Square: The First Intersection Repair

That little teahouse led to the first intersection repair. It was in Sellwood, half a block from that teahouse. It was a case of all those neighbors who had been connected by the teahouse going out into the intersection of SE 9th and Sherrett and converting the intersection into a village square. This, again, was an intervention.

When we were doing this teahouse project and we had built the capacity to take this idea into the larger neighborhood, the next thing to do, naturally, was to take it into public space. The idea was to take patterns of sustainable villages that are planet-wide and insert them into the development of westward expansion; again, the idea was that this was missing, and if we brought it back, then it would have a restorative effect and all these people would start to know each other again.

The idea first came about from my mother, who first brought that awareness to me. She had taken me to Europe after I graduated from architecture school. She was a teacher in Southern California, and she would take groups of California kids to Europe to do projects in villages so that they could learn about the cultural role that the public commons plays.

If you grow up in California, you think of a street as a place for cars, but by going to other countries, you can learn about the idea that the pathway is a public cultural continuance, not just a roadway. So I learned from her and her extensive studies over something like three decades. I learned from her about the idea that the piazza is most fundamentally an intersection.

I introduced the idea to the community. I try not to talk about that too much, but that's the truth. If I talk about it in a way that's too self-referential, people don't have a sense of ownership. This is an ancient idea that everyone owns. We just simply said, "Look at villages and the way the intersections are piazzas; they're plazas." In every language, there's a word for intersection as gathering place; in French it's *place*, in German, it's *Platz*. There's a corresponding word for place, and they have to do with intersections in village cultures around the world.

And I said, "Oh my God! Look at the intersection. It's a void."

So it was really very simple. We just said, "We will put back what should have occurred if not for the fact that developers don't really have any cultural training and don't care."

We installed concentric rings of color on the street; we were trying to create a focusing effect, visually, so there would be a united effect rather than a divided effect. Normally, you look at an intersection, and you don't perceive anything there, so we were trying to create a sense of "there" there. Where in a piazza you would have a very strong sense of defined space with the architecture around the perimeter, the walls of the buildings defining the form of the exterior space, we decided to put little interactive, functional sculptures on all four corners of the intersection that would offer the kind of functions that a village heart, or the center of a village, would offer.

Let's say you go to an Italian village. You'll find a bookshop, a café, a marketplace, cultural institutions, places to sit. So what we did in our first version there was to put in a community chalkboard; that was very simple and crude, but it was a place for people to write poetry and put up messages. Then there was a trading station where people could put out old toys or shoes or jeans or whatever they wanted to, even vegetables or something. On another corner, there was a place for books, for people to just give away books or to take books, to borrow or donate books.

Then there was a place we called the twenty-four-hour tea station, and that was in lieu of having a café. On the other corner, we built a kids' clubhouse, and also a chalk dispenser for kids to be able to draw on the sidewalks.

Every good piazza has a very strong open space that does not have a public monument in it so that people can gather and speak and dance without dodging a sculpture or something. Then around the edge of the space, there are active edges with activities that compel people or attract them to the space. With this in place, these kinds of amenities, this is really how human culture came together and sustained itself over time. So we were saying this would be an attractive node that would just help people to build community simply by wanting to come here.

But before we actually painted the street, we went downtown, and we said to the Portland Department of Transportation, "We would like to present an idea to you. It will slow traffic, raise visibility, make the streets safer, and all these good things that benefit the people that live right here."

They said, "Absolutely not. That's never been done before. Besides, that's public space, so nobody can use it."

We asked, "Wait a second, did you hear what you just said?!"

So we did try to work with them before we actually did it without their permission. We didn't want to be troublemakers, and we certainly weren't interested in getting in trouble. But we realized that we had engaged the issue in a way that was probably beyond their training as traffic engineers.

So we went ahead and did this illegally. At first, it was pretty simple. We had this idea, and we just started off by building a few of the things on the corners before we actually painted the street. We built the tea station, and we built the place for chalk, and we built the chalkboard and the little library and things like that.

That was all easy, because the neighbors just said yes. I knew that what we were doing was illegal, because you're not allowed to put things on the grass in the space between the sidewalk and the street. You can plant a tree or you can plant some bushes, but you can't do anything in the way of erecting a structure; that's not allowed. But from my architecture and planning background, and also my time in villages, I knew a couple of things. I knew it was essential to have active edges to the public commons. I also knew that in villages, authority is localized so they can decide for themselves what they can or can't do. But in American neighborhoods, your authority is not localized—it's held by people whom you probably have never met. In Portland, it was held by the mayor and the city council. They ultimately have a say over what every other person can do, especially in the commons. So I knew that creative local civil disobedience was the only way to take the issue forward.

The rest of the neighbors just thought, "Oh, this is fun. We never thought of that." But they also never realized that they couldn't do such things. We built all these things on the corners, and then on September 8 of 1996, we painted the street and had a big block party, and all these folk musicians came. We had this fabulous event. And then the next day, we were in trouble. The Transportation Department heard about it, and they said that we couldn't do it. They issued threatening letters to all the neighbors on the corners. They said, "If you don't remove all these things, you will all have to pay something like a thousand dollars a month or twenty-five dollars a day," or something like that.

Half the structures were removed, and half of them weren't. We had to fall back a little bit, but that was OK because we kept at it, and we were very persistent, until finally we were able to give a presentation to the city council.

Along with two other neighbors, a young woman and a young man, I presented before the city council. In part, we simply presented what we had done. We had nice pictures of the corner stuff and the painted graphic, and we showed the people at work on the day that we painted and that we were out singing and dancing. As I recall, we presented aerial views of villages; we highlighted intersections. We showed the town of Siena because my mother has documented that one extensively. We had a count of the number of outdoor gathering places, and then we pulled something off the internet about their low crime rates. The most persuasive thing was just showing them Portland neighbors recreating in the commons and obviously having a good time doing it.

We held up the golden objectives of the city for neighborhoods, like slowing traffic. We showed them our goals and objectives as a city. We laid a sheet of paper in front of them, and then we gave a visual presentation.

We said, "This is how we are meeting these goals, how we're slowing traffic, and this is how we're making the streets safer for kids and women, how we intend to make sure that the neighborhood is cleaner."

They could see the evidence that we were meeting all of these goals and that we didn't need any city money; we didn't need any work from them. But then we also showed views of the Italian villages, and the crime rates that they were experiencing as opposed to American neighborhoods, and they were just amazed—they almost couldn't believe it. The city council didn't even let us finish our presentation—they became so animated—and within a short period of time, the city actually passed an ordinance that lets people convert street intersections into public squares.

It helped that I coordinated the presentation, because I had a professional background in design and planning. Another bit of the story is that my father was the founder of the urban design division of the

Portland Department of Planning and Urban Development. So when I went in there, people knew that I was connected to my father and that I probably knew what I was talking about.

But when I went in there—this is a sort of funny thing—I went in there looking as much like a professor as I could. I even wore fake theater glasses. I had square glasses, but I went out and bought these little, round, kind of Le Corbusieran-looking theater glasses and wore those—as when, for example, sometimes a professor is talking and they'll take their glasses off and chew on the plastic—just to try to seem as smart as I could. That helped with the presentation.

After the presentation, it went to the council for the vote, and they voted unanimously to legalize the project and to turn it into a precedent for the city. This was in early 1997. So that was great news.

But then, some opponents stood up and started to complain. I mean that they called in; they wrote letters to the city council to try to get them to rescind their decision.

It might have been six months or so after the ordinance passed, and we found out that these people in the condominiums down the river were upset, and they had contacted the city council and said, "We want you to revisit your decision. It was too hasty, you haven't included our voices."

None of us had thought that they cared, because mostly, they would drive so quickly through the neighborhood and never seemed to care what happened there. So suddenly, they were saying it was their neighborhood too.

There was a polarization; people got mad at each other. I felt at the time that there was a lot of value in getting mad—it would give the neighbors some practice in feeling their power. Ordinarily, I really like to bring people together to be nice to each other. But in the case of the neighborhood residents, as opposed to the condo residents, the neighborhood residents had rarely had a sense of power in their lives. They hadn't participated in public-involvement processes; they hadn't much experience with public speaking or anything like that. They really didn't know how the city worked. So the idea of people being mad at each other was just fine at first.

In fact, I was mad, too. How dare these people who live behind closed gates, who have pools and spas and things, how dare they tell these lower-income people, who don't even have a park much less anywhere else, "No." How dare they tell them what they can and can't do.

The anger charged people up and helped them to get off their couches and go to public meetings and hear the things that were being said by the condo owners. The condo owners were saying, "This is compromising property values. It's embarrassing for our visitors."

The condo owners were very conspicuous in their wealth; they were wearing pearls and very nice clothes. The people from the lower-income neighborhood were witnessing this, and they were realizing that these people were saying that the thing we had created was an embarrassment. And the neighborhood people *knew* that it wasn't lowering property values. Then they realized that these other people were being dishonest. That was very motivational for them, because then they went out and organized the rest of their neighbors; they felt that something unfair was happening. That motivated them to get more involved, to become more passionate, to speak up for the thing that they cared about. People who had never done any public speaking, and even people who didn't care that much about the project, definitely knew one thing: the wealthy people they were exposed to in their lives were mostly their own bosses, and here was their chance to actually stand up and oppose that kind of power and feel a sense of power. The project ended up being propelled a bit by long-standing issues that were already in the community—internal and external resentment—but it ended up being creatively focused.

The beautiful thing is that at the end of the process, most everyone had shifted, and the neighborhood had learned a lot. None of them was interested in excluding anybody; that's the nice thing about most neighborhoods—that they're pretty inclusive and open. We took the constructive ideas of the condo owners and used those ideas to kind of uplift and modify the project. We changed the paint scheme on the street, we upgraded the structures on the corners, and we started to get compliments from some of the people who had previously been opposed.

The situation we had before was terrible: the condo owners speeding through the neighborhood and almost hitting kids. What we ended up with—through what I call an intervention—is that suddenly, these people who would just speed through the neighborhood suddenly had contact with it, and suddenly, we were creatively engaged in this process and ended up building relations with them that hadn't existed before.

One of the things that came out of all this was that we realized that one of the biggest problems was connected to the very issue we were addressing: we simply had nothing in common—or so we thought. We did not have an active commons, and once we engaged in the commons, we created a common dialogue that led to a stronger common culture.

Even the conflict with the condo owners eventually helped create a more cohesive community. It ended up involving people throughout the entire Sellwood neighborhood. Most people developed a sense of pride in the project. Even if they weren't involved in that controversy, once the news got out and the newspaper was reporting things, then people started to decide how they felt about it, and almost everyone was supportive.

In the beginning, there was a group of people that had become connected through that teahouse, and I think in the teahouse, enough of us were talking about this idea that we realized there were a lot of people who were excited about it. We also knew that we really couldn't tell the entire neighborhood. It was going to be kind of polarizing, and if we tried to get agreement on it before anyone had ever seen such a thing, we probably wouldn't be able to move it ahead.

Because we lived in the neighborhood and we knew the culture, I think we all felt collectively very strongly that once people saw what we were talking about, they would love it. We also knew our hearts well enough that we really weren't interested in getting away with a prank or hurting anyone. I think we were also flexible enough to change it if necessary.

The initial group of people was something like six to eight—maybe ten—families. We would meet at a house near the intersection. We were having fun with it. We thought, "Well, we're gonna do a revolution here." So we would have tea parties and talk about what we were going to do. It was a very collaborative process. We decided there what things would look like and how they would work and who would do what.

I brought plans of the intersection. I drew up the dimensions of the intersection, and I located trees and where the houses were and what they looked like, and I brought that to a meeting for us to discuss. I think I did bring a suggested design because I had something in mind, but that was never what we did, because a lot of other ideas were offered. The one that was most popular, that we discussed altogether, was the one that we decided to do—that had been proposed by my friend Robert.

So initially, this was a collaboration between those six, eight, or ten families, but on the day of the intersection painting, all the other neighbors were involved. We put out the word, and all these people came. We flyered the neighborhood, used a lot of word of mouth, and we also knew that as we were painting, people who normally went through the intersection would see that something was going on and probably jump in with us.

What's interesting is that nobody seemed to even ask or to realize that what we were doing at first was illegal. It was just fascinating to watch. I mean, people just walked right up in glee and wanted to join in. I stood there; it was an epiphany for me. My heart was full, and I was watching these people do this, and I was saying to myself, "This is our birthright. It's our birthright to do this creative collaboration in the commons. It's the commons, after all." It was amazing that nobody seemed to be scared of doing the idea, they all just stuck to it so naturally that I thought surely this must be natural for us to do.

Before painting the intersection, though, we had to get consent from the neighbors on all four corners. All of them had come to the teahouse except one. He was very reclusive, but we managed to get his support—we just sort of showed him what we wanted to do.

Well, that was a funny story. At first, I went over to his house, and I said, "Hey Brian, we have this really cool idea. We'd like to plant some sunflowers and flowers on your corner and paint these circles in the street and put this little self-service library on your corner," and he kind of looked at us like we were crazy.

He was a pretty large, auto-mechanic guy, and he said, "No way! Go away. Don't come back." So I went back diagonally across the street to the house where I lived—I lived on the northwest corner—and this young woman, a friend of mine named Emily, was there waiting for me on the porch to find out how it went.

She asked, "How did it go?"

I told her. She was just outrageously beautiful—and very confident, sort of like a European model. She also understood something of her power with men, as a woman.

So she said, "I'll handle this."

She went across the street in a bikini, knocked on his door, and she just kinda talked to him, and then she came back and she said, "It's fine."

Brian came out of his shell, and he became a public speaker. He stood up to the condo owners, and he went to the city council. I'm sure he struggled in school all of his life, but he became an eloquent and passionate public speaker. At one point, though, after a few years, he said to us all at a potluck, "You know that thing that happened one time when Emily came over? I know what you guys did, and I'm really glad you guys did it, but don't ever do it again," and everybody laughed.

* * *

Since then, the *American Journal of Public Health* has published articles on the intersection repairs in Portland. It's been established that crime, at least at the ones that have been studied, has lowered ten percent, and that mental and physical health has increased by measurable amounts.

I didn't know exactly what all the effects would be, but I figured if we're experiencing isolation because of an absence of place and we have all this violence endemic to the culture, then by changing important broad patterns and going from a kind of "no-place" to a place, we're probably going to see a lot of sociological and physiological effects. That's what I pretty much figured from the start. But I didn't know exactly how it would work. This was corroboration of the power of the premise of all this work—that it would literally come down to these measurable effects. What place making does for communities is give you a place for the social culture to actually start to weave together. What it did for this neighborhood, to create that gathering place, was that it brought back the place that it was missing and enabled people to connect with each other to build new relationships.

Surveys found after the fact that people actually perceived the world differently. They said that they felt safer, that their world, their neighborhood, had become a safer place. They felt that the neighborhood was becoming a more sustainable place. A lot of this just has to do with perception. Nothing had changed, and yet they felt less fearful because they knew the people around them; they were coming out of their isolation.

So there's increased friendship, definitely more community cohesion, higher quality of life, a sense of belonging, and just all the good things that come from living with a sense of community as opposed to isolation.

Probably every American city has the exact same goals and objectives as Portland's basic community-development objectives. But Portland is unique in a certain way in the sense that we're ahead of the curve in knowing that citizen participation is key to everything.

If you have a group of specialists in charge of the society but whose range of life experiences is limited to their own, they won't know how to solve people's local problems. Every person, even a homeless person, is the only one who really understands their own challenges. So getting them involved so that they can have the power to take those challenges and turn them into opportunities—that's the key.

That's why the word *democracy* has meaning to us, because it means that we have a voice and we have power. The thing about design and planning—design tools and planning, short- and long-term planning—these are the tools that enable a democracy to function. But in order for it to function, you have to have participation, and there has to be literacy in the population around *how* to design, *how* to plan. If it's only in the realm of specialists, then the rest of the society isn't equipped to do the analysis of a context, to understand their economy.

In Portland, we're super participation-heavy. It's only getting stronger and stronger all the time. But this is the way that every city probably has to be if we're going to be a sustainable society. You've got millions of people with these ideas, and if they don't learn how to express them, then you're not tapping into this inexhaustible well of power and creativity. That's opposed to the way I used to think, which is that the architect knows best, and if only those clients would just be quiet. But now I know better.

Now I know that I will have a better time, the project will get better, I'll end up with friends, and I'll also get more awesome jobs if I will have a creative party with these people, enjoying ourselves through the process. At the end of it, they will all know more about design that they can take into their lives, whether they're cooking something or making a party happen or formulating a new way of doing something at school or where they work. Explaining those creative tools is the job that I have now as an architect. Being the creative facilitator is really the role. It's not to be a creative dominator; it's to be a facilitator.

To create an environment that fosters high involvement and creativity, the main thing to focus on is having fun. It sounds like a big revelation, but in design and planning school, we're taught about ideas and theories, but we rarely sit down together and have tea or cookies; we *can* just sit down and have food together. But the thing that brings us together, in a way where we really care about each other and listen to each other is when we sit down and have some kind of cultural ritual, like sharing food. The key to all of this work, the key to building City Repair itself as a social culture, was to always come together around celebration and food, to prepare ourselves in the process to be whimsical. After having fun, the collaboration and participation just came naturally.

If you don't have enough money to pay people to do things, then they have to volunteer. But they're only going to come back and volunteer if it's enjoyable, if it's meaningful, if it's rewarding. For all the investment and time that people put into this work, if there isn't pay for people, there has to be something. It just so happens, very beautifully, that the basis of a sustainable society, a bioregional economy, begins by building relationships between people and places. Building a relationship of interdependence relies on a sense of connection, and that happens through fun and celebration. So we were on the right track—we were building a bioregional economy without even knowing it.

Here's the really important thing. From the very beginning, when I came back from those village cultures, I had learned a lot about what a partner society, in which women and men have more equality between them, is like. When I came back, I looked at our culture. I came back to Oregon and I felt, "Oh, my God. I finally understand."

Everything around me was designed mostly by men between the ages of thirty-five and sixty—the economy, the impact on the ecology, the entire physical environment that I see, most of the colors that I see. Most of the vegetation was probably planted by women, but almost everything else I saw around me was the vision of the men. It doesn't reflect women. So it was, How do you save the world? How do you evolve the society? You've got to enable a partnership mentality. That would mean more fun. A broader spectrum of emotions would be expressed. With white men between thirty-five and sixty, it's mostly so serious.

But for everybody else, it's beauty, love, a sense of humor, irony, metaphor, all of these things that really don't get employed in the skills in the world of design. Even in green architecture, it's serious, but with a smaller CO_2 output or something.

At the start, I knew that there would be all these things going on that I couldn't foresee. I think mostly, I was just delighted by everything that happened. I tried not to have too many expectations.

I think the condo owners were the big surprise. One of them said, "Oh my God! It's so dangerous. The intersection's clogged with children at seven o'clock in the morning. How can you drive through it without hitting a kid?" That was so untrue. Or the idea that someone would claim property values were more important than community development— that was pretty surprising to me. I can't relate to that kind of value. To me, embracing that mindset would be like committing suicide. I couldn't ever go there.

There's this principle that I think is important for everyone to learn: you're your own worst enemy and ultimately your own biggest challenge—you stand to get in your own way. I mean, even though we were fighting with these condo owners, the thing that's been most difficult over the years at City Repair has been our own internal culture. We talked about changing the world, but for a lot of people, it's news to them that they have to change themselves as well.

I think that's true for me, too. I've known that—in words, I know that—but it's figuring out how. My wife was saying to me yesterday that as the leader of this stuff, I'm the one who has to change the most; I'm the one who has to be the most patient, basically like a saint. Even when people project stuff onto to me, it's my job to stand there and model sustainability in my behavior and listen to them even if it's unfair. Even if they're horrible to me, I have to stand there and weather the storm. I wish I would have known that more in advance. Maybe I wouldn't have even wanted to do any of this—because it's just painful sometimes!

But the main thing is that the benefits of this work far outweigh anything negative about it. It changed my life in every single way: as a designer, as an architect, as a planner. Before, I would dream of just working with people who were respectful, and I would hope to do things that were relevant to the culture, and now, I'm overwhelmed with things that are coming at me where people want what I have to give. Being treated with respect—I don't even have to think about it at all anymore; it's just the way it is. There's just no end of creative collaborations that are possible, and that's just because I started to follow my own dreams.

But the most negative things have just been really the interpersonal difficulties and how, sometimes, perfectly wonderful friendships can be lost because of a meltdown. Just when someone gets so stressed out by something, they take on more than they can handle. We have to help each other and support each other, and when somebody is really distressed, it's time for some really direct communication, even if it's tough love.

We've all probably seen this over and over again. People avoid conflict. If someone's pissing them off or has hurt their feelings, they would rather avoid them than speak to them directly. Some people would rather give up friendships than deal with the hard stuff of telling that person how they really feel. So I think that there are a lot of patterns that Americans in particular have to relearn, because we are so out of touch.

That has to do with things like continuing to care about other people in spite of disagreements you get into, saying to them the things that you feel and the things you think they need to hear, but in a way where you're really careful—so that they can hear you, and you're not attacking them, but you're saying it in a loving way. These skills take a while to acquaint ourselves with, but they're very important. Those are the kinds of things I wish I would have known more about at the start.

I have played many roles in this process. I'm still quite youthful, but I'm also something of a granddaddy in a way. Most people that are involved in activism are in their twenties. So I'm kind of like a role model and kind of like a mentor, like a teacher, but I'm not comfortable with that, so I'm more like a brother and sometimes a father. But I'm a punching bag, too, it seems.

I'll have an interaction with someone, and I'll kind of wonder, "Are they thinking I'm like their high school principal or something? Because that didn't really feel comfortable, and I don't know where that interaction is coming from." Maybe they're thinking I'm some kind of authoritarian.

A lot of times, I feel like people have expectations. I don't really feel like they're interacting with me as who I am being present with them. I'll come to the table, and even if I'm working with kids, I'll think of us as equals. But because I'm pretty well known in the community, I'll sit down with someone—and particularly this is true of other males—and there's this competitive energy. Or they won't really want to look at me, and it feels like maybe they're intimidated or something.

So I will have to do a little bit of work to reassure them that I'm not trying to be dominant, or I'm not interested in their girlfriend, or something like that. There's just a real strong tendency that people have—to project their fears. I have to do a lot of work on that. I never even realized this at the start. This is the sort of stuff I wish I had known in advance.

The best way to overcome those situations, frankly, is to listen and listen and listen, and not react, not get defensive. I'm not always so good at it. Sometimes, it's flat out unfair. But the best thing is to just listen and be as sure as I possibly can be that they feel comfortable that I have heard them, and maybe wait for another time to create clarity or to get to have my say.

4

Bridging Minnesota and Wisconsin with Twenty-Eight Stakeholders

Michael Hughes's Practice Story

Editor's Preface

This case involves a place-making conflict that had gone on for thirty years. Environmentalists were pitted against transportation engineers and economic-development interests. Historic preservation advocates fought to protect a historic, even iconic bridge across the St. Croix River separating Minnesota and Wisconsin. Local, state, and federal officials were all involved, with any one agency not always knowing what the others were doing.

Mike Hughes brought a training in land-use planning to his early involvement in mediating environmental conflicts. He was no stranger to multiparty negotiations, including those involving race and ethnicity, public health, and community and economic development. Here he faced the challenge of negotiating his own breathing room as he worked to design and carry out a process giving twenty-eight significant stakeholders voice and information, design and decision-making power. If ever there was a story about managing conflicts between engineering and design sensibilities, this is it.

Once It Could Be Wonderful, It Could Be Possible

I came to mediation work while I was working in local government, in a planning department for a county. The county commissioners were wrestling with a significant increase in applications for sand and gravel mining, and those were kind of new to the county. The county had no mineral extraction plan or regulations.

This was in Colorado, in the county between Denver and Colorado Springs. The county commissioners declared a moratorium, and they put in one room all the people who had been yelling at them—either to open the county to sand and gravel mining or to close the county to sand and gravel mining. Then they got two mediators whose organization had been leading a minerals roundtable, locally, for the adjacent towns. I was supposed to write the mineral-extraction plan and put the county regs in place—to codify things in draft. The mediators were supposed to keep the peace and make things go.

We got a draft plan, we got a county policy, and then there was one hearing at the planning commission, and no one spoke in opposition. That was great, because I was essentially the client.

So I would meet with the mediators to discuss their agenda and approach and to prepare the technical information. We'd distribute the agenda and the technical information in advance, and we would meet for dinner right before the evening task-force meeting to talk strategy and make sure we were all ready. Then we would go into the meeting, and I typed and did the meeting summary. I got insight into their strategy, and we became friends. They finished the project, and as soon as the contract was done and the last person was paid, I thought, "OK, I'm no longer your client. Here's my résumé."

I went to work somewhere else, because they didn't hire me. But they did say that to get into the field, you needed to be trained. So I took their training, and then a year and a half later, they hired me when I wouldn't stop asking for a job. That's now twenty years ago, almost twenty-one, and I've been mediating and doing a range of public policy/public mediation ever since.[1]

So let's go to this case. The St. Croix River crossing was placed on a White House list of thirteen high-priority transportation projects for what was called then, in the Department of Transportation, "environmental streamlining." These were thirteen projects that had been dead in the water. People had been trying to get these roads built, or projects done, for a long time. They had been stalled in one way, shape, or form, and the top thirteen got vetted and put on a list, and the White House produced the list. This was the first term of the second Bush—George W's first term.

Then the Department of Transportation started to figure out how it was going to break these deadlocks and move forward on all thirteen of these projects, and they moved them in different ways. One of them—or *at least* one of them—was slated for a conflict assessment through the US Institute for Environmental Conflict Resolution [ECR].

A staff member at ECR hired a former transportation commissioner from Massachusetts, I think, to help him with the assessment. The two of them wrote an assessment on the St. Croix River crossing, and they published a report called *One River, Two Bridges.*

In that report, among the many findings was the need for two separate collaborative processes, run by a hired mediator, and a recommendation that the mediator should be selected through the ECR roster. That recommendation went forward, and federal money was allocated to the two states of Minnesota and Wisconsin to work with ECR to hire a mediator to start that process.

That conflict assessment was to identify the reasons for the conflict: What are the underlying issues that are keeping this problem alive, that are keeping people from settling it? That's mostly done by reviewing the background information—What's the history of this conflict in its written form?—*and* asking, What are the perspectives of the key stakeholders?

So there's analysis of the documents—there was a whole pile of NEPA [National Environmental Policy Act] documents that had been generated, for example. But also, there were interviews with key stakeholders to be done: the two secretaries of transportation for the two states, their lead staff people, and then key stakeholders who had been battling with each other, or suing the state, or in some other way engaging directly in the conflict over this question of the two bridges.

For example, there was the Minnesota Center for Environmental Advocacy and the Sierra Club; on the environmental side, those were the two most active. There was a set of preservation organizations that were mostly interested in one of the two bridges, because there was an existing bridge on the National Register of Historic Places, and there was a historic landmark district. So historic-preservation organizations—locally, statewide, and nationally—were part of that stakeholder group.

There were also transportation advocates, economic development people, people who had been weighing-in either for or against a new bridge and for or against different options for what to do with the existing one. All the local governments were there. Minnesota has a requirement for local concurrence for transportation projects, which meant that local governments had to essentially sign on to state-funded transportation projects running through their jurisdiction. So local governments were part of that as well.

The idea of assessment is to interview the stakeholders, or the people who have claimed some interest in this question or set of questions, and then to sort out what their perspectives are, what their needs are, why they are concerning themselves with this set of issues, and what they hope for.

The title of their conflict assessment was *One River, Two Bridges.* They did not answer the question about whether or not there would be a second bridge. What they said was that there should be two processes: one to sort out whether to build a new bridge, and one to sort out the future of the existing bridge. It said that there was a conflict over these things, here's the nature of the conflict, these are the people who have attached themselves to that conflict, and processes of consensus building and conflict resolution should be used to get answers to the "whether" question for both bridges.

We offered our services as the mediators for both of those processes, which were bundled together. Both processes were expected to be led by a single mediation team. So we responded to a request for proposal, and we were short-listed by the institute. They short-listed us, but then the stakeholders interviewed the three short-listed teams.

I was at RESOLVE at the time, and Robert Fisher and I were the two who were interviewed. Robert Fisher was a senior mediator with RESOLVE in the DC office and an attorney at the Department of the Interior, in the Office of Conflict Assessment and Dispute Resolution.

Robert and I were two senior mediators, and we told them that we had administrative and associate level support, that we had behind us—though not in the interview—a team of people who could handle contracting and note-taking and all the administrative and contractual tasks. But Robert and I would be the two lead mediators, and we would presume to each lead one group or the other and to work together as co-facilitators, depending on how the stakeholders ultimately wanted to set it up.

The competition was formidable. I'll confess that one of the three finalists was, in fact, the guy who wrote the assessment, a former commissioner from Massachusetts whose name escapes me now. He joined with others to create a team, I think, but he was essentially the lead mediator or would have been. The second team was Howard Bellman and Louise Smart. Louise Smart was the mediator in the Douglass County mineral extraction mediation, and she had been my mentor there. So that was the competition.

It turned out to be a two-horse race because the stakeholders—although we didn't know it at the time—had not liked the assessment report. I'll come to that in a minute, because it formed a major part of what we did. But that report, *One River, Two Bridges*, was not embraced by the stakeholders. So despite the fact that its author had been short-listed and got an interview, he was never going to be selected as the mediator because of that.

So it was between Louise and Howard and Robert and me, and I discovered only much later, once we had the project, what had happened. I asked people in meeting five or six or somewhere, in some casual conversation over a year later or so, "How did you not take Louise and Howard? I mean, given their reputations, given Louise's transportation experience—she was senior to me, and Howard is senior to everybody—how could you not choose them?" Howard was very accomplished, formidable, and we had watched them go into their interview. So we were like, "Oh my God! We have to follow Howard Bellman!"

The answer was, we seemed to have so much more energy and stamina, and we seemed more optimistic, and in the face of what they thought was an intractable conflict, we didn't seem like people who would give up. That's what carried the day. It was a conflict that seemed intractable to them, but we thought we could really make a difference there.

The only thing that we had to go on was the report, which said it was a very solvable kind of problem. These were the key interests, and these were the things that had been done that had gotten tangled up. There was so much at stake here environmentally, and in terms of historic preservation and in terms of transportation needs, that an answer needed to be found. Their report had said that the urgency of the problem required that some solution be crafted, and people thought that it was so urgent that people could do it. I think that people also believed that being placed on the list of thirteen would create a very different approach in Washington, DC, and in fact it did. Federal agencies that had been taking opposing positions were now feeling compelled under one administration to break their own federal-level disagreements about Section 106 and historic preservation, about NEPA, and about the environmental issues.

Because this involved a designated wild and scenic river, the National Park Service had the responsibility, under the Wild and Scenic River Act. They and the transportation agencies had fought over this, and the thought was, if you break the federal deadlock, the local stakeholders will come together and find answers that could work for this place. But although the report had suggested it was solvable, the report was then rejected by the stakeholders.

So we were selected, and we wrote a scope of work that presumed a very, very short introductory period—not really what I would call a convening, but an introductory period where we would have very short conversations with each of the identified stakeholders and then launch into a first meeting, presuming that situation assessment had in fact served as an effective convening and that we would step right in and start going forward.

That was our proposal. But six months later, we hadn't had the first meeting!

What went wrong? Well, the proposal was based on the premise that this report, *One River, Two Bridges*, was the basis for beginning, and in the first three conversations we had, we asked people which of the two groups they would be in. Did they want to participate in the new bridge group or the old bridge group? The first three people all said, "Well, that's a stupid premise! They're interrelated, and we want to be in *both* groups. So if you are stupid enough to form two groups, we want to be in both of them."

So we sat down and said, "Maybe there aren't two groups. Maybe there's one group—or there's one river, two bridges, but one group."

When I said that to about the fourth person—"Look, the first three people said they wanted to be in both groups, maybe there's just one group"—the fourth person—whoever this was—said, "Oh, thank God. We thought it was an idiotic idea. We never agreed to it. We think there should be only one group, and we think that that group has to deal with both bridges—if for no other reason than the National Park Service has a 'non-proliferation policy' on wild and scenic rivers, which means that if you build a bridge, you have to take out a bridge. So these things are, as a regulatory matter at the federal level, inextricably linked—and we want to be in both groups."

Our objective in these first four interviews essentially had been to introduce ourselves and sort out who was going to be in which group and really hit the ground running, using the convening report as a basis for constructing two groups. There were deadlines, and people wanted to see progress, and this needed to move quickly. And we bought into that and said, "Hey, fast is the order of the day. Let's go fast."

But it took six months to see this wasn't going to work. So we went back to the lead person from the institute who was the co-author of the report that people didn't like. We had to very carefully go back and say to our client, "This isn't going to work, and we need more time before the first meeting, and here's why."

Then it became clear that there was a second problem that also was part of taking us this long. We wouldn't have had to wait six months, because it would have been easy to construct one group and to move past that problem with the report, had that been the only problem. The second problem was much more difficult. The departments of transportation were under the presumption that they had been given another tool, and I'm going to have to use *tool* in its most pejorative sense—a tool to get the stakeholders to agree to their alternative. The transportation people misunderstood what it meant to hire a neutral mediator, and they thought we worked for them, that we were going to help them get *their* preferred alternative, which was the alignment that had been put forward.

They only cared about the new bridge. They were fine to blow up the old bridge or to convert the old bridge into a pier to leave it in place. They didn't care, as long as somebody gave them some money to take care of it. They figured that they could get their hands on the money, given that it was one of the top thirteen priority projects. They thought, "Well, we don't care what happens to the old bridge. As long as we get enough money to take care of whatever the answer is, that's fine. We want a new bridge, and we want it here, and we want it to be *this* much, this cost."

They were saying to us essentially, "So you're going to help us get that answer, right?" And Robert and I said, "No, we're not going to help you do that at all. We're going to help you engage as one party among twenty-eight"—there were twenty-eight people at the table—"one party among twenty-eight, and you're going to be at the table, and you will have to negotiate to advance your own interests, and you will build consensus on what the alternative is, all the way to the possibility that maybe there's no new bridge at all."

They looked at us as if we were insane. They were outraged, and they felt betrayed, and they were suddenly mortified that we could possibly be so crazy as to presume that the answer wasn't already known.

How did we handle that? We were in meetings with seven, or eight, or ten department of transportation people at a time because both states had to be represented, and both states had multiple people in the room. We were at a meeting that I still recall all these years later, where we were explaining this to them, and they were turning all shades of purple. In that meeting, there was a man named Rick who was senior to the project manager from the Minnesota side. (Wisconsin was not equal in this. Minnesota was going to put in more money and had been much more the proponent of the project. This was near the Twin Cities, and it was a much more urgent problem on the Minnesota side, and they had more money. So Minnesota was essentially the lead.)

The project manager was the one who was purple lipped, who was the most outraged. His boss, Rick, was in the room. So I called Rick and said, "This won't work. You know, you have to either help the project manager change his perspective on what we're going to do, or we're just going to keep running into each other over and over again."

He said, "Well, what do you propose?" And I said, "I propose that we name *you* as the designee from the Department of Transportation of Minnesota, and not the project manager."

He said, "I can see where that would be advantageous. Let me see what I can do about it."

I think he understood it, and I think he agreed with me. He turned out to be one of the heroes of this story. He was—*is*—instinctively collaborative and was willing to push his own agency to do things that they had never done, and I think this was the first of many successes to come on this project. I think he had a history of being innovative and being a problem solver. So I think we were lucky. I mean, we got Rick, and when I asked Rick to do this, I think he understood it.

But Rick was no altruist, no pushover—God no. He was one of the toughest negotiators I've seen in public policy circumstances. He knew when to face the group, as we were in this months and months later. There were times when he would say to the group, "What you want is not possible, and I'm here to tell you that if I go home and ask for this, it will not happen. So we need to find another way." Then there were times when he would say, "I think this is going to be a hard sell, but I will go home and try to sell it, and there are constraints on my end, and you need to just understand that as I go and try to do this." He was magnificent and not a pushover at all.

He was very effective, and his ego was very much intact. He didn't need the approval of other people. He wasn't particularly concerned with being liked. He wanted to find an answer, and he had a hunch that the answer did lie in the group rather than in his agency—and that was pretty monumental. But it didn't happen immediately, because I needed one more thing before he would do it.

The project manager had resisted being displaced in this way, and I started to get some even harder pushback from their hired NEPA consultant, their transportation consultant, who also thought the stakeholders were a bunch of idiots who didn't understand that the right answer was right in front of them. She was very condescending and unhelpful.

I made the decision to go even higher. Minnesota, to save money, had given a second job to their lieutenant governor. In order to reduce the number of agency heads with six-figure salaries, the governor had named the lieutenant governor the secretary of transportation as well. Her name was Carol Molnau.

I had interviewed Carol earlier, and one of the things she had said to me was, "If you ever need me, give me a call." So in this six month period, as I was asking Rick to step up and before he had said that he would, I called Carol and said, "You told me to call you if I ever needed you. I need you now." And she asked, "What's the problem?"

I started to explain that the agency was treating us like a hired gun, not like a mediator, and that I would be happy to come to Minnesota and explain this and to talk through what to do about it. She said, "Get on a plane."

So I got a plane ticket, and as a good agency lead, she notified people that I was coming, so the project manager knew I was coming. He called and said, "We have to have a pre-meeting, before your meeting, because you don't get to just appear without my knowing what's up."

We had a very difficult meeting—the project manager, the hired consultant lead, and me—where I said, "*This* is what I'm going to say to her," and they said, "Well, we're going to say *this*. We're going to give her our side of the story, essentially, about what we want out of this process and what we think you should be required to do." So I said, "OK, that's great."

They said that they were going to say that the facilitator should be led by the technical information from the consultant and the project management approach of the project manager and that we should be taking our direction from the two of them.

So I got into this power struggle—honestly, that's what it was—a power struggle between the project manager and me. They insisted that I put together a PowerPoint of what I was going to say. I agreed to do that. I gave them my PowerPoint, and they put together a single slideshow of their perspective followed by mine, and then we went through just the oddest meeting.

We walked through the PowerPoints in the pre-meeting, which was very tense. They said, "We are going to do this, and then you are going to say these things, and then, you know, Carol will pronounce," and I said, "OK, let's go."

So we walked into a room—we got there early—and we were in a very large conference room with a hollow square. The project manager and the lead consultant set up their computer to project their PowerPoint, and they were at one corner, projecting on a screen that was sort of over to the side near the corner of the room. They set it up, and the Power-Point was on.

I was—just by happenstance—sitting pretty far away from them because I wanted to be far away from them. The door opened exactly in the opposite corner from where they were, and the lieutenant governor/secretary of transportation—Carol—walked in and immediately sat down in the first chair available to her, which was in exactly the opposite corner from where the computer was. They immediately said, "OK, we're ready to begin. We're going first." So they stood all the way across the room and stood at the computer and did their PowerPoint thing from way across the room.

They finished. They turned to me and said, "It's now your turn," and I moved next to her, and I sat down very close, and I looked up, and knowing exactly what I was saying, I said to the consultant, "Can you advance the slides for me?" So I turned her into a minion, and I knew exactly what I was doing, and so she had to advance the slides for me from across the room.

The two of them stayed across the room—a huge mistake. And as the slides came up, I turned to the lieutenant governor and whispered, "Carol, I think this is what's happening. This is where we are, this is what I've done."

"Next slide."

It was awful. It was as condescending as I could make it. So I went through the little dog-and-pony show, and I was sitting with her, and I remember it like it happened yesterday. We got to the conclusion, and I said at first that I had one question, and then there was something I wanted to say.

She said, "OK, what's the question?"

I said, "How's it going, doing things the way you've been doing them for the past thirty years on this project?"

And she said, "Not so well."

I said, "They want to keep doing things the way you've been doing them, and we can see where that's gotten you. So now, here's what I have to say: you should turn me loose or you should send me home." And she looked at me and stood up and left. She said, "OK, I've got it. Thanks so much. Thanks for coming," and she walked out. She just left the room.

I thought, "I'm fired." I was sure I was fired. I was *so* sure I had gotten myself fired. So I now was left in the room with the person whom I had turned into a slide advancer, who looked like she had swallowed eight pounds of thumbtacks. She was furious. They drove me to the airport in silence. I got on my plane, and I flew home to Colorado. I got home, and there was a voicemail on my phone at work—I checked it when I got home—and it was the lieutenant governor. And she said, "Get to work." It was amazing.

I thought, "There is a real chance that these two agencies, particularly this one on the Minnesota side, will get out of their own way and will get this project done because it has been causing so much pain. They have been getting in their own way, and maybe now they're going to get out of their own way and get this done."

As if by flipping a switch, everything changed. I had Rick at the table, I had the project manager and the lead consultant sitting in the last row of the observer chairs, to be called on when asked. I made it clear to them: you will answer questions when you're asked, you will come to the podium when people need you, and you sit in the back otherwise.

Carol had said, "Get to work," so we wrote a five-page set of protocols on the basis of the new interviews we had done over the course of that six months. Essentially, we shifted all the most important conclusions from the *One River, Two Bridges* report into a five-page protocol that said, "This is the problem, these are the stakeholders (as agencies or organizations), these are the individuals who will be at the table on behalf of each of the organizations—the individual's name and their organization's name—and these are the ground rules. This is how this is going to go." I sketched out a schedule that said, "We're going to do *this* in meeting one and *that* in meeting two," and it was sort of very high level, meeting by meeting, major objectives.

The universe of stakeholders had been pretty well described. This had been going on for thirty years. Thirty years prior, the department of transportation had said it wanted a new connection across the St. Croix River at this point, just south of Stillwater, Minnesota. In that thirty years, it had fought about it on and off. And there was lots of *off*; there was lots of time when it just wasn't on the list, it just wasn't a priority. This went on for thirty years, and sometimes it flared up and got lots of attention.

Then there was a whole NEPA process, and it had gone to lawsuits, it had gone to court; the court had nullified the environmental impact statement and thrown it out because of the wild and scenic river problems. The department of transportation had actually acquired houses and relocated people, only to be told that they couldn't have that alternative, that their alternative was not viable, and they threw it out. So there were lots of processes and lots of efforts made. So the stakeholders' universe was really well described, and everybody knew who should be at the table.

What we did in the protocol was describe why it was one process, why this group of twenty-eight were the right twenty-eight, and then, what were the issues? That was a part that we did differently from the guy who hadn't gotten picked. We vetted that document and got consensus on every semicolon in it before we said, "We're ready to actually begin the work."

We discovered that there had never been any attempt to build consensus on the earlier conflict assessment. The guy from the institute and the guy from Massachusetts had simply interviewed everyone and written a report with their own view of things, and there had been no attempt to build consensus on its conclusions or its content. We had full consensus on that five-page document—to the semicolon.

This was all part of the six months. We wrote a draft purpose statement, we named all the stakeholder organizations and who we thought was best fit to represent them; we did it in *draft*, laid out the draft schedule, and then went back to them. We distributed it and then went back to each of those stakeholders and said, "You know, this is *totally* reworkable, and if we've drawn some conclusion that you think is wrong, we're happy to revisit that. We will both try to construct this protocol so that you as a group own it and so we aren't just passive in it—we know about some things that are good process, and some things that are not so good, and we will offer our process advice, and if we really have to insist that the only way we would do something is *this* way, we will tell you that. But let's work together to get a process that everybody thinks is the right one and that's encapsulated in these five pages."

So we did interviews with each person after it was drafted to rework it and to tweak it and to change the language about it. Then in the very first meeting, we spent some time actually confirming it. Section by section, page by page, so that everyone, face to face, could actually see that being done.

In the first part of the first meeting, they were agreeing to a process, and to this set of protocols for conducting that process. It identified the duties of each of these named participants, that each person will bring information to the table, will work together to gather credible information about the bridge and its impact, will operate in good faith, which means *this*: that they will tell the truth, that they will disclose information if necessary, that they will listen carefully.

It was all ground rules—like "no spitting, no chair throwing"—and all those were based on the things we learned in the six months. They had said, basically, "People have been dishonorable in these ways," so then we wrote a protocol that said, "Well, that's not honorable, so we're not going to do that."

It included our responsibilities. This was going back to Carol's charge to us: "Get to work." It clarified what the mediators were for—that we were neutral with respect to the existence of a bridge or the future of the existing bridge. We did not care whether they had one, two, none, eight. But it said that we were going to keep things fair and enforce ground rules and build the agendas and try and break deadlock and help people communicate. So it said all of those things: who does what and when, what are the responsibilities in the process, and what are the ground rules.

To reassure people that this process could now go ahead, we did several things, depending on the individual stakeholder. For some, they were sure that they were going to be arm twisted, and so one of the things that I would say to them was, "Look, I'm not in the arm-twisting business. You will not find me very much of an arm twister. I am here to *prevent* your arm from being twisted. So if you feel some-one is behaving badly, twisting your arm, you get to say, 'Stop it!' and then you get to look to me to make sure that I stop it. And you *certainly* get to look at me if you think I'm doing it. So there's not going to be arm twisting, and I will be the police of arm twisting, but you also have to make sure you keep me honest, too, because I can get carried away. If you think I'm twisting your arm, you get to say so, and I will stop. I'm beholden to the group, and you all own me, and you own our presence here, and we are not tools of the department of transportation. We are here for the twenty-eight of you, and what happens and what we do is yours."

Some people thought we would be tools of the department of transportation. It was their full expectation that we were just going to come and try to hammer down the bridge in a new way. They were sure of it. To cut through that suspicion, I think that what we really did was say, "The proof is in the thing itself, that it becomes self-evident. I will tell you that I am not anybody else's tool, but you should only believe me *when* I'm not. So it's a testable hypothesis. You watch my behavior. If you find my behavior questionable, you question it, and I will correct it or explain it and we will work through it. And if I'm, at any point, tipping toward one stakeholder, then you throw a flag and we deal with it, up to and including dismissing me. That's my commitment to you."

I said that, and I say it all the time. I *always* say that; I didn't just say it in this case. I always say it, that I'm outta here if you don't want me; I serve at your request. I say it all the time: "My responsibility—my duty—is to the group as a whole, and if at any time I'm not serving the group's interest, you need only to say so, and we'll deal with it. And if you all say, 'You're the wrong guy for this show,' then I go."

I think that the whole of the twenty-eight would have had to fire me, but any one of them could have raised that I should be fired. But the group had to decide whom they wanted to work with and how they wanted to work. The same was true with every key element in the process: "It's not done *to* you; it's done *with* you and *for* you, and if you ever think it's not being done for you, then it has to be done with you, and you should stop me if you don't like it."

I had said to them often in the first three or four meetings, "You are going to plow some old ground, and I'm sorry that you will have to, but you *will* have to, because there's something in here that you haven't unearthed yet. So we're going to plow some old ground. Now each of you, as painful as it might be, as many times as you have repeated it over the last thirty years, tell me why you are here. Tell me what you care about and why you have a stake in the outcome of this—and don't just tell me that you want a bridge or don't want a bridge, but tell me *why* you want what you want."

We went through the interest scoping that way so that everybody could hear it, even with the eye rolling. And I said, "I know you're rolling your eyes. You've heard this all before. You need to listen, and you need to really tune in and pay attention, because you've missed something. If you haven't solved this problem yet, you haven't figured it out. So open your mind and try and discover what you haven't learned."

So we did the basics. We scoped all the interests—the whys—and then I wrote them all down and condensed them into what is still one of the most eloquent one-page summations of interests that I have ever constructed, and we worked it. This was another time where we said to the whole group, "We want your consensus that this is an accurate and articulate statement of the interests of every stakeholder. You will see items on this list that you don't care about, and you don't get to take them off the list. But rather, we want you to look at this list and say that it is, in fact, a perfect reflection of the needs of all the stakeholders."

We translated those interests into a set of criteria for judging bridges and judging all the elements that are attached to bridges—the criteria for judging whether we had the right answer or not. For example, one of the criteria that they really liked was that the answers—whatever the answers were—had to satisfy *all* regulatory requirements. I said to them, "That seems obvious to me, but your reaction to it is a strong one, so that means something. So what does that mean?" People said, "One of the reasons why this has gotten so stuck is that we have all of these competing agency mandates, priorities, regulations, and rules, and no one has been able to build the puzzle to satisfy all of them."

Here's who we had at the table. It was ridiculous. It made this puzzle really complicated. We had the National Park Service, the Environmental Protection Agency, the US Army Corps of Engineers, the Coast Guard, the Fish and Wildlife Service, and the Advisory Council on Historic Preservation (the national-level one). We had six federal agencies. Then we had two state departments of transportation, two state historic preservation offices, two state commissions of wildlife—because this was an environmental controversy. It was believed to threaten an environmental crisis if this thing got done, so there were two environmental agencies, two historic preservation agencies, two transportation agencies (one from each state). Then we had local governments, and we had the concurrence rule in Minnesota to say that all the regulatory requirements would have to be satisfied—which should be a threshold, not a high bar—but it turned out to be a pretty high bar. No one had been able to solve the puzzle that way.

So when we put it all in the criteria list, people said, "That's right. It has to meet park service regulations, wild and scenic river regulations, and the Endangered Species Act. It has to do all that." And then we had about forty other ones that were just as intensely felt—protecting endangered species, advancing the local economy—and there were lots of aesthetic criteria. Things had to be beautiful, and we would have to protect the history of the region.

What gave me the hope or sense that something was possible here? What made me not want to stay home in Denver? Well, I almost stayed home early on, because it turns out that culturally, I'm not very upper-

Midwest. In the first couple of meetings I would say, "So, let me just test this question: It seems that the sense of the group—or *my* sense of the group—is X; is X good for everybody?" And there would be silence. And then I would go on. There would be something a little procedural, like, "Can we have lunch at 12:30?"—I mean, it could be anything—and I would say, "Is 12:30 OK? Any objections?" Quiet, quiet, quiet. Then I would say, "Great. Next," and I would move on, and move on at my pace.

After meeting two, one of the Lutherans pulled me aside and said, "We don't do things like that here."

I asked, "What are you talking about?"

He said, "That quiet part."

And I said, "Yeah? The part where I made sure nobody disagrees, and then I move on?"

And he said, "Yeah, you gotta stop doing that."

"Really? Why do I have to stop doing that? Because that's kind of how I do it, so what do I need to do instead?"

And he and another person said, "No, no. People aren't going to speak up if they disagree."

And I said, "Ohhh, *that's* part of the problem here, isn't it?"

And they said, "Yeah. So we make nice in meetings, and then we go home and we disagree. But you don't disagree out loud."

And I said, "Oh, OK. *That's* good to know!"

I was thinking, "Well, I don't know what to do with you! I don't know how to get through, because if you don't tell me that there's a problem, I'm not sure that I know how to help you solve it. So what am I going to do?" So I did what I always do: I made fun of myself. I asked them for help training me to not be my usual speedy "Everybody OK? Let's keep going" kind of self. And they thought I was pretty funny.

It demonstrated to them that I didn't hold myself above them, or that I didn't hold myself out as something fancy or tricky or mysterious or any of that—that I was willing to say, "Look, I do it this way. That doesn't really work here. I'm prepared to change. You tell me how to figure out or ascertain whether you agree or disagree about something." It demonstrated that they could then teach me how to help them, and in doing that, it let them relax with me. And then it let them observe their own behavior—including behaviors that had gotten them into this trouble in the first place. So I was able to say to them, "Is that part of why you've had such trouble these thirty years?" And they would laugh and say, "Well, of course it is."

I did this with the whole group, out loud. All to further say clearly, "I don't know what I'm doing here. So you're going to have to help me understand how to help you and how to conduct myself here and what you need from me that is different from what I'm doing." I said this out loud—in front of twenty-eight stakeholders and a whole room of reporters and observers and staff people from members of Congress—in front of all of them.

It went great, because it made the whole thing less fancy, less high-falutin'. It just made me a normal person. It made this more of a straight-forward, "Look, we're just going to have to figure out how to figure out what we disagree about. We're going to have to start to talk. We're going to have to give this poor mediator some signal—or he'll just be lost."

It let them not feel like they were bad and that I was there to give them an F, but that what they did was OK, and that I needed to figure out how to help them, given how they are. It let them feel that how they are was *fine*. I didn't need to judge it; I just needed to figure out how I was going to change.

It turns out that they thought they had had agreements in the past, and they hadn't—that they were, in fact—many of them—furious with one another for having, in their view, defected on agreements they had had in the past. The person who appeared to be defecting had some plausible deniability: "I don't know what you're talking about. I never actually agreed to that," and they sat quietly and stoically—as they do. This uncovered a whole set of behaviors that were both *acceptable*—because this is just the culture of the place—and that were also *dysfunctional* and that needed to be changed. They needed to see that, to see that they were in fact *in their own way*.

Fascinating? It was fun. But it was frustrating, like, "These Lutherans are making me crazy, and I don't know what to do with them! They won't talk, won't say when they disagree, and I don't know how to help them!" But I never *really* wanted to go home; you know, I started to kind of fall in love with them.

So anyway, first we did "interests." Then I built into these criteria that this was *yours*, and that this was the test for whether there's an answer here. The next thing I did was that I said, "If you thought the interest thing was going back to basics, you're *really* going to hate this next one. Looking at those interests, what are your options? Now, I know you've been through NEPA analysis of alternatives, and I know you've had proposals, and there's three architects over there who've just designed their own, and you're all fighting about which one is the right one—but just suspend all that."

"Let's put all the options on the table *again*"—and they rolled their eyes—and I said, "What are they? So there's the existing alignment, and then there's *this* one, and then there's *that* one from the study in 1972. And then there's *this* one."

There were several efforts, including some big transportation guru dude who would come in and tell them what the answer was, which was a *horrific* idea. It was so stupid. But he had ridden in on a white horse and said, "Here's your alternative," and then left—and everybody hated it.

But we put it back on the table. And then I said to the consultant, "You have to analyze all these alternatives now, again, or present the analysis you already have on all these alternatives." And they were *furious*—"We've already done this work."

I said, "Well, you're going to do it again, or you're going to at least *present* it again. You're going to have to redo the work again, because we have to understand each of these alternatives as we balance them against this set of criteria—and I know you don't want to do it, but you're going to. I'm not asking, I'm telling ya. If these are the alternatives that belong to the group, you're going to do your work to help them understand them. And I don't care if you don't like them or you think they're crazy—*too bad*, you don't run the show here—help these people out." So we put all the alternatives on the table.

There were five or six really viable, or potentially viable, options. There was one that was so obviously not viable, but one participant was so deeply attached to it that I knew we'd lose him if we got rid of it too soon. So I kept it around for a while and made them work on it and made the group talk about it, and people went, "This sucks. This is not going to work because this . . . nah, nah, nah," and I would turn to Stan and say, "Stan, you're hearing this criticism, right?" and he said, "Yeah, I hear it," and I said, "You've got to try and improve your alternative."

So that's the next thing we did: if people could point out the way that each alternative failed to meet one of the criteria, then that alternative had to be improved in order to meet *all* the criteria, if it were possible. So we moved into, "Improve every one, lift every boat, make each option its best, and then if there's one that simply *can't* meet the criteria, ultimately you'll be able to discard it"—and one by one, they fell.

This all happened over the course of a year, in monthly meetings, two days each. I'd never met for so many hours in my life. Throughout the whole first year—we met once a month, and then we had two eight-hour days—we'd fly in on Sunday, we'd meet Monday and Tuesday all day long, and then I'd fly home Tuesday night, and then a month later we would come back—for the better part of a year. I would say probably for ten meetings, it was every month. We'd be in touch with a bunch of people in between, absolutely.

I knew, in meetings four or five, that in fact, we were going to be able to find the answer. I knew it because the conversation shifted very subtly from *whether* to *how*. I had said to the group, over and over again, "We imagine that we solve problems by asking whether to do something, and then deciding how to do it," as in, 'If I want to go on vacation, I decide to go on vacation, and *then* I decide where to go and when to go and all that stuff.'"

"But in reality," I said, "here's how human beings actually do it: we posit, temporarily, the *whether* question, and then we answer the *how*, and then we go back to the *whether* question because the *how* might eliminate the choice."

So we say, "Well, let's go on vacation," and then we start to think about, "Well, when might we, and how much is in the bank account?" and then we say, "Well, you know what? We actually can't afford a vacation this year."

You come back to the *whether* question once you've examined *how*. So I said, "That's how we're going to do this. We're going to examine the *how* questions, and we're going to always come back to *whether*. So, "What's the best possible new bridge to build?" and then, "Should we build it at all?"

In the earlier going, in the first few meetings, every time we started talking about how—*how* might one build a bridge that responded to these criteria—someone would say, "Wait a second. I don't want a bridge."

Then—it must have been in meeting five—we changed the game. The way the departments of transportation, especially the federal Department of Transportation or Highway Administration, had played the game typically was this: You say there's a transportation purpose and a need. You then analyze the alternatives to address that need. Then you select the most viable alternative, and *then* you go into the design phase, where you say the particulars of what it will look like. So it's only after the NEPA decision, where you file a "record of decision" under the National Environmental Policy Act, only then do you start to design the final project!

One of the things that had gotten them so hung up for thirty years that they hadn't really articulated in quite the right way was that the departments of transportation kept saying, "Sign on to an alternative, then we'll file the record of decision, and *then* we'll design the bridge. Then we'll decide how tall it is, and what's it made of, and what color it is, and all that stuff."

So I said to the transportation people, "You can't get across the finish line in this way. You have to change the game."

They said, "In what way?" And I said, in meeting four or five, "You have to put it in front of this group—you have to let *them* design the bridge. Because part of what I've heard—and if you haven't heard it, you haven't been listening—is that they hate your design, or they don't trust you to design it later—and so they want to design the bridge *before* they say that they will have one. So you have to do this much of the *how*: How will it look? How tall will it be? How will you build it? What material will it be made of? Only *then* will they answer the *whether* question. So you have to take the design phase, and we have to move it up."

There was a representative from the Federal Highway Administration, and they were at the table—Cheryl Martin. I said to Cheryl, "I know you don't do it this way, but you have to change the game. You cannot leave design until later. You have to put it on the table now. So I need you—if you have to go to Washington, go to Washington—to get approval to do it this way."

She said, "You know, I'd like to throw you off a cliff, but OK." So she got the go-ahead to participate in the design process. She did it.

Then I said to my friend Rick, "Your bridge office isn't trusted to be the one to do the design."

He said, "You're kidding."

I said, "No, no. The stakeholders don't want me to bring your bridge people to the front of the room to help them design. That's not going to work." And I said, "You have to let me hire; you have to give me the money that you haven't given me yet, and you have to let me hire a consultant to come in and help with this design, and it can't just be any old engineer; it needs to be an artiste. I need somebody with artistic skills."

He said, "Impossible. The meeting is just coming up. We can't get anybody on the contract that fast."

I said, "Look, these are the problems to be solved. Tell me how you can solve them." And he said, "Well, maybe we've got an on-call contract where I can just tap somebody," and he went and got the list and said, "These are the consulting firms that are on our on-call list. The only way to get somebody here for meeting five is to pick one of those."

So I started to research the firms that were on the on-call list, looking for the right one. I found one—and my shorthand for this person was that I needed a guy with a pink tie. I knew that they needed someone who could give them the *artistic* rendering of their image of what a good bridge would be. So I said, "I don't want a bridge engineer. I need an artist. I need somebody who can hear what they're saying and translate it in artistic terms."

Rick said, "I think you've lost your mind."

They were thinking "engineering," but so many of the stakeholders had said that Stillwater, Minnesota, is this stunning, beautiful, exceptional place, and that the existing lift bridge is iconic, and it's beautiful, and it has meaning for us. Its image was on the side of the police car, the Stillwater town police car. If you went into the little gift shops in Stillwater, Minnesota, they were selling photographs of the bridge.

So I said to the transportation people, "You can't give this community a new bridge that is any less exceptional. The new bridge has to be so good that people will want to un-paint the police car and put the new one on it, so good that people in gift shops will sell pictures of it. That's how good this has to be. Because you're replacing something people adore, and you can't do that except by replacing it with something people will adore."

I said, "This has to be beautiful, or you're never going to get through this gauntlet of twenty-eight stakeholders. They'll never let you build it!

And the truth of that is in their not having let you build it yet. So I'm just telling you what people are telling me. You can't get there from here—unless it's beautiful."

So I found this guy at Parsons Brinckerhoff [now WSP] who had an engineering degree. But he also had an art degree and an architecture degree. He was like the triple threat. So I called him—he was in the San Francisco office of Parsons Brinckerhoff there on the short-list. I said, "We can get you under contract. Can you come?"

He said, "What do you want me to do?" And I said, "I just want to start a conversation and let it run for the better part of the day, about what beauty is in this place—what the beauty of the existing bridge is and why it's iconic and what it means. Then, if there were a new bridge, what kind of beauty would it have to represent?"

I told him that on the phone to San Francisco, and I said, "I just want you to listen to this conversation, and then I would want you to draw a picture, or pictures, of what a bridge could be if it did all that, if it sang in the way that they need this bridge to sing."

And he said, "No problem."

I'd said to him that this bridge had to *sing*: "I want you to be able to draw a picture of what it sounds like, how the bridge would sing."

He said, "No problem. I'll bring my pens, and I'll come."

I asked him, "Do you have a pink tie?" And he said, "What are you talking about?" And I just said, "Wardrobe is important here. Is there any chance you happen to own a pink tie?" And he said, "No, I don't own a pink tie."

I said to him, "Oh never mind, Scott. Just come as you are."

I was after the non-engineer. None of their bridge engineers wore pink ties. They all wore blue shirts and khaki pants and ties that were mostly blue striped.

So he came. I said to them, "We have to take these really lofty ideas of beauty and we have to bring them down to earth. So I want you to talk about what is beauty, but I also, then, want you to talk about how you put that on the ground—or how you put that across the river, in this case mass, height, volume, texture, color, historic reference."

I just listed every kind of objective manifestation of an object that I could think of. I said, "Talk in lofty terms, but then also talk in practical terms: How tall is too tall, how short is too short, how wide is too wide, how thin is too thin, how brown is too brown—height, color, mass, texture, all of it."

People said, "Oh, OK, well, we'll talk."

I really just turned them loose, and he started to draw. He said, "Well, you could do a bridge like *this* . . ." and he would draw these pictures. He would say, "Now this would be *this* tall," and he would say, "At two hundred twenty feet tall, that's *this* many stories."

People would say, "Well, the tallest building in Stillwater is *this* many stories—that's too tall." Then I would say, "That's tall?" And people would say, "Yeah, it's too tall." "Well, OK, good; that tall is bad."

So we just went through it like that, and he drew pictures. At one point, he drew a suspension bridge like the Golden Gate Bridge. Someone had said, "Suspension bridges are the be-all and end-all of all bridges, and they're fantastic, and we love suspension bridges."

Rick asked, "How expensive is a suspension bridge compared to other bridges?" And the guy with the pink tie said, "Five times more expensive than any other bridge you would build."

Rick said, "Give me an order of magnitude. So if this bridge were a boxed girder bridge and it cost, say, fifty million, then a suspension bridge is two hundred fifty million?" And he said, "Yeah."

So Rick said to the group, "I know you thought that a suspension bridge was kind of pretty, but can we take that one off the table? Because I don't think I can do that. I don't think I can justify that it's five times more expensive than the basic bridge. Five times is too much."

So people said, "Yeah, no problem. We don't need a suspension bridge. It was kind of cool to think about, but let's take it off."

I mean it was just that easy. We went back and forth: "What can we have, and how would it work?"

So at one point I was talking, paying attention to the group, and I looked over, and there were these weird sort of slashes on the flip-chart as Scott was drawing. Then I would look back at the group, and I would look back again at Scott, and pretty soon there was a drawing—in perspective—from one side of the river to the other, and he's got a vanishing point. I mean, the drawings were stunning and *live*. People were like, "No, that's too much!" or, "That's not enough!" or, "That's *this*." And then we really dug in.

At one point, he took out a green marker, and he put a little green along one side. And then he took out a purple marker and highlighted some piece with the purple. I asked, "Why purple and green?" And he answered, "Well, this is the Minnesota side; this is for the Minnesota Vikings, and this is the green for the Packers—and people were laughing, and I could just feel that they were going to design a bridge that they wanted, and that the whole *whether* to build it question was going to simply disappear.

Once it could be wonderful, it could be possible. Even the people who objected most to the idea of the bridge began to see that it might be wonderful. Then it just changed everything. So they agreed on a basic design, and I went home.

The guys from the Sierra Club had been the most adamantly opposed to the idea of a bridge, because it was a wild and scenic river. So here was the tangle that had hooked them, one of the many tangles.

I began to talk in these terms, too, that the stakeholders could readily have two of the three major items (environment, history, transportation) that they wanted. They could have environmental protection and transportation, because environmental protection translated as only one bridge over the wild and scenic river. You could have one bridge and take care of the environmental question and the transportation question by blowing up the old bridge and building a new bridge that would make the transportation part work—but the historic preservation people would be left out. Or you could do any other combination of two of the three major interests: transportation, historic preservation, and the environment. You could never do all three.

So the Sierra Club guy, who was the most "I don't want a new bridge," said to the group, "If you're going to sin, sin greatly. If there is going to be a bridge—and I'm not sure that I will sign on to there being one—but *if* I were to sign on to there being a bridge, we'll never do better than this."

I said, "OK. I'll take that for today. We're only in meeting five. That's enough."

Everyone else was more positive than that. So that's pretty far. And I thought, "We are going to find an answer to the *whether* question. This is something people are going to want eventually."

Then it was a matter of putting all the pieces together. The big regulatory trick was that the Coast Guard had to call the two "bridges"—if they existed, they had to call them both "bridges" for purposes of their regulation. But if you took the historic lift bridge and you took all the cars off it—and you made it bike-pedestrian only—and linked it into a loop trail that went onto the new bridge on the Wisconsin side, across the lift bridge with no cars and then back onto the Minnesota side, in a loop trail, and linked it to the St. Croix River—which had been designated for recreation, one of the major reasons it was designated a wild and scenic river—then the historic bridge could become a "recreation facility" for purposes of the National Park Service's wild and scenic river evaluation. Then for the Park Service, there wouldn't be two bridges; there would only be one.

In regulatory terms, there would be only one bridge, because there would only be one place for cars to go. The National Parks Service representative said, "I will go to Washington, and we will write the letter that says this alternative does not violate the wild and scenic river regulations because there is only one bridge with cars on it."

The Coast Guard guy said, "I'm going to go back and make sure that my agency is still comfortable that operated in the proper way, these are both bridges, and they will be regulated by Coast Guard rules for navigation. For us, it's two bridges." These two people looked at each other and said, "You do it your way, I'll do it my way, both regulations are going to be taken care of, we're all good"—and the regulatory problem went away.

This option arose because of the conversation about what to do about the Wild and Scenic River Act compliance. How do you have two structures here and not two bridges? One of the participants said, "You just take the cars off," and it was so obvious. It was so easy. Once people got out of their own way and said that the problem was solvable, they said, "Well, what about this? Let's just try it that way," and *poof*: the alternative was so obvious.

So that became the preferred alternative, and there was just a matter of working out how it was done and whether everyone would sign on on the environmental side. They were the ones who felt the least taken care of—and they were right.

The transportation agency tried to sweeten the pot with mitigation as much as they could. Ultimately, the Minnesota Center for Environmental Advocacy said, "If you give us *this* on water quality, *this* on growth management on the Wisconsin side, *this* on the endangered species, we will sign on." And they did.

The Sierra Club stood aside temporarily and then changed their mind. So we ended up with a consensus agreement that then unraveled in the last meeting when we ended up with all but one. The group signed an agreement. The Sierra Club guy, at the very last, withheld his signature. The departments of transportation went forward with it. The Federal Highway Administration signed the record of decision.

The Sierra Club sued about the Wild and Scenic River Act, and then the most unbelievable thing happened. All the other stakeholders went to Congress and got written into a piece of legislation that this bridge is exempted from the Wild and Scenic River Act, and Congress passed it—and President Obama signed it. That's how much these stakeholders came to believe in their alternative—that they actually went to Congress and got it in a bill. This was after we were done and I was gone. The agreement was made. The department of transportation kept the stakeholders together.

There's a visual-impact oversight group to make sure the design continues to be upheld. They basically said at the end, "We don't trust you to just send us all home. We're going to stick with you." And when this suit came up from the Sierra Club, the stakeholders themselves all got together and said, "We're not going to let this fail. We worked too hard. We think we got the right answer. We're not going to let this go."

They went to Congress. It didn't hurt that at the time, the members of Congress on both sides of the river were both from the same party. So both the Wisconsin folks and the Minnesota folks were like-minded on this one.

Looking back, I think that the reason they hired our team turned out to be pretty insightful. They needed someone who kept telling them, "No matter how many dead-ends you find, no matter how many road-blocks—no pun intended—you run into, there's an answer here. If you just work harder, if we just keep trying, if we just stay at it, you will find your way to dance around this one. It's there if you want it."

I think they needed me to be that. They knew they needed it. I was that voice for them over and over and over again. We would get stuck, we would have to go back, they would come back and say, "Oh, that didn't go very well. I didn't like that very much," and we would go to work and say, "OK. Well, then we've got to figure out what we're going to do about that, and how to respond to it, and whether something can be done about it."

Frankly, having it on the list for national priority helped. When I needed to, I could elevate things in Washington to a very high level. Then the agency flexibilities came about. There was a lot of pressure from the White House, from the top level of the agencies, to handle all of the projects on the priority list. So that was a huge difference.

Keeping them at the table even when they hit those, what turned out to be temporary, roadblocks was important, just keeping them going and saying, "You know, you can do this—you can figure it out." Giving them the whole problem, I think, was really essential.

In every iteration prior to that, the department of transportation had kept some part of the problem for themselves. They would say, "We don't really want you to put together the mitigation package," or, "You don't really get to do design." There were some elements they kept from the stakeholders, and I refused to let the department of transportation keep *anything*. They had to give it *all*. This way, the group owned the solution instead of having to trust the agencies. I think those were the big lessons.

But I kept them at it *not* because I think absolutely anything can be mediated at any time. But I thought in this case that there were so many choices. When you stack up the numbers of variables they had to play with—the design of the bridge, the width of it, the placement of it— there were so many things to trade and move and push and do. There was such willingness of the people who were there to try to put their problems on the table, or to put their authority in play, or to put the stuff that was in their jurisdiction in the game.

Rick kept saying, "If you want something that's not what we usually do, then I'll go fight for it. I'm with you. I'll try. If I can't do it, I'll come back and tell you why we can't do it, and I need you to be willing to accept that." And the park service guy was crucial—his being willing to help his own agency define the two pieces of infrastructure as something that they should sign on to. That was actually beneficial to the wild and scenic river evaluation; that was huge.

PART TWO

Engagement and Difference in Place Making

Introduction to Part Two

As in part 1, part 2 also refuses to reduce urban design and place making to the often romanticized creation of the public square or piazza, where old and young congregate, where families meet as children play, where people of diverse backgrounds comingle and recognize one another in public. We see now how place making comes alive not just in space but in time. What happened here yesterday matters: Did realtors try to break up the neighborhood? Did banks refuse to loan here? Have residents been served well or poorly by city services? Have religious or cultural or ethnic differences mattered here?

Place makers must wrestle with the legacies they inherit in this or that place. Past events like earthquakes or hurricanes may have done widespread damage, but so have past deeds, whether block-busting by realtors or disinvestment by employers or redlining by banks, to take well-known examples (Sugrue 1996). Many urban places appear, then, not with blank slates but with traces of racism and uneven investment, traces of past displacement or community building, past layouts of transportation corridors or zoning designations (Agyeman 2020; Parkinson 2012).

So place makers will often work in cities and neighborhoods marked by histories of contentiousness and disorder, spaces scarred by poverty and inequality (Amin 2002; Hou 2013). In these very real places, where residents' minds and memories and hopes are no more blank slates than the streets they use every day, place makers need to think not only about spaces and possible places, about what can happen tomorrow, but about what has happened here yesterday (Cannavo 2007; see also the afterword to this volume). In many places, residents' mental maps tell them

"We don't go there" or "It's not safe here" or "You have to be careful there if you're seen as Muslim, or South Asian, or Black, or . . ."

In the face of these complex cultural and economic histories, today's place makers know that yesterday's residents have been displaced, or have walked and lived in fear, or have felt themselves poorly served by their city administrations. But as recent work in Detroit, Brooklyn, Los Angeles County, and the United Kingdom shows, careful place makers can contribute to community building, to improving ranges of public and social services, and to transforming dangerous spaces into safer places hosting networks of support and safety, solidarity and mutual regard, and recognition (Bose et al. 2014).

In part 2, we see that place making can involve cultivating gardens as well as organizing communities, creating convivial public spaces as well as assembling well-publicized interfaith coalitions. We see the painstaking work of learning in communities as residents and staff do door-to-door surveys and build trust as they do. We see the design and convening of workshops in which participants grapple together with racial stereotypes and with their fears of local violence. This work is not simply social but spatial, too. This land is cultivated for and by community members; these empty lots become recreational areas serving and maintained by community members. These congregations and community centers become not neutral spaces but places of safety and welcome. All this work happens in space to re-create and reclaim, to redefine and transform places at hand in Detroit, Brooklyn, Los Angeles, and Oldham, England.

Again, these chapters present the work not of heroes and geniuses but of sensitive and skillful, committed and responsive citizens working with others to improve the places in which they work and live (Hou 2010). If these chapters in part 2 rarely mention the concepts of design or planning, that should be instructive; it tells us more about the languages of different disciplines (landscape architecture, political science, social welfare, and sociology, for example) than about the actual work of assembling land and building the organizational capacity to develop urban agriculture.

We might ask, as a result, what kinds of spatial imagination, planning, and design has actually been brought to bear in the place-making work that follows, as it involves community organizing, interracial recognition and relationship building, and development of interfaith coalitions (Anguelovski 2014). By considering these cases more carefully, along with many others like them, we might reimagine both spatial planning and place making less narrowly than we have traditionally imagined them.

Part 2 begins with Karen Umemoto's account of organizing a community workshop for residents and officials of the city of Azusa who were faltering in their efforts to address recent hate crimes. Similar challenges of judgment and strategy then appear in James Brodick's story of building community capacity and a community justice center in Red Hook, Brooklyn, in the wake of racial violence there. Father Phil Sumner's story broadens our view from race and poverty to immigration and religious conflict as place-making imperatives and challenges. Malik Yakini's story, last but hardly least, shows how place making and white privilege, food security and political empowerment, can be closely interwoven in an urban context like Detroit. Throughout, we see that local capacity can be enhanced as city residents reclaim space, overcome distrust, and re-create safe and culturally rich places in their own cities and neighborhoods.

5

Dispute Resolution, Deliberation, and Racial Violence

Karen Umemoto's Practice Story

Editor's Preface

Karen Umemoto knew from her own family history how precariously political any place called home could be. Her parents had been among the "resettled" Japanese citizens incarcerated in American concentration camps during the Second World War. Growing up in postwar Los Angeles, interested in community development and social justice issues, she had been doing doctoral work in planning at MIT when she found herself invited to Azusa, California, the site of recent racialized hate crimes and gang-related violence.

The city-council-appointed human relations commission needed help in addressing its own agendas as well as local residents' senses of fear and hopelessness. In the face of inequality, distrust, and candidly acknowledged racism, Umemoto's carefully developed workshop employed practices that can work to foster safer places, complementing the related efforts of education and recognition that these re-created places require.

Navigating Hope and Fear, Learning about One Another

This work was more a result of my life experience than of any study. I grew up at the intersection of the Harbor and the San Diego freeways, the two busiest freeways in Los Angeles County. At the time, Watts was Black, and Torrance was white, and I was right in the middle, in Gardena. I call it a buffer-zone community, because it is at the intersection of the freeways and freeways are like the railroad tracks that racially divided one group of people from another.

It was along the freeway intersections that you found the most diversity of people, because that's where Black and white communities met, and Latinos and Asians could be found as the buffers between Black and white communities. So every time you'd go under one of the freeway overpasses, you'd be in a different world.

I grew up code switching and seeing that people lead such different lives; people listen to such different music, the smells are different, the slang is different, the style of dress and the way people soup up their cars—it's so different. My own code switching within Gardena meant that I could just be a regular, all-American, ten-year-old Girl Scout kid and YMCA camp counselor, but the minute I walked onto the grounds of my grandmother's church, my voice would go up an octave and my head would lower, and it was, "Ah, *yoroshiku*" (nice to see you after all this time) and all that.

Code switching is shorthand for using a different dictionary to make sense of what people are saying or for using a different lens to see what you're viewing. So you're aware that different actions, different words, have different meanings to different people. So for example, when a Black person says the N-word, it's a very different thing than if I or a non–African American uses the word. That's a very simple example, but that's true for a lot of gestures and a lot of words that people may use, or even the kinds of celebrations that people have.

It's knowing that there's a different mindset, that there are different ways that people interpret the world and events and the words that you need to be conscious of. I grew up doing that all the time—constantly code switching. So sometimes when someone says something, I'll think, "Oh no, they shouldn't have said that," because I know that it's not going to be received by others in the way that the person intended.

I was involved in a lot of movement politics—at that time, a lot of it was Third World coalition politics—both as a student and as a community activist in Little Tokyo, which was undergoing redevelopment and gentrification at the time, through the struggle against evictions in Little Tokyo, along with all of the other things going on in the movement at the time. Because the Soweto uprising took place at the same time, there was a divestiture and anti-apartheid movement, and the farmworkers were on strike in California. I was a freshman at UCLA at the time. When you're involved in one movement organization, you get asked to support all these others, so then you get exposed to all these other kinds of progressive activities in the country.

I grew up in Gardena, where in the seventies, people did get along better than they do now. There was a lot more integration in student government and classes and social activities. The Girl Scout troop was mixed; everything was very integrated. I grew up in a high school where it was twenty-five percent Black, twenty-five percent Latino, twenty-five percent white, and twenty-five percent Asian, and while there was still some voluntary segregation, it was probably one of the most socially integrated periods and places of that time. I really saw the best of race relations growing up in Gardena, and also during college in Third World coalition politics and progressive coalition politics where you're working with everybody.

Then I moved up to the Bay Area and finished off at San Francisco State, and I was involved in the statewide Asian Pacific Student Union. I moved in 1978 or '79. I was in a leadership position in the statewide Asian Pacific Student Union. We worked with MECHA (Movimiento Estudiantil Chicano de Aztlán) and the African/Black Student Union. MECHA was a Chicano student organization, with a network statewide.

During the Jesse Jackson campaign, I was cochair of the LA Rainbow Coalition in the '88 campaign, as a student. It was safer to have students, because it was so politically factionalized, so I was kind of thrust into this because we weren't seen as part of any political faction. So I was co-chair of the LA Rainbow Coalition at a fairly young age, alongside being a MECHA member.

Through that, I continued to work with a lot of different organizations across the rainbow, so I had a very positive experience both growing up and in doing progressive movement politics. So when there were increased tensions growing in Los Angeles, ranging from some of the publicized tensions between Blacks and Koreans in South Central to the tensions between new immigrants and long-timers in various neighborhoods, I became concerned more and more about the future direction that race relations were taking, at least as I had experienced it.

I got my master's degree in 1988 in Asian American studies at UCLA. I did my master's thesis on the San Francisco State strike and the role of Asian students in the strike. Through that, I also studied the Black Panther movement and all the related kinds of activities that were going on at the time. An article based on the thesis was published soon thereafter in the *Amerasia Journal*.

After I graduated—actually, even before I graduated—I was working full time at the UCLA Asian American Studies Center under professor Don Nakanishi. We were involved in a three-year battle for his tenure. Anyway, I was working there as the coordinator of student/community projects, bridging the town-gown gap, setting up internships and research roundtables to pair researcher interests with community needs, and things like that.

I really thought I needed to get more education to do the kind of work and research and policy-oriented activities that I wanted to do. I felt that I had reached my maximum capacity in terms of what I could offer. I wanted to get more involved in the development of policies that had to do with issues I saw as pressing from the standpoint of local communities. One was improving race relations, and the other was really helping, or working with, those historically disenfranchised to create policies that would really help empower minorities and historically disenfranchised communities in terms of economic development and all that. Anyway, my advisor suggested that I go to MIT or UCLA. So I applied and got into both, and I decided to go to MIT just because I had been at UCLA and I wanted to broaden my life experience.

In 1992, I was in my dorm room at MIT watching TV when the news came on about the riots—the civil unrest and the Rodney King decision. I turned on the TV, and I saw LA in flames.

My family still lived in Gardena, and the flames were pretty close. I felt a real personal sadness about the whole thing and concern for my friends and family, as well as this bigger concern that told me, "Oh no, this is really bad in terms of the racial fallout that this represents," and what would also result from what happened. In a city that's got so many problems already, this was the last thing it needed. But I also had felt that way when I saw the videotape of the beating of Rodney King. How could this still go on?

Rodney King was the motorist who was pulled over by Los Angeles Police Department cops in a patrol car, who then called in reinforcements and, unbeknownst to them, were videotaped beating Rodney King to the point of his not being able to even open his eyes. They had pulled him out of his car and beaten him with batons. They circled around this man who was on the ground, and one by one, they would poke their batons at him and hit him and kick him, and it was obvious to most viewers, in my mind, that this was use of excessive force. Yet the defense lawyers were able to convince the jury that it was not use of excessive force, and the jury acquitted the officers in a trial. It was upon the announcement of the acquittal that LA started to burn. There were—I don't know how many—over a hundred fires set across the city.

There were other atrocities that were also committed in the course of the civil unrest. On one hand, it was a bread riot. I mean, there were a lot of stores that just got everything stolen out of them and burned. There was a motorist, a white truck driver named Reginald Denny, who was pulled out of his truck and beaten by African American young men, and that was also caught on videotape, as well as a story about several other African Americans who saved Reginald Denny and picked him up and took him to the hospital.

That was in April of 1992, and I came home two months later. I had to stay in Boston until the end of the semester, and I immediately came back to LA and interned with the LA City Human Relations Commission for the summer. So several months after the civil unrest, I felt like this was where I needed to be. This was where my research needed to be relevant, and interning at the Human Relations Commission, I thought, was important to give me a sense of what could be done. What could cities do in the face of all of this?

I ended up going to a lot of community meetings and events and talking to a lot of people and just helping to be a kind of eyes and ears for the commission as they tried to figure out what to do. That summer, I learned how difficult it is to facilitate a deeper understanding among communities that are both geographically and socially so far apart. I learned how we really lack an infrastructure that would help facilitate communication in these kinds of crises—whether it's big, like the civil unrest, or small, like the other publicized conflicts between Korean storeowners and African American residents. We really didn't have an infrastructure.

I just wrote an article called "Towards a Human Relations Infrastructure in California" [*California Politics & Policy* (July 2002): 59–77] because I really feel that our cities are not well equipped programmatically and policy-wise. We traditionally don't see race relations as part of a city's responsibilities, or the responsibilities of city and state government, or government in general, for that matter.

I worked using the Community Coalition as a model. They started as a community coalition, mainly composed of Black and Latino residents, but who also had the involvement of some Koreans and other Asian Americans and whites working in South Central to lower the number of liquor stores and improve the quality of life.

There was also a group called the Multicultural Collaborative that grew out of that period. I found those types of models hopeful, especially the grassroots work that really engaged people in positive, forward-looking activities where people were able to build an identity inclusive of racial difference, an identity built on making a change in a place that everybody will benefit from—because people can have multiple identities. And in light of the beating of Rodney King and the civil unrest that followed the verdict, race was far and away the most salient identity boundary among them for most people, especially those living directly in the affected areas.

What the Community Coalition was doing was reinforcing or bringing out the salience of other identities, so that an identity of you and I working together to get these liquor stores out that are really hurting our community would matter—whether it was as a member of Community Coalition, or as a member of a movement, or through some identification with this group of people who were trying to do something positive. That was to acknowledge, not to downplay, the salience of race, but to also be inclusive of a progressive political identity.

It was an additive approach to coalition building. We weren't simply African Americans, or Latinos, or Koreans. So knowing that there were going to be racial divides and differences, we could work through them, and we could build upon the unique contributions that people might bring with them because of their differences in experience.

I lived that way. I have a Japanese American identity, for sure, but I was also a Mohican at Gardena High—the school mascot has since been changed to the Panthers—and I was also a Girl Scout and a member of the Y. And so there were many identities that I wore. At the same time, I was involved in a lot of Japanese American community issues and understood the gravity of race as a marker in American society. But they were never in contradiction.

I decided, at that point, to do my dissertation on race relations in LA somehow. I returned to LA in '93 after I had done two years of my MIT coursework, exams, and all that, and I started looking at different cases. I was going to do a comparative case study of different forms and arenas of racial conflict.

Down the street from where I lived was the housing project where there had been big fire bombings of Black residents' homes. So I started looking into that and a number of other issues. One that was close to my house became most convenient, most fascinating, and most dangerous, so I knew that I couldn't do more than one. If I was going to choose that, I would need to focus full time on it.

It turned out that this involved a gang war between a predominantly Latino gang and a predominantly African American gang. It started out as a fight over the drug market, and then it spread to Venice, and then it led to this whole cycle of racial polarization. So I did a participant observation study starting from the early stages of the gang war.

I did two years of fieldwork in Culver City and Venice. My husband and I lived in Culver City at the time. I didn't work directly with the gangs, but I did my research and work with several community organizations in those communities. I began my research in the Mar Vista Gardens housing projects in Culver City, less than a mile from my house.

The two gangs there were the Shoreline Crips and the Culver City Boys. Then the Shoreline Crips were run out of the projects after the fire bombings and gun battles and everything. It was really bloody. They fled to the protection of their cousin gang in Venice, just several miles down.

But there was a Latino gang there in Venice that was different, the Venice 13, or the V-13s. The V-13s and the Venice Shoreline Crips got into it, too, and that's where it led to a much bigger, wider conflict.

Newspaper headlines would read, "Bloody Venice Gang War Turns to Race War." There was just a lot of fear, racial distancing, and polarization. No one was on the street. No one could walk the neighborhood. People had doors and refrigerators on their front porch so that bullets wouldn't go in the front of their homes. People bedded their kids in the bathtub at night for fear of flying bullets.

There's a neighborhood in Venice called Oakwood where most of the violence was centered. I did two years of fieldwork studying that whole phenomenon, and I interviewed gang members, probation officers, police officers, ministers, community organizers—the whole gamut of people—to see what was going on. True to life in my neighborhood where I grew up, no two people had the same story of what happened, because people interpreted it in very, very different ways. So my job became finding out how people made meaning of different actions and events and how those actions, along with the interpretations of them, helped to explain racial distancing and polarization over time.

Because Venice is in the city of LA, I was able to share—with the guy that I had worked with at the LA City Human Relations Commission—what I thought were some insights that I was getting, so that some of the community efforts to get a truce, and then to support a truce, could be supported by the city. Because I had interned there before I had begun my dissertation, I still had that connection with Ron Wakabayashi.

Ron had since then moved to the LA County Human Relations Commission, where he had a bigger staff, and one of his staff members was also doing some work in Venice around this problem. He had all these federal agencies, from the FBI to Alcohol, Tobacco, and Firearms, involved. You had guys from the FBI who had just been brought back home from Russia and who didn't know north from south, running around with FBI T-shirts in the middle of the day doing things that seemed odd in the eyes of people who would see them.

There was a lot of attention being paid to Venice. In addition, Venice is the second most frequented tourist attraction in LA County; it relies in part on tourism. So there was probably extra attention paid to this battle. Over a ten-month period, seventeen people were killed and over fifty injured, mainly in about a one-mile radius centered around Oakwood.

So when I was asked to do this workshop in Azusa, it was based on work I did for my dissertation. Because of my training at MIT, I also had done GIS—geographic information systems—mapping of all of the incidents that took place in Oakwood during the gang war.

I shared this map with different people, and Ron Wakabayashi said, "Hey, those are neat maps. I have hate-crime data for the entire LA County. I wonder what it would look like to map those!" I was, at the same time, trying to find out, "Where else in the county are these types of phenomena taking place?" So with the data from Ron, I mapped over a thousand hate crimes in LA County.

I mapped over thirteen hundred race-bias hate crimes. I mapped these by race of victim, by race of perpetrator, by types of incidents, so that this became a map of LA County with the dots and the locations of the hate crimes. This was color coded by race of victim. We found out which neighborhoods were experiencing more intense racial conflicts, including gang-related conflicts.

One such city was Azusa, which is on the eastern edge of the county. Here, there was a concentration of Black victims who had been attacked in racially motivated crimes by those identified by police as Latino.

I showed the maps to people at the County Human Relations Commission, to the city, to the police department, and to others. They found it useful in various ways, especially the Human Relations Commission, who could use this information to ask, "Where are the hot spots?" and, "How can we look at a particular area and use this data to help figure out what's going on and where we might allocate our resources?" I had done this mapping, and I was trying to figure out other applications of mapping technology for human relations work.

After he left the county, Rob Wakabayashi was recruited to work at the US Department of Justice, and he was appointed as the western region director of the DOJ's Community Relations Service. He knew about some of the things that I had been doing, so he had me do a training for the entire Washington, DC, staff of the Community Relations Service of the Department of Justice. They had regular trainings and meetings where they'd bring all their people from across the country to Washington, DC. I did a presentation on the use of GIS for identifying hate-crime hot spots.

After that, I talked to him about the role of planning, because I really believed that planning could play an important role in trying to address these problems, because planning could work with people in communities to try to figure out how they want to solve the problems they're facing. I really don't believe, with this type of problem, that any person or agency could solve the problem from the outside. You really need neighborhoods and cities organizing together with the help of external resources to figure out how they want to address the problem of racial violence.

The city of Azusa was one of the cities that the LA County Human Relations Commission was working with, as well as Ron, because, as anyone could see from the maps, there was a big cluster of African American victimization by Latino gang members. There were two murders. Usually in places like this where you see a cluster, a lot of the initial incidents are name calling and people just harassing each other, and then you have beatings, and then you have arson, and it usually climbs the ladder of severity.

There were a couple of murders, and at that point, the city of Azusa passed a resolution to set up a task force to come up with a plan for how the city should deal with this. So they appointed an eighteen-member hate-crime task force, and they were mandated to come up with recommendations. But for seven months, they had various false starts and internal problems within the committee. Because there had been political appointments by the city council to the hate-crimes task force, there were a lot of issues that people raised about who was on it, what right did they have to be on it, who did they represent, was it representative, and all that.

* * *

Ron and people at the LA County Human Relations Commission were afraid that this task force was ready to fall apart after seven months. So they asked me if I could do something, if I had any suggestions or if I could help. I suggested that a strategic-planning retreat might help get it back on track and help them produce a set of recommendations; otherwise, nothing would happen.

At this point, I was teaching at the University of Hawai'i, so I was not able to have any meetings prior to the event itself with principals in the task force. What I did then was to work closely with Marshall Wong of the LA County Human Relations Commission and with Ron Wakabayashi of the Department of Justice. They played the role that I would have played myself in consulting with people on the front end, doing the individual consultations with people, clarifying expectations, working out an agenda, making sure everybody was fine with it, and making sure people would come.

I was in consultation with Marshall and Ron—by phone mainly and email—and we worked out two things: an agenda for the meeting, which, of course, I didn't stick to, strictly; and a pre-retreat questionnaire. I set what I thought could be the goals of the retreat. There was a process-related goal, which was to build a stronger foundation for the human-relations infrastructure. The task force had changed their name to Human Relations Commission. One goal was to build a stronger foundation for the Human Relations Commission based on mutual respect, shared understanding, and common direction.

There were three stated goals; one was process related and two were task related. The task-related goals were to generate innovative solutions to the problem of racialized violence and to develop a framework and outline for the strategic-planning report and present it to the city council.

I only knew the participants based on this pre-retreat questionnaire that I had sent to them, but it was very, very helpful. I asked them in advance, "In your opinion, how widespread is the problem with racial prejudice and animosity among the following: among the Azusa-13 members in the gang, among the adults, among the youth, etc."

Then I asked them, "What do you think have been the major causes of animosity, and what's your understanding of the history of race relations in Azusa?" Then, lastly, I asked them to list resources that might help address the problem by suggesting effective solutions that they might have. I collected this from all the members of the task force, and they were all supposed to be at the meeting.

I tallied and summarized the results of the questionnaire, and that gave me a good sense of where the similarities and differences might lie between members of the task force. So I had some feeling of connection to them prior to the event.

I flew in and checked into a hotel in Azusa. You know how to psych yourself up for an event. You've done all the preparation you possibly can. You have all your rollout paper all marked up. You have all your big sheets of paper printed out with the agenda. We had the Ten Commandments of Consensual Dialogue—kind of ground rules—and all of those props.

That was the evening before, drawing the last lines on the graphs and making sure I had enough Post-it notes and all that. But really, there was more—meditating and trying to center myself. Anything can happen in these kinds of situations.

After I had read the results from the surveys, I realized that there were some deep differences in terms of whether or not some people even thought there were racial tensions and what the sources of those were. This was a microcosm of the nation in terms of the differences in ideology, in attitude, in racial attitudes, and in backgrounds.

Half of Azusa is flat and half is on the mountain. You have million-dollar homes on the mountain, and you have barrios—poor, very low-income, high-density neighborhoods and apartments—in certain neighborhoods down below, not in all of them. You have some people who just don't think race is a problem, that there isn't racism—even in the face of the murders and everything else—even on the task force. Robert Blauner had written a book I knew, *Talking Past Each Other: Black and White Languages of Race*, arguing that people have such different lived experiences and perceptions of the problem, and, whether or not there even is a problem, that it's hard to get people into the same room face to face, confronting each other's beliefs and attitudes.

In a situation where there's so much pain because people have experienced the racism or the deaths of friends or family, it's a highly emotionally charged environment. People are so sensitive to the touch. And you could have the same type of polarized debates. Some are saying, "The problem is that we have single mothers who don't watch over their kids, and that's why we have this problem," and on the other hand, people will say, "It's poverty that's causing this, not single parent families."

I was anticipating all of this from within the commission itself—and all that was likely to come together, through divergent views, experiences, attitudes, and points of view—converging in one room around an issue that was so highly sensitive.

I had learned from Puanani Burgess how to do guts-on-the-table, which is an exercise that helps bring people together face to face in a somewhat disarmed or disarming way. It allows people to sit and listen to one another without making assumptions about why they're saying what they're saying and jumping to conclusions about what they might mean. So I started the retreat just giving a little background about how I got asked to do this, and I commended their efforts. I started off by saying, "I commend you for what you're doing. These problems exist in other places, but I think this is really the first place that a city is trying, in some official capacity and in some systematic way, to deal with this very serious problem that we as a whole society face. I think that what comes out of this committee can potentially serve as a model for other cities. So what you're doing is so important and very difficult."

I tried to lay out what I thought were some of the goals and to see if there was consensus around the goals for the two days and how we might go through a process together. We had an evening and a day. I thought there were two things that we needed to do on the first night so that on the second day, we could focus more on the plan.

So I devoted part of the first night to the exercise guts-on-the-table. I laid out some grounds rules. First, everything said in this exercise was to be kept in this room, and the identities were confidential. Second, once you wanted to talk to somebody about what they said during the exercise—after the exercise was over—you had to ask their permission first before raising it, because maybe that was the only place they wanted to talk about it. Third, if anyone wanted to go to the bathroom or leave or do something else, we would stop the entire exercise and wait until she or he returned, because everyone's story is important. Fourth, silence is just as meaningful as words; there are times you don't want to say anything, or if you don't want to say anything at all, that's respected. Fifth, whoever convened or initiated guts-on-the-table had to go first.

Then I gave them four questions: What is the story of your name? What community are you from? Why are you here? and What is your gift?—*gift* being different from skill or talent, but something you can give. I went first. I told the story of my name, my community, why I was there, and what I thought my gift was. It was very emotional, and I felt I really needed to center myself so that I could start. I knew that if that exercise didn't go well, the rest of the retreat wouldn't go well. In fact, I had visited Puanani Burgess the week before I left for LA just because I felt I needed to go through guts-on-the-table with her once because I hadn't done it in a long time. You really have to let yourself be vulnerable, and we don't do that on a daily basis as faculty. So I had to get myself in a somewhat different mindset and be able to open up in front of a group in that way. In telling the story or taking my turn, it was very emotional. I did choke up at times.

Now, this could last days—just doing guts-on-the-table—so I did something that Puanani does, which I think is very effective. You have a set amount of time that you want to spend on it, and you divide that time by the number of people there. You give everybody so many minutes based on that calculation, and then the person next to you holds a watch. When you've reached your time, they hand you the watch without saying anything, and you are now taking someone else's time symbolically. So people really end, because they don't want to use up the next person's time. I think we only had three or four minutes each, because we had a group of about twenty-four people. Everybody would speak to all four questions in about four minutes. But it's amazing what you can do in four minutes. I've done it with six people over two hours, and this was very different.

To backtrack a bit, when I got into the room, the room was set up just like a classroom; it was a big room, and we were only using a third of it. The chairs were set up around round tables, almost like a banquet. I wanted a horseshoe, or a circle rather, almost a circle.

They also had chairs behind the tables for observers, and they were marking a difference between task force members—Human Relations Commission members—and observers. Other people had been invited to come to observe, but they hadn't been invited to participate.

But my feeling was that we needed everybody's participation; if you were there, that meant you were concerned and you could contribute. So I had them change everything right on the spot, right before we started. We pushed all the tables back, made one big circle, and invited everybody into the circle. Some people were viewed by some of the commission members as troublemakers, and that may have been why the rows of chairs had been separated, but I rearranged them to be all together in a circle.

As the exercise progressed, I developed my own connection with each individual there. I saw other people dropping their guard and developing connections with one another, even though there was a lot of distrust between certain members of the commission because they had been appointed by politicians.

Each council member, I think, had appointed a couple of people. So all the divisions between council members was passed on to these commission members—not to all of them, but to many of them. There were just some council members who were more supportive of this task force than others, and people suspected that someone who didn't really care just appointed someone who also really didn't care about this problem. There were all these kinds of presumptions being made, so including everyone helped to temper these assumptions that people had.

There was an African American young man who was working for a church and who was doing a lot of youth outreach, and some people had suspected that he was part of the problem, that he was fanning the animosities. He told a very moving story that showed that he was concerned in a very deep way about this issue and that he had something to offer in terms of solutions. Another person, who people thought was a bigot, who didn't care, shared his history, which was apparently very different from what people thought his history was. And one high public official talked about how she had been a radical in the sixties and why she'd come to feel this was important. A lot of people distrusted the mayor's intentions. In another instance, a Latino woman said, "I'm here because I don't believe in color, and my boyfriend is Black, and we go around everywhere in the city scared that something is going to happen to him or something is going to happen to me." And then the Latina elected official shared, "When I was in law school, I clerked for a judge, and this judge helped me become of who I am, and this judge was a Black woman judge."

So people shared things about their history that helped them connect across the color lines. One guy said, "I have to admit, I'm a bigot. I don't like Black people." He was on the task force. I don't know if he said this in the guts-on-the-table exercise or if it was later in the retreat that he admitted that. People felt really good about sharing, disclosing all this together, so I felt good about that depth of conversation.

People were talking to each other. There was so much buzz after the exercise ended that people were shaking each other's hands and walking across the room to approach each other to thank them for sharing their stories. People were feeling like they were included in this process. People who were formerly asked to sit in the chairs in the back were feeling that they were part of the process now, and others were feeling like, "Yeah, we should include these people in this process." So I was trusting that my decision to include them had been the right decision.

This was halfway through the first evening. By reading the surveys, I also knew that not everyone was convinced that there was really a problem.

I had spent the earlier part of the day with the police captain getting a tour of the whole city and the places where different incidents had taken place. I asked her to describe to me what incidents took place in what places, so that I could, through her, live through some of the experiences that people had lived through. I also did an interview with an African American family that she referred me to so that they could tell me their stories, because two African Americans had received death threats and couldn't participate in the retreat because of fear for their lives. So I felt like that voice wasn't going to be represented in the retreat—the African American victims' voice.

The task force was maybe half Latino, half white. The African American commissioners couldn't be there. There were other African Americans who ended up coming who were not commissioners but who had heard about it and came. But not knowing that anyone of African American background was going to be there, I just felt, walking into it, that I needed to interview people to get their voice and to be able to share that voice at the meeting if the situation called for it.

So I did those two things beforehand. What I structured after guts-on-the-table was a presentation by a panel that I had asked Ron and Marshall to arrange. We talked about who we would invite on the panel—for example, a police captain of Azusa, along with a probation officer. I thought a probation officer would be really important because probation officers have access to the minds of youth that other law enforcement people don't have, and they're in touch with the people who are getting arrested for these things. We had a youth worker. So they presented on the panel.

The police captain had done her own GIS mapping, so we had some of the Azusa maps. She presented the maps; she described the incidents and what happened and what they had tried to do. The probation officer did interviews with the kids in preparation for his presentation to the panel, and he gave verbatim quotes of what they had said about what they thought the problem was and why this was going on. He even quoted using the N-word. He said the word itself, and that created some problems later on that I can talk about.

The youth worker talked about the positive side of youth and what youth are trying to do in positive ways, because there were some people on the commission who had very negative views—especially some of the people who lived up high on the hill have this view—about inner-city "barrio" youth, an overly negative view of these kids being thugs, just violent, disrespectful kids.

The guts-on-the-table exercise accomplished what I'd hoped—that they would put their defenses down, be more open to each other, give each other a little bit more benefit of the doubt, see the positive, the good in each other, and see where their aspirations were shared. I'd hoped they would see beauty in each other in whatever way they might define beauty—that they would be able to appreciate each other's gift, because they had heard each other's stories and appreciated, I guess— and Pua said it best—the humanity of every individual and the gift that they brought to this process and problem. So this developed into an appreciation for one another that didn't exist before and a greater willingness to see if people could work with each other.

The panel evened out the plane of understanding about the nature and scope of the problem, which didn't exist before. Now, people were better able to approach the planning and the planning process based on a shared understanding of the nature of the problem.

Then we regrouped the following morning, and I showed them my maps of hate crimes throughout the county. I tried to put Azusa in a broader context so that people didn't think that there was something wrong just with their community and so they could see that this was a larger phenomenon. I shared that we don't understand why it was going on in these specific places, but that it had to do with things like the phenomenon of race-bias hate crime, gang-related hate crime, and that also had to do with what was happening in the California prison systems— with the prison gangs such as the Mexican Mafia and the Black Guerrilla Family and the Aryan Brotherhood and the race riots that were taking place in the prisons in the late eighties and throughout the nineties.

The Azusa gang, the A-13, was connected to the Mexican Mafia. The Mexican Mafia was the Southern California prison gang that had extensive connections to most Mexican American/Chicano gangs in Southern California. In Northern California, it's La Nuestra Familia that is their counterpart. The prison gangs have heavy influence over the street gangs because street gang members often get sent to prison, and the prison gangs control the space within the walls of the prison in many ways, in terms of privileges, rights, safety, protection, and all of those things. So they exert a certain amount of control, and they're also allegedly involved in a lot of the drug trafficking. A lot of that works through the prison.

So it was really important for everyone to be able, somewhat, to de-personalize what was going on and to see that what was happening in the community was not their fault per se, to see that there were other, broader social phenomena that were connected to this.

Then I gave them a review of "What is a strategic-planning process?" because most people don't know what a strategic plan would even look like once it's written. I wanted them to know that they could do it, that they didn't have to be a planner to be able to come up with a plan. The way that I explained planning was that it's a way of figuring out who's going to do what, when, where, and in what order so that they felt comfortable that they could embark on a planning process and come up with recommendations. That's just what they had been asked to do, but there was just a lot of confusion about what a strategic plan is.

Then we spent the morning doing an assessment of the problems. I shared the survey results, and we had a discussion about that. Then we did an exercise, a morning exercise on strategic actions. I had a big piece of paper saying "Peace Making," "Peace Keeping," and "Peace Building" on the left column, and then across, I had different areas of work that could be done—whether it was peace making, peace keeping, or peace building. So there are activities that can be done that are peace making; for example, getting the violence to stop. The other is peace keeping, maintaining peace. Peace building is creating the relationships and programs and activities so that a peace could be long lasting.

So they did a "how to do it" exercise, and they had to think about, "What can law enforcement do? What can the schools do? What can community organizations do?" They had to think, "What can the churches do?"—and to consider all these categories of players.

Now we had the walls covered with suggestions of what they could do. Then we did a kind of a Delphi technique where they voted for the top three or five that they thought were good ideas. Before that, we had taken a lunch break, and during the lunch break, I had clustered the ones that sounded similar so that there wasn't a lot of duplication on the sheets. Then people started to rank them.

But before we did the ranking, we had a short discussion on "What ideas do you think are the best ideas?," "Which ideas are bad ideas?," and "Which ideas do you need clarification on?"

But earlier, after they had put up all their ideas on Post-its, I had them go back and read everybody else's ideas. The good thing about Post-its without names is that there's no attachment of that idea to a person, as opposed to what happens when people verbally share their ideas. So people judge the ideas on the merit of the idea as opposed to who suggested it. Only then did I have them write down which ideas they thought were the best ideas, which ideas were bad ideas, and what ideas they wanted clarification on. Then they sat down.

When they sat down, I asked them, "Let's start by answering two of the three questions from this discussion, and we'll start with what you need clarification on." So people needed clarification. Second, I asked them, "What do you think are bad ideas?" People said, "This thing about rounding more kids up and sending them to prison is a bad idea, because this is where the problem is coming from, it's from the prison gangs—so how are you going to da, da, da . . . ?"

Talking about the bad ideas didn't get other people's backs up against the wall, because they didn't know whose ideas they were. They were criticizing the idea, not the person. There was no attachment between person and idea. The people who had written them didn't get defensive; they listened to what the people were saying because they didn't feel they were being attacked. Then the third question: "What did they think were the best ideas?" I asked them then to put their stickers up on those Post-it notes so they could vote with the stickers for the best idea. The rest of it was just working on how were we going to narrow it down. So we narrowed it down, and they came up with a plan.

But before the end of the day, the mayor had actually run out during her lunchtime, because she had asked me, "Do you have a closing exercise?" I said, "No, that's something that I have options for, but I haven't really decided what the best way to close is." She gave me an idea, and she said, "I'll get it for you; I'll get the supplies for you." So at the end of the afternoon, she had a box filled with sand and there were different jewels buried in the sand—jewels, just from a craft store. So at the end, we just went around, and everybody reached into the box of sand and pulled out a jewel and then had to say what they were taking from the meeting, from the retreat. It was really wonderful. The self-proclaimed bigot said, "You know, I came here as a bigot and I . . ." he almost cried.

He said, "Hearing your stories about what's happened to you, I've really come to change my mind about all of this."

There had been different periods where I just went off the agenda totally to deal with some of the personal issues that were coming up, like the N-word. I heard through the grapevine, through Marshall, that someone was really having a hard time and wasn't going to come back, because she was so offended. But she did come back after his encouragement. So I built in time to deal with those issues.

For example, we had taken a time-out. After getting her permission, we asked her to share what offended her the previous night. She told the story about how she's a Black woman and a victim of hate crimes in Azusa as a resident and what had happened when she opened her front door one day and her kids' shoes were set on fire—and how that N-word the evening before had evoked her fear and her knowledge of the lynching of Blacks and, historically, all of those kinds of things all came up. She told this story in the early part of the day, because I'd felt that we really needed to take the time to do this.

These things are going to come up all the time, and part of the success of what you do depends on how you're able to talk about these things with each other—because they are going to keep coming up. I had said this to everyone at the retreat, too: "We can't ignore these things just because we don't know how to deal with them. How we process these critical moments affects how we will relate to one another in the future. If we can model good processing of racially sensitive issues, we can take those lessons to new situations that will invariably arise. The success of this group is going to depend on how the group is going to be able to resolve many things like this that come up and how well we can talk to each other about how these things affect us and how we want to change the way we do things."

At the closing I said, "I wish I could have taped that," because people were very moved by everyone else's reflections. People said "I didn't trust you" to the mayor or to somebody else and "Now I have a lot more faith" or "I was ready to quit this committee, and a number of us were, but I feel like this has renewed my hope, and we can actually get something done here that's meaningful."

Someone had said, "Yeah, I was a bigot and da, da, da, and now my eyes are open more to what my problem is."

The mother of the youth worker came, and she said, "My daughter—I'm afraid for her. She's trying to do something, but she could be the next victim just because she's trying to solve the problem, and I really feel like this committee is so important because it can't just be my daughter who's out there trying to do this."

So that helped reinforce everyone's sense of importance of the work that they were collectively doing as well. Then I shared my own feelings about the meeting and what I was taking from the meeting and the inspiration that the group gave me and the aloha that I felt and that I thought would help carry the group on.

Then that was it, and they figured out a time for a follow-up gathering. I was very surprised because after it, all, one by one, they came up and gave me a big hug and thanked me. And they were hard hugs, and I gave them hard hugs back.

Looking back, I don't think I would have done anything differently. Maybe I would have done closer follow-up about the actual production of the plan, and I wished I had done a little more to help problem solve the rest of the process of getting the proposal passed and implemented.

It went to the city council, and there was a discussion over how much resources were going to be available to give to the commission, and in the end, I don't think they got quite enough in the way of resources, so that was a problem. But I don't know exactly what they got, if they got a director or if they got a staff person or something.

Overall, it was one of the most fulfilling things I've done. It was stressful. But actually, after I did my fieldwork for my dissertation on gang violence, very few things stress me out.

6

Developing the Red Hook Community Justice Center

James Brodick's Practice Story

Editor's Preface

James Brodick went to work in the Red Hook neighborhood of Brooklyn, New York, at a time when the local news was all too full of drug related violence in this low-income, diverse community of color. His efforts to develop a local community justice center involved very much more than the criminal justice system, especially because public sentiment regarding local government and local governance programs registered in the vicinity of "trust in local officials: 12 percent."

Brodick had his work cut out for him. He had little budget to work with, but he had AmeriCorps recruits from the community. Working to transform the siloed community justice center into a program closely connected to job counseling, drug counseling, and other local services, Brodick built trust, overcame suspicion, encouraged community buy-in and ownership, and, not least of all, developed youth leagues for recreation—all for the recreation of Red Hook as a newly safe place.

Place and Race, Community Development, and Crime Prevention

Let me tell you about how I started. When I graduated from St. John's with a bachelor's in business, I took off for about a year, and during that time, I was trying to figure out what my next steps were going to be. I actually got involved with an organization called Victim Services, which later changed its name to Safe Horizon. Victim Services was one of the leading victim's assistance agencies, not only in New York City but in the entire country.

While I was working with them and doing some consulting, they started to have this conversation about Red Hook. They were talking about how Red Hook was in the process of having some dialogues about a community court. Victim Services was working with the Center for Court Innovation and also with the chief judge of New York at the time, Judith Kaye. They wanted to start to get people to go out into the Red Hook community and learn about the neighborhood, the feasibility of a court, and what having a court would actually mean—would people be open to it.

So one of the first projects that I was responsible for was helping them start up what was known as the Red Hook Public Safety Corps. It was actually an AmeriCorps program (AmeriCorps was President Clinton's domestic Peace Corps). But unlike a lot of AmeriCorps programs where you recruit young, smart college kids to come to a community to do good work, we wanted to go with a different model. Our model was to recruit people from the community to serve the community.

So my initial position with Victim Services was to recruit a team of fifteen residents who would do things like community needs assessments, but who also were trained in conflict resolution, mediation, and facilitation skills. These groups of people could do survey work at local schools, etc. That was the beginning of my having contact with the Red Hook community.

After I did that for a year, I left for two years and did some consulting work for the department of education, again starting peer-led mediation programs. Then, in 1998, I came back to Red Hook, and from that point forward, I've been working for the Center for Court Innovation, and I have been part of the court planning team as far as supervising a lot of the programming that now takes place at the Red Hook Community Justice Center.[1]

Along the way, the strangest thing happened to me. I think the reason why I took off that year after St. John's was to try to figure out what I wanted to do. I had this idea of getting my MBA or going to law school. But as a kid, I always did a lot of volunteer work, and then as I got older, I coached Little League. I coached youth basketball. I was really into learning more about community development.

So when I got this opportunity through Victim Services to work on that project for a year, I think there was a shift going on in my mind; obviously, you want to earn a good living, but at the same time, I wanted to be entrenched in some kind of movement. I really felt that working with people, working with a community, was something that was interesting, and that year working with Victim Services changed my scope, so much so that later on in life, I went on to get an MPA, to do public administration, instead of an MBA in business administration, because I felt like that was now what I wanted to do. So I think it was partly growing up wanting to do volunteer work, wanting to be part of the neighborhood in communities, and that one year experience with Victim Services really shifted my thought process about what I wanted to do with the rest of my life.

Let me take just one step back for folks who don't know the Red Hook story. Red Hook is this isolated community in Brooklyn. It's surrounded on three sides by water. It's separated by an elevated highway, so it's physically isolated. And during the late '70s and almost the entire '80s, it went through a horrific crack epidemic, where many people called Red Hook the crack capital of the world.

There was gunfire every day; people were getting killed. It was the type of community that you didn't go to unless you lived there. It had a really scary reputation. In the early 1990s— '92, actually—a local principal looking for a student got caught up in crossfire and was killed. When that principal was killed, there was this outcry, both in the community and in the media; if a neighborhood can't keep principals safe, then what chance do the kids have, what chance do the residents have? That's what really sprung this idea of bringing justice back. The DA of Brooklyn, who was Charles Hines, said, "We're going to bring justice back. We're going to prosecute the killers to the fullest extent of the law."

But then the question was, what happens when the case is over? That's really when the momentum started; even with that being said, even though people wanted justice, what does that mean?

In the first year of the Red Hook Public Safety Corps—1995—they did a community survey, and in that survey, about seven hundred people responded. In that survey, we asked questions about perceptions of safety, programs that community members would like to see, and their feelings about the criminal justice system. Only twelve percent of the people gave a favorable rating to the criminal justice system and the courts. As somebody who was part of a planning team wanting to bring a court to this community, that was a scary number to hear.

We weren't naïve enough to believe there was going to be a seventy-five percent favorable rating, but we also didn't believe it would be twelve percent. So we went on a major campaign to engage community residents in what a community court is, to get them engaged in the planning process, to go to a lot of community meetings, to get them involved in talking about what services would be in place.

From the very get-go, we had a community advisory board and a bunch of stakeholders, and we had them participate in the planning—that was the most critical thing. Also, I think, having the AmeriCorps program out here, delivering some early wins, helped. Not only did they teach conflict resolution and mediation, they painted over graffiti, they cleaned up local parks, they worked in the local health center, and there was this feeling that community residents were interested in taking back their neighborhood.

The Public Safety Corps really set a foundation for us. It made our work less scary, so people said, "OK, well, I'm not quite sure what that court is going to do or what that court is going to mean, but I do see this good work by the Public Safety Corps members—and actually the Public Safety Corps member is my neighbor, my friend." So watching them do some good work made some people feel like at least there were some positives that could come their way because of this program.

Two years later—and this is before the building opened in '97—we started a teen court, where we trained local teenagers to hear really low-level cases referred to us by police, and they would give out mandates or sanctions, like community service or letters of apology. In both AmeriCorps and the youth court, they got a stipend; they got paid, they learned new skills, and they were doing busy stuff that made them feel good about their communities. There were a lot of early wins, both in creating new programs for this neighborhood and in making sure that the stakeholders realized that we weren't coming in to arrest people, we were coming in here to try to help solve problems. I think that was the shift that was made, that they didn't see this court as a negative, but they started to appreciate that this court could potentially bring in services that were long overdue.

We identified community leaders by going into communities and asking around. So here in Red Hook, this included the two association presidents for Red Hook East and West, one of the largest housing developments in the county. You had people who sat on the local community boards. You had police captains. You had the local principals. You had the clergy and religious leaders from the churches. And then also, if you asked enough questions, you started to hear certain names that kept popping up, people who were activists, people who were trying to do some good work on their own. So we created a list of people, based on positions and titles and then based on word of mouth and on hearing names over and over. That led to our initial stakeholders' advisory board—the kind of people who we went to because there already was a forum for us to meet them, and it allowed us to communicate what we were trying to do.

The AmeriCorps program helped us to get to that underbelly, the people who don't normally get involved but who actually did know a lot about their neighborhoods; for example, the grandma who looks out the window all day and knows what's going on. The AmeriCorps program, because we grew to fifty positions, allowed us to tap into a new group of community leaders. As a result of getting to know those AmeriCorps members—who, again, live here in this neighborhood—they will also then say, "Oh, I know someone else who would be good as well. We should invite them." What it became was a kind of word-of-mouth approach to, "How do we start to get more and more people involved?"

We did the community surveying because even if you welcome people in, even if you invite folks, there are still people who don't want to participate. The surveying, in which we weren't asking for names, was confidential, but it allowed us to get information from people who normally aren't the ones who are speaking the loudest.

So we went down all of those avenues, starting with the people who were identified as stakeholders, the AmeriCorps members, the underbelly, and then the surveying. I think that's truly how we started to get to know and get involved in this community, and that's why it wasn't people like me doing this survey but instead the AmeriCorps members, since they lived in the neighborhood.

If you lived in a building, you tended to know more people in the building. So they would knock on the door and say, "Hey, Ms. Jones.

I'm working on this new project. They're talking about bringing programs and services here to Red Hook, but before we can do that, I'm going around asking people questions, and I wanted to know, 'Would you be interested?'" And again, people are more likely to do surveys if it's like a familiar conversation: "I'm doing this for you because I know you. If I got a random phone call, I probably wouldn't be doing this." It's the same model with our surveying; we involved people who lived there, who already had connections to community residents, so it became much easier to gather this information. So in doing the planning for this project, we had to do the planning with community residents as part of the team. That's why we were able to get back so many surveys.

Having AmeriCorps members conduct the surveys did not necessarily give us legitimacy. Early on, I think what it helped was that people were going to be honest and that they would actually answer the questions. Because AmeriCorps members were doing the surveys, that's how we found out that only twelve percent of the people felt good about the criminal justice system.

It wasn't really about them feeling like the product or the end game was going to be something positive. Really, we wanted to get honest information from as many people as possible. We think that because of the way we did the surveying, we got honest information from a lot of people. That really was what our goal was. Once you get the information, then the next part of the planning process is to ask, "Now what do we do with it?" And that's what we worked on.

Here's a perfect example. As an outsider who came to Red Hook—again, my first time out here was in '94—we would say, "Oh, the drugs." When we were doing the community surveying, though, people said drugs were an issue, yes, but so were the lack of educational opportunities, employment opportunities, and the lack of programs for young people. So getting together all this information is what helped us decide what the justice center was going to look like and what programs were going to be here in the building.

We are a court, first and foremost, but we are also a community center. Not only do we react to crimes that happen, but we also work on programs to prevent crime. We offer interventions. We offer ways for young people to come in through the front or voluntarily to get engaged. All of these things came out of the survey. That's why we have a job developer on-site, and GED [General Educational Development] classes, and youth programs—because this is what the community said it needed. So if we never did that survey, we would've come in as a court, and we probably would do a drug treatment court out here because we knew the use of drugs was a big issue, but it wouldn't have resolved or solved the real issues community residents had.

We asked, "What can a court do to resolve some of the issues that have been brought to our attention?" This court is about a couple of things: it's about accountability, but also about rehabilitation. We feel like the small things matter. So we were going to deal with low-level crimes—the low-level felonies, the misdemeanors. We knew that a lot of the people who were going to be coming through were going to need things like drug treatment, and they were going to need housing help, and they were going to need services. So the first question was, Were we serving that population that's going to come through the front door just because, unfortunately, they were arrested? Or do we have the wrap-around services in place to address these other issues?

The next step we took was to ask, "OK, who are the people we need to have working here?" Besides the judge and the court officers and lawyers, we also have social workers. We also have job developers. We also have educational specialists. We have housing specialists.

Then the next question was, What other community organizations are already working in southwest Brooklyn, and how can we see if they are interested in working with our population? Then we started to reach out to other community-based organizations, either saying, "Can we make referrals to you? Can we send people to you?" or, "Would you like to have a staff person located in our building so you can have more direct contact with this hard-to-reach population?" So on-site, we have sixteen different agencies working here, and that came out of the planning, too.

After we figured out what the court needed, the next question we asked ourselves was, "Why do people have to get arrested to get these services? How do we make sure that people walk in through the front door voluntarily, so they seek out services so they're not involved in the criminal justice system in the first place?" That's when we started to write grants to develop programming.

Just as I talked about the AmeriCorps program and the youth court earlier, we wrote grants for an HIV and substance abuse prevention program for teenagers where we trained peer educators, with arts programs on-site, with photography programs. We also have web-design programs on-site. We have a computer lab on-site—because these were the things that this community lacked, and this is what came back in our surveying, and so then we started to add those programs here.

A lot of what the planning was about was to figure out, whichever way somebody comes into this building—in the back door in handcuffs or in the front door voluntarily—"How can we make sure we have the services and the staff on-site to address the issue?" That's what we spent the next year and a half doing, before the building opened.

We got word out about these services through the brilliance of the AmeriCorps program. Fifty people a year came through that program. These became our outreach specialists. These became the mouthpieces of the justice center. These are the people who said to other residents, "You know what, you can actually trust them. It's a good organization." I think a lot of what happened was having those folks coming our way and doing this good work for us. I can't overemphasize how important the AmeriCorps members and the original stakeholders were in passing the word out.

In the first years, my job was to supervise the AmeriCorps members. It's one thing to recruit people, but it's another thing to make sure they have the skills to go out there and actually perform—to know how to do surveying, to know how to ask questions in a neutral way. We also trained the AmeriCorps members on issues around domestic violence, around conflict resolution and mediation. My direct role for the first year was supervising these people and making sure that they were well equipped to do the work they needed to get done.

When I came back in 1998—at that point, we had started up all these community programs that I've mentioned—my job was to supervise the community programs, to make sure they were running smoothly, and to make sure the community was engaged in them. I went to community meeting after community meeting after community meeting, meeting folks, introducing myself, talking about the organization, talking about our goals, talking about our future. I did that hand in hand with a lot of the AmeriCorps members; that's what I focused on during the planning process. And over the course of time, before the building opened, I did a lot of the community planning, community program supervision. Then, when the building opened, I went from overseeing all our community programs—when every so often we added things, like a mediation center, or a housing research center—to becoming, a few years later, the deputy director and then being the project director of the building.

One of the challenges of supervising and recruiting AmeriCorps members was that not only did we want them to be service providers, but they were also service recipients. For a lot of them, this was the first job they ever had, or they had been out of the workforce for a very long time. So some of what I was teaching them was not only the skills to be effective at their job, but skills of how to separate your personal life from your professional life: What happens when you have a sick child, but you also have to go to work? How do you manage those things? How do you manage when you're struggling with something or you're not comfortable speaking in public? So a lot of what I did was coaching, a lot of staff development, a lot of teaching people not only how to have a job but how to keep a job. In part, I was really trying to be a support for people who, like I said, for the first time in their lives were either working or had been out of the workforce for such a long time that they were getting reconnected.

Now I think my job is different. I feel like I'm responsible for three missions. First, outcomes matter. Our courts don't only have to process cases; we can come up with good outcomes that not only hold the defendants responsible for the crimes that they committed—and we try to make the community feel responsible, as well as the victim—but at the same time, we try to make sure that the services are in place to get this person rehabilitated and get them back on track. My job is to make sure that we have those things, that they're running well, that if there are any gaps in services or things that they are not happy with, either from my staff or from service providers, those things are being addressed immediately. I also work very closely with the police to make sure that the police feel connected to what we're trying to do. This is a hand-in-hand effort. This is community policing, prosecution, and court all working together to try to solve crime and disorder. So that's number one.

Second, I'm trying to change the perception the people have of the criminal justice system in communities like Red Hook. This court serves over two hundred thousand people, but because of our proximity to Red Hook, because we're smack in the middle of it, we do a lot of community education, we conduct a lot of community meetings, we try to invite people in for trainings. We've been so effective that in that same survey that I spoke about—we do the survey every other year—now seventy-five percent of the people give a favorable rating to the justice center. So it went from twelve percent back in '95 about the criminal justice center to about seventy-five percent of the people feeling good about having this court in their community; in 2008, over ninety percent of people surveyed reported feeling good about the community court. So that's job number two: the public relations of this work.

Third, we host visitors from around the country and around the world to come to hear the Red Hook story, so they can see what might translate to their jurisdictions. Currently, there are thirty-six community courts in the United States. There are about fifteen or twenty internationally. We have worked directly with the UK government, and they've started ten community courts in the UK. We're now working with Australia; they just opened one, and they'll open up a second. We're working with Vancouver, British Columbia, Canada. That's some of our international work. Then nationally, we are working with San Francisco right now, and we're working with New Orleans. So this model that started out in Midtown Manhattan first and then Brooklyn is now really taking place all over the world, and people come here for guidance as to how to get a court like this started.

But there are, of course, obstacles. I think the obstacles are that people want to see for themselves. Seeing is believing. It's one thing for us to say that this court is about getting folks back on track, that this court is about serving people. We don't want anyone saying, "You engaged us to get the doors open, but once it was open, you forgot about us." We've made a concerted effort; we have quarterly advisory board meetings or we have people from the community come in here and talk about issues and what's going on with them. We have issue meetings. For example, graffiti was a major issue in Red Hook. We had a task force around that. We have a task force around illegal dumping. We've also done some work with the local businesses to make sure that they're getting services that they need in regard to community service and payback. So we have not stopped engaging the community from the very get-go.

The court has made a big difference. We have higher compliance than the downtown court. We have fewer people getting rearrested. We have more people going to treatment and getting the services that they need. Then, more importantly for me, we have more people walking through the front door voluntarily to access services.

So when I think about why we were successful and how we overcame barriers from the very beginning—we overcame barriers because throughout the whole process, we always included the people who helped plan this place; that's the community residents, that's the AmeriCorps group. To this day, in many ways, they are a driving force behind what we do. It doesn't mean that everything that the community wants we do, but it does mean that there's a conversation and that there's a process about how we go about our business, and we're very transparent, unlike the court system. If you never worked in the court, you probably don't know what the hell goes on in there. I can tell you that most people in Red Hook have a sense of what goes on in this court. And that's because we want to be transparent, we want to talk to them about what's going on, we want to tackle issues, and we want to include them. It's a very inclusive process, and whatever barriers a community court can or will have, I think some of them are dealt with by just making sure that people are at the table having conversation.

I think the most difficult thing for me was that feeling that we haven't cracked the nut, and we're still trying to figure out how to; there's still a certain population, that for whatever reason, doesn't trust the court system—which I understand. It makes sense to me. But you hope, after being open for seven years, that we can change some of those people's perspectives. But it's been challenging.

We do family court here as well, so this is a multijurisdictional court that does criminal, family, and housing court cases. With the family court cases, I'm often surprised, even to this day, how hard it is to get the family engaged in the process, or even, when we're doing community programs outside, how challenging it is to get parents to be more involved; that's still something challenging, even to this day.

One of the lessons learned, for moving forward, is that even to this day, there is still a group of people, still a population of folks who, for whatever reason, we haven't reached. One of the biggest populations right now is out-of-school, unemployed youth, the seventeen to twenty-one year olds.

That's something for us that we're constantly trying to think about—how to get them more engaged. I don't think we've done a really good job tapping into them. When I look back, we probably should've been doing a better job in the high schools when we first opened up, because we should've realized that if these young people are not doing well in the high schools or are not engaged, or if they fall out of high school, then more than likely, we're going to wind up seeing them coming through the criminal justice system. So we've made a major point over the last several years to collaborate with as many middle schools and high schools in this community as possible, because the correlations between criminal justice activity and education are high; if you drop out of school, you're much more likely to be involved in the criminal justice system.

The fact is that we're trying to fix the educational system, but sometimes, as an outside organization assisting the schools, we've found that we've been able to get kids transferred into other schools, get them transferred into better school placements. If there's a lesson learned, we probably didn't think about the group of older teenagers, who are at a crossroads, and we, as a court, probably could have engaged them more or done some more programming earlier on. We're trying to do some catch-up at this point. That's something that I kind of look back and lament a little bit. But in regard to community organizing, community needs assessments, engaging the community advisory board—those things I'm very proud of.

I have also seen the impact from working with middle and high schools. There are two programs in particular that we're working on. One is called "attendance court," where when a school identifies a young person who is missing too many days, instead of referring them to a program—where, quite frankly, the city is overwhelmed with these cases—they refer them to the attendance court. In the attendance court, we have a hearing officer who works with the school, and we work with that family, not to say that they're in trouble, but to ask, "What's going on that's causing this young person to be missing from this school?"

Now we're talking about fourth, fifth, and sixth graders, so it's not kids who are cutting school to go smoke a joint; we're probably talking about kids who are missing school because of health-related issues, because a parent maybe has a substance abuse problem, something like that. So we have a hearing officer, and we have social workers work with those families on identifying the underlying reasons why their children are missing school, and then we're trying to get them services that help.

That project's only in its first year. And in that first year, of the twenty families that we've worked with, every one of them has gotten up to a ninety percent attendance. And that's what the goal is: that they're going to school ninety percent of the time. These are kids who were at the brink of getting the city involved in their educational neglect. So that's a very big success.

The second program is for our family court kids between the ages of ten and sixteen; some of them are in middle school, and some of them are in high school. For every family court kid who comes through, we have a family engagement specialist and an educational specialist, and our job is to make sure that the family is engaged and a part of the process, that we're trying to deal with whatever issues they have there. We're also working with the schools to make sure that these kids are in the right school placement—that if they needed an IEP [Individualized Education Program], or if they needed some kind of evaluation done by the school, that that would get done. And if they're in the wrong school, we work on getting them transferred.

That also has been very, very successful. Of those kids who have come through in the last year alone, we've gotten forty-seven kids back into school who had dropped out; it was forty-seven out of about seventy-four kids who came through at the time who weren't in school. Now it's not perfect—you can only do so much—but we are working very closely with identifying family and education as a need, and then working with the department of education, because by law, these kids deserve educational opportunity, so we're working with them to make sure that happens. Those are—to me—our major successes.

In regard to other things we've done in high schools, we've partnered with four high schools now in our area: the School for Law and Justice, John Jay, and two other smaller high schools. With all those high schools, we go in there, we talk about our community programs, and we try to get them engaged—for example, with our youth court. If there are issues that arise pre-suspension, they're sent over to our youth court, where we hear the cases and we give out sanctions and mandates. But it keeps the kid in schools while at the same time holding them account-able for their actions, because so many times kids get suspended. Not only are you suspended; that's number one. But number two, they are not learning during that time, and number three, there's not this real sense of accountability, because some adult has just told them, "You know what, you're bad."

But here, it's other teenagers hearing their cases they're referring. And we have also worked with some schools on starting peer mediation pro-grams and youth courts within the school itself. So for kids now in these high schools, they feel like they can be part of programming in a positive way by joining, or if something's going wrong in their lives, both they and the school have an opportunity to get this situation resolved using us as a referral source.

So the court, over the past five to ten years, has moved into doing ser-vices for both adult and younger generations. We've always worked with young people, but usually we waited until they had already gotten in trouble, and it was a response to what had happened. I think what we've emphasized, especially over the last five years, is that we as a court need to do more preventative services, that we shouldn't wait for somebody to get arrested—we shouldn't wait for somebody to start to smoke mari-juana, we shouldn't wait till somebody starts to drink alcohol—that if we can get out into the schools, if we can run programs, if we can start peer education programs, and if we can model positive behavior, we have an opportunity to stop crimes before they even happen.

We also run a baseball league, a youth baseball league, which has gone for ten years. That's another way of having something positive in this neighborhood. Many people from the court volunteer their time as coaches and as umpires, etc. It gives young people, especially males, a connection to other role models. A lot of what we're trying to do here is prevent crime from happening in the first place. That's not a typical role for a court. A court by nature waits for things to happen. Obviously, we know that's one of our responsibilities. But I feel like another responsi-bility is to work within the communities that we serve to prevent these things from happening.

How did we guard against complacency? Well, I think when you fi-nally let people know that they can come here and tell you what they're not satisfied with, they will. I think that's what keeps us motivated. I often say just that at a community meeting: "You may not need the justice center now, but if something arises in your life, I want you to go to your address book, I want you to pull out the justice center listing, and I want you to give us a call. Whether it's something that's happening personally to you, whether it's in your household, or you lost your job, or if it's a community issue, I want folks to call us."

Now, ten years later, the phone calls don't stop. I consistently get visits from community residents coming here, bringing up concerns and issues; they come to our community advisory board meetings. I think the reason why we aren't complacent is because the community doesn't allow us to be.

That, to me, is the biggest blessing of everything that we've done— because they actually think that we can help solve problems, and that feels really good, that when people are going through something in their life, they will stop and think about calling the Red Hook Community Justice Center to get them resolved. I think that's what keeps us going.

I also think part of what keeps us going is that because internationally we are being duplicated, we want to show the best product that we possibly can. Not long ago, Jack Straw, who was the third highest guy in the UK government, was here. We wanted to make sure that we were performing at a level that somebody like that would want to come see us. That's another part of what keeps us going.

Then thirdly, we have an amazing staff. And these are people who have heard about us, either through the documentary that was on Channel Thirteen [PBS], or reading law journals, or reading a book. But somehow or another, they heard about problem-solving courts, and they've come from around the country to try and seek employment, and so their desire to do well, too, has kept us fresh and kept us going.

All of those three reasons, for me, are why every day when I come in here, I'm not sure what to expect, but I do know there's things expected of me. So we have no choice but to be at the top of our game.

You always have to guard against brushing off a complaint or grievance as just another complaint. Sometimes it's a complaint, and sometimes it's a real issue, and so you deal with it in different ways. First of all, any community resident who comes here with a complaint, they will get an opportunity to speak with somebody and be heard. That doesn't mean something's going to get done. But being heard, sometimes, is what people need. That's first.

Second, when we hear a concern or an issue, one that comes to my desk or to a staff person's desk, or somebody comes in, we have a meeting with a researcher. We try to gather some statistics that say that this is actually, really true. Just because Jeremy came to me and complained about illegal dumping doesn't mean illegal dumping is an issue.

That actually happened once. We had a resident come in and say, "Justice center, what are you doing about illegal dumping?" The first thing that we did was, actually, two things: we developed a community-wide survey, and we had people survey an area where supposedly illegal dumping was happening. We had some people go out and survey and see what people really felt. At the same time, we contacted the department of sanitation in the place to see what the numbers were like. Was sanitation getting more calls about illegal dumping? Were police writing more summonses? As a result of that, we then decided if that was an issue we should tackle. That particular issue was something that we learned was a concern to a lot of people, and so that's how we convened a task force.

But there are also a lot of issues that people bring to our attention that maybe we're not the most equipped to deal with, and then we give them a referral to somebody else, or we try to set up appointments for other people. There are some complaints where people just want to complain, and my feeling is that you hear them out and you be realistic. We can't solve every problem, but they are heard. And then there are some complaints that are real issues, and then we try to figure out how as a justice center—because we consider ourselves conveners—to solve those issues.

The lowest days actually concerned construction of this building. It took five years for this building to get ready. We took community residents around in a bus, and we drove throughout the neighborhood, and we were showing different locations that we thought would be good for a community justice center. Pretty much unanimously, they picked this building, which had been an old parochial school. It was abandoned for over twenty years. But they said, "If you're going to take back our community, why don't you start with this building, this eyesore," because it also physically sits right in the middle of Red Hook. So we did.

The construction started, and once we started the construction, there was a lot of asbestos. There were a lot of things; you don't know what you're going to find until you start picking at a building. For a project that we thought was going to take a couple years, it wound up taking us five years. There were many days where we felt like, "Is this really going to happen?" And the longer it took, we had this feeling like, are community residents going to say, "They're just talking shit. It's never going to open up."?

I think those were some of our low days. We had this idea that we're going to be up in two years, and two years would come, and then somebody would tell us, "Another year!" Trying to keep that energy going, where we really didn't have the space—we were working in apartments in a housing development, and we were trying to run programs and run services, but it wasn't conducive. So we were worried that the momentum would run out.

But I think maybe it was a blessing, in hindsight, because of the grassroots approach that we developed and because we were in the neighborhood. Because we had a two-bedroom apartment, and if somebody complained about noise, I knew what it was like to have a noisy neighbor, and how thin the walls were. There was really a connection. As a result, what we thought was a negative at the time probably was in many ways the best thing that could've happened. But keeping staff motivated, keeping the AmeriCorps members motivated, that was challenging, because everybody wanted to believe this building was going to open up and offer all these great things that we promised, and constantly getting the delays was challenging.

* * *

As difficult as it was to keep staff motivated, it was even more so to keep the community motivated and confident. One way we tried to keep the community engaged was that, again, every year there was a new AmeriCorps group. They had these bright-red shirts, and they were out there cleaning graffiti and cleaning up parks, and they were doing community gardens, and they were running a youth baseball league, and we ran National Night Out against Crime in a park. The point of the matter was that even if a court never came, I think what the community said was, "Hey, what they're doing is pretty cool, too."

So it wasn't the ultimate endgame, but it was something that people felt proud about. They saw that the community was a little bit cleaner, that there were more programs for kids. I think at the end, they said, "You know, it's not the big prize, but it's not a bad one, either."

I think that's what got us through the community's feeling like, "They're just talking a lot of game." A lot of the motivation was just for us the planners to say, "OK, you know what? We have to keep moving. We have to keep moving, and we have to figure out how to make this work with the limited resources we have."

Also, we started both of those programs, and we thought they were instrumental to keeping the community engaged. The baseball league came out of this idea of Red Hook having these beautiful fields and parks, and what we were most surprised to learn was that most of the people who were using the parks in the mid-1990s were coming from other communities. So the kids who lived here in Red Hook weren't using this great outdoor space. So we started to talk about what we could put in place that would get people excited. There were already basketball leagues that were happening out here, there was a football league that was happening out here, and at the time, I loved baseball, and there were a couple of staff people who loved the game as well, and we said, "Hmm, a baseball league?" Really, it started as simple as that: "Why don't we do a baseball league?"

We've turned the baseball league into something where not only do we raise all the money and engage the volunteers and do that stuff, but all the kids who come through the league have to do at least one community-service thing, they have to come to National Night Out against Crime. So we use baseball as way to get them civically engaged in other aspects of their community, and they have to do one community-service day. So for us, it was a win-win, because we got a chance to put a baseball league where kids were going to be participating and staying out of trouble, enjoying their neighborhood, and it got them more involved in their community, and then they started to take pride in where they lived. That just started out as this idea of underutilized space that turned into a real plus for us.

Similarly with National Night Out against Crime. It's a national event that happens throughout this country, but nobody was running one in Red Hook, and so every year, on the first Tuesday in August, we do a big party in a local park, convening police, and fire department, and residents, and there's a barbecue, and there's a community softball game, and there's a resource fair, and there's a DJ, and it's just about making people feel good and feel like this is a place that they want to live. So those are two projects that we started. Again, the best work that we've done has taken place outside of the four walls of this building. I couldn't agree more with the statement that the outreach programs made the court seem active and have a friendly community face.

The impact of the court is bigger than I ever thought it would be, frankly. Sometimes I take a step back and reflect, and I ask, "Has this court really made this big of a difference in this neighborhood?" When I'm here on a Tuesday and Wednesday night and I see hundreds of kids coming in for programming, who are all here for positive reasons, I think, "Wow, that blows my mind," because I never thought we would get so many people coming in through the front door.

When I look at the court part of it, I knew we would be better than the downtown court, but I didn't realize how much better we were going to be—on everything from compliance rates, to getting people back on track, to lower recidivism. That blows me away, and quite frankly, the national and international impact we've had on the justice system—there's no way I would've thought that was possible. Not only is it possible, but it's being duplicated. If you would've told me ten years ago that this is what would've happened, I would've laughed at you. I would've said that maybe one of those things would've happened, or maybe parts of those things could have happened. But all of three of those things have happened, and they've happened in such a big and meaningful way. This has by far exceeded all my expectations of what this court can do.

These things happened because, first, the community justice center is a good idea. That's number one. It just makes sense. Because you can do outreach about a project that's crap. But this one, it makes sense. It's what courts should be doing. When I talk to other people about it, I say, "Forgive me if it sounds like common sense, but it really is." Engaging community and police in the process of what happens in the courts— that's number one.

Secondly, for me: having community participation and having community members have a say in any project that you get into. So whether you're a not-for-profit or if you're coming into a community to open a warehouse or a factory or something—I mean, having the community as part of the process, I think, has really been beneficial. Some of the reason for our success is the really smart, early-on planning, and then some of it is that it's just a good idea.

Not knowing I would be working in a court when I was younger, and now coming through this, I do think sometimes, "Why hasn't this happened earlier?" It's just that the court system is very traditional, and the court system has always chosen to deal with things after they happen, and not too many people knew about what was happening. The court system had to catch up with the rest of society, had to catch up to the community's expectations, had to catch up with what police were trying to do. Police are now trying to deal with these low-level offenses; the courts are trying to deal with twenty-first-century problems using twentieth-century solutions. That just can't work, and it just caught up.

The most meaningful impact is changing the community's perception of the court. I get that feeling every day. I get to walk in Red Hook, and somebody comes over and thanks us for something or is asking me questions about how we can bring a new initiative to this community. I think I'm most proud of that because I get the feeling every day.

But then the most important impact is being watched, because I just feel flattered that people from around the world make so much of a product that we helped plan and are producing. But the number-one thing is the change in community perception.

It's actually humbling to be asked for help. At the same time, when any visitor leaves and we just spent the day talking about our jobs, I think it just makes us feel better about what we do. Because as great as I'm going to talk about this place, there are issues that we deal with, and there are people who are worn out and feel that they're overworked—all the typical things that you feel on the job. But when you get to brag to somebody about something that you're doing, and when they leave they say they're going to take some of the things that you do and bring them back to where they live, it really does make you feel good.

Moving forward, we need to continue working with the seventeen-to twenty-one-year-old out-of-school youth who are out of school and unemployed, and we need to still be working on services and programs and making sure we're doing everything we can to keep them on track and engaging the families and working with schools and working with employers. That will be a big emphasis for me over the next year or two in regard to what we're seeing come through the court.

Taking that to the next step, in regard to the court system, is really figuring out how—even though we've gotten a lot of national recognition—we can take this model, even more so, out there. And not that everybody needs to have this independent building like we have, but how can you take the best practices that we've learned in this court and bring it to the main courts? In the Bronx, they're doing something called the Bronx Community Solutions Project, and that takes the best of problem-solving courts and brings them into the main courthouse. Over the next few years, we're going to be working with Manhattan to set up a similar project. We're doing it with some other jurisdictions around the city and the state. So I think for us, in regard to the criminal justice movement, that's probably the next step.

7

Community, Belonging, and Place Making

Father Philip Sumner's Practice Story

Editor's Preface

Place-making practices often assume a level of peace, an absence of violence and hatred, that will actually enable residents, users, and even tourists and passers-through to feel safe. But this seemingly obvious prerequisite simply does not exist in many spaces, in many historically contested and otherwise dangerous places, in cities and regions around the world. Just as Karen Umemoto and James Brodick worked to foster conditions of safety and justice in their communities, Father Phil Sumner had been working on contentious interracial and interreligious relationships for many years in Manchester, England.

Father Phil, as he came to be known in the press and media, was then asked to lend his insight and experience to residents and congregations in nearby Oldham, where relations between ethnic and religious groups had frayed badly. People of color, immigrants, and members of non-Christian faiths had been attacked on the streets. The question at hand was this: Could Father Phil work with local residents, leadership, and diverse congregations to build peace, to create safer places for residents of Oldham?

Father Phil's story depends far less on financial resources than it does on untapped local capacities for social organization and social recognition, for networking and learning, for mutual education and shared activities. His work shows all too vividly how the creation of place depends on the social and political relationships we have as we live in the spaces available to us. We see here the significance of visibility and publicity, of outreach and relationship building, of slow, daily work to overcome stereotype and presumption, to show clearly what we can be together and how we can live together. Father Phil's story of place making might seem unconventional, but that is likely to be because it is so fundamental, because place making so deeply requires these measures of community building and public safety.

Addressing Immigration, Ethnicity, and Religious Differences in Oldham

I am a priest, and I was working for twenty-five years in Moss Side, greater Manchester. That is an area with many people of African descent—I would say about fifty percent. There were riots back in 1981. A community forum was established through which local people tried to work with the various authorities to address the issues. I was elected as the press liaison for that forum, and I learned so much from the African-descent communities. I learned, for example, how to nurture identities through the education curriculum and how important this was in terms of giving equal access to that curriculum, to people of all different backgrounds.

When there were riots in Oldham in May 2001, my boss asked me if I would come to Oldham to do similar work to that I'd done in Moss Side. My bishop sent me as a sort of Catholic response to the disturbances that had taken place in Oldham. We appreciated, of course, that the issues in Oldham were very different from those in Manchester; in Oldham, to put it simplistically, it was Christianity and secularism versus Islam, whereas in Manchester, it had been people of African descent versus a white-dominated system.

Oldham and Moss Side are eight miles apart, but you don't leave a place after twenty-five years without some sadness. My years of training in Moss Side had prepared me in terms of understanding the importance of identity for building good communities and enabling people from different backgrounds to feel that they belong. One of the things I did in Oldham was to become the chair of the Community Cohesion Advisory Group. Several years later, perhaps for reasons of political control, this body was subsumed into the Community Safety and Cohesion Partnership. I continued to serve on it until my responsibilities as a judge in the diocesan matrimonial tribunal conflicted; both met on the same day at the same time! I'm still in Oldham, and have been here since I arrived on the day of 9/11.

When the riots occurred in 2001, it had reached a point where the Muslims and those who referred to themselves as Christians were rarely speaking to each other. The matter in Oldham was not so much contention as it was segregation. The communities lived almost completely separate, and unfortunately, the Pakistani, Bangladeshi, and Kashmiri communities lived in the poorest areas in the center of town. As the Pakistani or Kashmiri communities moved in, many residents of the white communities would move out.

So you had what we called "white flight." Blight would then occur in a particular area, and businesses would move out. We had lots of cotton mills in this area at one time, but many of these have gone. There are very few cotton mills around now, and people who had come in from Pakistan and Kashmir to work in those cotton mills were left unemployed when all that work disappeared. Often, due to either racism or a lack of cultural awareness in the businesses of the town, it was difficult for them to get employment, except in things like taxi driving, small shops, or as their own bosses.

It's that sort of thing that was creating conflict—the poverty itself. So one of the major areas we had to work on was making people—in fact, making Oldham—more prosperous, and then making sure people had equal access to that prosperity.

I am still a priest, so I am responsible for a church. But I'm also a person who goes beyond my normal responsibilities, in that I take on positions in the wider community or in the local strategic partnership of the town. When I came here, I immediately made it my business to stretch out a hand of friendship to people from different backgrounds to let people know that I cared about building relationships between people and that I wished to be involved in that process.

After the riots here, it became obvious that there was no meeting of even the principal workers within the religious communities. The imams and the priests were not meeting, so in response to a challenge by David Ritchie, the author of the government report on Oldham after the riots, we immediately set up an interfaith forum for the area in February 2002, and that interfaith forum included all the groups in the town that had a place of worship. The three main groups were Hindus, Muslims, and Christians, and I became the first chair of that interfaith forum.

In my last place in Moss Side, I'd already developed a modus operandi of attending wider community meetings, listening to concerns, and attempting to find shared solutions, rather like what I understand to be the role of a community organizer in the United States. Initially, these meetings were full of anger, and I saw some women with great credibility in the community take local authority representatives and others down to size. I had kept my head down.

Then, at one such meeting, which was full of people, a young Black guy saw my priest's collar and came over to me and said, "You should have something to say here." He physically took me by the arm to the dais and asked the chairperson to let me speak. I can't remember now what I said, but it was the beginning of my being much more high profile.

In Moss Side in the 1980s, more than eighty percent of Black men between the ages of eighteen and twenty-five were unemployed. So with the ministers from the different Christian denominations, we set up a churches' work scheme. They elected me as the chair of this organization, and as such, I had three hundred fifty people who worked for me on community development projects there—for example, refurbishing and reupholstering furniture. The completed products would then be simply given out to people who were in need. There were other projects, too, like light engineering and small construction projects. That was a way of the church being alongside the local community in creating jobs.

When one of the churches in which I worshipped each week was going to be closed down by the local Catholic diocese, I feared that it would become a symbol of dilapidation in the center of an impoverished community. It was a listed building and could not simply be demolished. In my capacity as chair of what was then named Firmstart (Manchester) Ltd., I bought the church from the diocese for one pound and then attracted three hundred thousand pounds to create managed workspaces within the church. It then became a very visible symbol of economic regeneration in that area.

There were several people who worried about whether I was doing the right sort of work or if I was just a glorified social worker. Every church in this country at the moment—well, not every church, but almost every church—is reducing considerably in size in terms of the number of people attending. If you're just going to have a maintenance approach with the group of people you have coming to your church, that's going to be an ever-aging group of people and an ever-reducing congregation. So there has to be a much greater sense of mission, entering into the wider community without the power and status given to the priesthood within its own community, but only with the power of your own abilities. There, the aim is to listen and then to work to build up relationships and be a sign of being alongside people.

Since my initiation in that huge public meeting in Moss Side, I have always been very vocal, and I had a high profile even before I came to Oldham. I was often seen on television. I also do work with the BBC as a presenter for a radio program called *The Daily Service*, and I'm often contacted by the BBC to do interviews on various issues having to do with ethnicity.

In more recent years, I have been a witness on *Moral Maze*, a combative program that sees a panel of four "intellectuals" challenge a witness on a topic. I was a witness in favor of multiculturalism and, on another occasion, in favor of decolonizing the curriculum in universities. But before that, I was being asked for a community response to yet another murder of a young man in the local community or for suggestions as to how that community could extricate itself from its problems.

When I came to Oldham, therefore, on 9/11 day, before anything had happened in the States, I was followed by a whole group of press—by the television cameras, by the radio reporters, and by the newspapers. It was, for the local press, a sufficiently important story that I was being sent here. Of course, most of that interest rightly disappeared once the Twin Towers were attacked.

There was, however, a note on the front page of the local newspapers on the day I arrived—"Father Phil Arrives in Town!" In that sense, I was starting off again, but I was still high profile. When anything happened in town, like the local elections for the local councilors, the press would come to me to do interviews again. At that time, the BNP [British National Party] were actually trying to win a place on the local council, but they never actually achieved that.

Straightway, people in positions of influence in the town were getting to know me. I'm able to express an argument, and I am able to get involved politically. I've also pushed in this area, within the schools that

I have responsibility for, that we open up our schools, which are faith schools, to people from the Muslim and other communities. Although the other schools in the area were very much single ethnicity or single religion, the schools that I had responsibility for very quickly became twenty-five percent Muslim or involved people from faiths other than Christian. So immediately, then, I established a certain credibility within the town.

Because I also was the first chair of the Oldham Interfaith Forum, I've been a driver in setting it up and establishing its objectives. I attended every single meeting and was also asked to represent the interfaith forum in what later became the Community Cohesion Advisory Group. This was a group set up by the town themselves to work in partnership with the local communities, and after two years, I became the chair of that particular organization. I am now on the executive committee of the local strategic partnership for the town as their advisor on community-cohesion issues.

Within the parish community here, we established a Filipino choir, an African choir singing in several different languages, and also an Indian choir. It all started one Christmas when I became aware of just how heartbreaking it must be for people to be exiled from their homes and families at that time. I asked one of the African parishioners if he could get a few of his friends together and sing a couple of songs from his own background during our Christmas service. As luck would have it, I had approached someone who'd been a director of a choir in his own country. Their music was appreciated so much that they agreed to do more, and a choir was formed. Immediately, the Filipino community approached me to ask if they could introduce some of their music into our services. Straightaway, the parish community, the way I ran it, became even more multiethnic.

But before I came here, it was almost all white, and I was the youngster. Now, that's completely changed. The demographics have completely changed so that there are many people who are younger than me. There are about fifty Africans, fifty or sixty Filipinos, and about fifty or sixty Indians. In fact, there are, at the last count, people from fifty-two nations worshipping in our parish each Sunday.

There are people within wider Oldham who are worried about this agenda, specifically the BNP and those who would follow that line.

You have to appreciate that sixteen percent of those who voted in this town—in the Oldham West constituency—in the year 2001 when I had come, had voted for the BNP. There were people who felt let down by the usual parties—the Labor and Conservative parties—and they were worried about the amount of immigration taking place.

Immigration became a major issue, and again, since the massive majority of the immigrant community here come from Kashmir and Pakistan, they become the focus. When there is racism and prejudice, good people generally like to disavow being racist and justify themselves on some other basis. In this case, they did that in terms of religion. My main fear was that the BNP would gain positions on the council in the town, but because of the work carried out in partnership, the BNP vote reduced to 7.4 percent in the 2010 election and to four percent in the 2011 bi-election. In subsequent years, they have failed even to field a candidate.

So with local people who were very clearly committed to the agenda that I was looking to develop, we immediately began to normalize in the minds of people that Muslims and Christians and Hindus mix together quite happily and could do so here in Oldham. When it came to the actual elections the next time, it was clear that people would then say, "We are speaking to each other these days, aren't we?" There was a MORI opinion poll, which was taken every three years for a while, and it showed that there was a considerable movement in terms of the number of people who feel happy to mix with people of a different ethnicity.

The interfaith forum is based on the ground floor of my home; I live on the first floor. It has only one and a half employees. The half employee is a mufti, an Islamic lawyer, who works part time, twenty hours in a week. One of his roles is to ensure good communication between the local authority and the different Muslim communities. The project coordinator has the responsibility for creating activities that bring the communities together.

Some of the obstacles we faced when setting it up involved the lack of coordination between non-Christian communities in the town. The Christian communities all seemed to have a structure, whereas the Muslim communities did not have a council of mosques, and they were not structured in a way that they could have representation. One of the main things we did was to get that structure in place and for our worker, the mufti, to enable and to facilitate that structure.

The other part was that when you're dealing with Christians and Muslims, the leaders of these groups tend to be men. So there was a question of how to bring more women into the interfaith forum as well. The way that we did this was to set up a women's interfaith network with the right to put people onto the interfaith forum itself. Something like six of their members have right of membership on the interfaith forum. In that sense, you get a more even interfaith group.

We also said that every faith group to be represented had to have a place of worship in this town, and they could send along two people from that place of worship to represent them. Generally, this enabled a broader group of people to be involved, but it doesn't always work. We only get about twenty sometimes, and other times, forty or fifty people.

Our goal for the interfaith forum was mainly just to get people talking to each other and to prevent the situation in which Christians say, "We don't talk to them, do we," referring to the Muslim community. When I came here, that was often being said in my own church.

There have been people in Oldham living parallel lives—with the Muslims in this community and the Christians in that community—and all the myths building up between one community and the other. There was very little mixing at all. The idea was to break down those barriers, to challenge myths, and to bring those communities together to enable them to engage as much as possible.

At times, we would just get the imams and the priests to get a cup of coffee together, a meal together, or to do a prayer together in one church building or a mosque. Especially during the war on Iraq, we prayed together for peace in the center of the town. We could have, for example, a group of imams coming out of a Christian church and being seen doing so by passersby in their cars. This happened on the occasion of the death of Pope John Paul II. The corner on which my church is built is renowned for accidents; a crash barrier was installed only in 2018. Thankfully, as several imams and Hindus left the church and engaged in conversation together, there was no one sufficiently distracted by the strangeness of the scene to cause another accident. But these events are symbolic gestures that start to prevent people from saying, "We don't talk to them, do we."

In doing all this, we tried to inculcate the values of respect for each other. It was important, too, that each of us was not there to try and convert the other but instead to try and understand what drives each of us in faith terms, and to respect that. So it isn't about trying to convert each other but rather walking down a road together on a spiritual journey. There, we discover the other person, and we begin to see what makes them tick and why that faith is so important—and we discover respect for them in that whole process.

One way in which we tried to overcome the barriers between the estranged communities was through shared activities. For example, we would take the major celebrations of the religious year, such as Eid ul-Adha, Eid ul-Fitr, Christmas, Easter, Hannukah, and all these different things, and we tried to celebrate them in a way that focused on one particular symbol. For example, we had Eid ul-Adha, Hannukah, Diwali, and Christmas—all celebrations that could let us talk about light and the symbolism of light. I know that's pushing it slightly with Eid ul-Adha, but we took the symbol of light and explored it with three or four verbal inputs from good speakers. As the celebration of Eid moved further away from the celebration of Christmas, we focused instead on the birthday of the Prophet (peace be unto him).

We took over a hall and invited people from all over Oldham to come, and there were over five hundred people who came. In between the speeches, we had entertainment—Indian dance, *nasheed* singing, singing of Christmas carols, and then a meal at the end.

Each year, we've done it slightly differently. Sometimes, we invite a young person's brass band to play some Christmas carols. By bringing the young people who were competent in playing brass instruments—brass bands are linked to this area, traditionally—you are nurturing the identity of local people, and you're also bringing to this event the parents of those young people who were involved in the band.

Generally speaking, those parents might not normally mix across ethnicities and across religions. So straightaway, we found different ways to bring people into an experience that was challenging but was also very gentle. One way was to have an interactive interfaith quiz before the meal, where, to get all the answers, people would have to ask those of another faith. Each year, by doing something different or going into a different area—but bringing some of the people who are already committed with us—you encourage people into an ethos where mixing is easy and where people do respect each other.

Another example of an activity that we do is "Any questions on faith?" events, where we go into a particular area in a community center or in the local sixth form college, and invite people to come and ask so-called experts in their faiths any questions that they want to ask. The inevitable question of a Muslim expert is usually, "Why do you have jihad?" For Christians, it tends to be, "Why do you believe in the trinity?" They're not easy questions to answer, but the panel does not take offense at the questions that are asked, and they honor them, and they try to come up with decent answers.

Those are just two examples of some of the things that we do. Another example was at harvest time, when this aligned itself with Ramadan. We invited the non-Muslims to join for one day at least in the Ramadan fast. That involves getting up very early in the morning—in recent years, at two-thirty a.m.—having something to eat, and then not eating at all for the rest of the day until the sunset—sometimes after nine p.m.—and then gathering in some community center to break fast together—*iftaar*. We had twenty-seven of the local police force who actually gave up eating for that day, and they joined in the fast as a way of trying to understand what it's like for a Muslim during Ramadan. Several years ago, this event was held just after the earthquake in Kashmir, and to fast seemed a very appropriate thing to do in solidarity with the Muslim community in the town, since so many of them were from Kashmir.

There's another element that's significant. We quite deliberately used the principles of John Paul Lederach, the American Mennonite, who wrote a book called *The Moral Imagination* in 2005. There he talks about the principles of addressing conflict, and one of the principles that he has is the "spider's web." He suggests that you don't need to work with the whole population but just with certain well-chosen anchor points. He calls this the "critical yeast" approach rather than a "critical mass" approach. If the spider is going to build its web, it finds anchor points in its geographic location across the whole area. After finding the anchor points, the web begins to form around it. In terms of building good relations between different communities, this meant finding people of influence in their own communities—whether young or old, Black or white, Muslim, Christian, or atheist—and bringing them together for a series of meetings to listen to each other's stories. It's almost impossible not to be affected as you listen to stories of the pains and injustices experienced by people, even if they are different from you. When these anchor points go back to their individual communities, the web of cohesion begins to form organically because of the influence of each of the anchor points. For example, the editor of the local newspaper was considered to be someone who could and did influence the minds of others.

During the disturbances in 2001, the local newspaper buildings had been attacked by the rioters, because the newspaper was seen to be part of the problem. When we were working with Mediation Northern Ireland, a particular group brought in by the local authority to work with us, using the John Paul Lederach principles, we were invited to choose certain people from across the town from all different backgrounds—right wing, left wing, the different political spheres, and from different areas of work. We brought these people together to share stories and to look at different ideas about what was going on in the town. So the editor of the local Oldham newspaper had been one of *those* people.

Just before the 2010 general election, a few years later, he wrote a vision for Oldham in his newspaper that was a wonderful piece about a multi-ethnic, multi-religious town. He was quite clearly suggesting that that was his vision, too. He was almost encouraging people to use their vote for that sort of Oldham—in other words, don't vote for the BNP! I would suggest that before the disturbances, he would not have done that. But by being involved in the Lederach process as an anchor point and listening to the stories from the various people involved—that had an impact on him.

In the interfaith forum, we've worked in a similar way with younger people. We've taken a group of eighteen young people from across Oldham on a trip for a multifaith experience. We had advertised in that same local newspaper for people to apply, to tell us why they would like to go to Srebrenica or to Auschwitz. During the process of our visits, we saw the results of extremism, and we were all massively moved by what we saw.

We also went to Westminster, where one of our local MPs gave us a tour of the Parliament buildings and faced questions from the group on interfaith issues. Then we visited one of the offices of the European Union in Brussels to see how the young people could engage with power at a European level. We also took the group to the Paris Central Mosque to see if Muslims find life easier or more difficult with an even more secular approach, the system of *laïcité*.

These eighteen people, in the process of doing all this, listened to each other's stories, and they saw the results of extremism. Once they returned, they worked together and became eighteen anchor points among other young people. Three of the young Muslim men involved were all leading lights in the process of setting up the Oldham Muslim Center. After they returned from the trip to Auschwitz and Srebrenica, they made sure that one of the six priorities for this center was to reach out to other communities and build good relationships. Two years later, the Oldham Muslim Centre was recognized, in an awards ceremony organized by the Oldham Mosques' Council, as the mosque that had done the most to build good relationships with non-Muslim communities.

So for the interfaith forum, there was a double approach, one being "the spider's web approach" for engagement and the other being to normalize interactions, or what we call "the critical mass approach." We recognize that if we carry out an interfaith event and get the press to cover it, people begin to think that mixing is normal. The press can have a negative impact when they cover disturbances taking place in one street; people begin to think that these disturbances are happening all over the town. But similarly, if we can get the press to cover examples of good relations across different communities, people can begin to think that this is happening everywhere. A while ago, another of my parishioners suggested that people from the different communities were talking to each other now. The reality is that they are not talking as much as we would like. But the perception that it is happening enables it to happen.

John Paul Lederach wrote about the critical yeast as opposed to the critical mass. You have critical yeast when you choose the anchor points from across communities and you enable the engagement between them to take place that addresses their differences. The critical mass approach is what you're doing when you normalize engagement. I believe that we have to do the two together.

In the community-cohesion agenda, there are three main areas that we work on. The first one is *identity*, and that splits into shared identity and other identities that we have, and those identities are numerous. So there's the shared identity of being an Oldhamer, but being an Oldhamer also includes people of differing ethnicities. The other identities that we have, that might not be shared with other Oldhamers, can include being of Bangladeshi origin or of English origin, and we need to be proud of that as well and nurture those identities.

By nurturing those identities, we come to the second element of our strategy, which is *engagement*. You can't engage with others if you don't feel confident of who you are. If you feel insecure, then the relations you enter into are not going to be good. So you've got to have your own roots down deep, and be proud of who you are, and feel valued in who you are, in order to be able to engage in healthy relationships.

This engagement has two parts. One is interaction between communities, and the other is participation in the structures of decision-making in the town. If people feel as though they are excluded from that decision-making, you can have people feeling disaffected.

The third area of the community-cohesion agenda is *equality*, and it's getting people to have equal access to the growing prosperity of the town. Those are the three areas that we work on—identity, engagement, and equality. Over the years, because of the negative reaction, in government circles and elsewhere, to what is perceived to be multiculturalism, there has been a change in how these terms are expressed. Now we tend to talk of "belonging" rather than "identity," but it amounts to the same thing.

So for example, the people of African descent in Manchester were often saying things like, "In the curriculum, when are we ever represented? Is there something of our story told in the delivery of the curriculum in education and the choice of the content in that curriculum?" They opened my mind to how everybody who is teaching a subject can nurture identity if they know how to do it. That doesn't just mean the African-descent identity; it means every identity to be found in the locality, but especially if these identities are stigmatized.

I gave many lectures to head teachers and principals of schools, in secondary schools around the country, to encourage them to nurture identity through the delivery of their curricula and their choice of the curriculum—besides actually having role models in the school who were also nurturing identity. This was one area that transfers very easily from Moss Side, Manchester, to the situation here in Oldham, even though one was about faith identity and the other was about ethnic identity.

I would say that in many towns with which I have had some experience—dealing with community-cohesion issues—they have looked at *engagement*. But they have only seen it in terms of participation in decision-making, and they have not worked enough on *interactions*.

I have also seen that they haven't understood the identity issues. But without addressing identity issues, you don't get to healthy engagement and then have genuine interaction taking place. That's something that I learned in my twenty-five years in Moss Side and, I believe, that I have brought with me here.

Because of my position in the community-cohesion advisory group, we were able to make sure that all that gets into every secondary school in the local education authority. For example, we had a group of lead practitioners from every curriculum area—from languages, or sciences, or mathematics—who went away with thirteen of our principles for how to nurture identities through the curriculum areas and to form lessons plans that they could pass on to other teachers in their curriculum areas.

Some of them made CDs with resources on how you could nurture— through delivery of mathematics, for example—what it is to be a Muslim, by recognizing the importance of Islam in the development of trigonometry, developing the idea of the zero, and all sorts of different things like that. In the literature curriculum, you can make sure that people of different backgrounds and faith communities can find their stories told in the literature that students study. Later, we formed an educational tool called the Oldham Story, providing lesson plans and online resources for enabling everyone to find something of themselves in the Oldham story. Sadly, though, because of austerity, the main officer leading on this for the local authority took early retirement and was not replaced. So teachers can no longer access these online resources. We keep trying to resurrect them, but so far, without success.

The Qualifications and Curriculum Agency in this country talked about the importance of identity, but then went to books from African-descended people like Ngugi and Achebe. Achebe is from Nigeria, and Ngugi is from Kenya, but the Black communities from these countries are usually Black British. So they have to find something from their own identity, not just somebody that goes back to their mother country or whatever. The task is to find literature that's right, that enables the story to be told and that enables the readers to feel valued in seeing that story.

We have also a shared identity as a town, where everybody is invited and where different communities are clearly valued. For a while, we had a diversity week or two weeks in summer where we would celebrate diversity together. We also had plans for high-quality developments, initially in an area termed "the West End of Oldham." We hoped to re-develop this area with good-quality, high-profile buildings in it. So far, a science center has been opened, which can tap into a regional need for more science experts, including people from the different ethnic and faith communities represented in Oldham. But so much that was planned has been allowed to wither on the vine.

There is, however, a university center now that has opened in Old-ham. We didn't have a university presence before, and with a university center going up, there is an economic base developing. I keep suggesting that we form what we call a "technopol," a collection of businesses that are associated with the knowledge that you have in a university and that are nurtured by that knowledge and understanding.

If there's an enemy in this town in this process, it is the BNP, or its ex-tremist counterparts. They would get involved in writing letters in the local press, so that when things happened, they would deliberately go and blow it up—and I don't mean with explosives, but bringing it into the newspapers and into the media, and making an issue of it. If there was an argument between young pupils in a school, they would descend on that school in numbers and start making a massive case about it, saying, "This is what the Muslims do. We have to get rid of them!" and lots of things like that.

The other thing that must be said is that there are people within the churches who justify racism, when it includes or involves Islam, on the basis of religion. We have to challenge at every available opportunity, as Christians or as Muslims, any sort of racism on the basis of religion— and again, to show that it's a matter of building respect for each other and seeing the tremendous dignity of each faith community.

The council in this area has been very genuine in terms of their desire to work in partnership. They were criticized severely in the independent report, written by David Ritchie in 2002. They were told that the leader-ship was appalling, and they were criticized severely in terms of the way that they worked in the town.

We had another independent report five years later, by a guy called Ted Cantle, and he said that Oldham had perhaps done more than any other town to address community cohesion, and he actually suggested that the political leaders had been heroic in their attempts to work on this. Maybe he'd gone a bit far in that, but they have been very genuine in their desire to work in partnership, and they have enabled people like myself to enter into positions of decision-making, even though I'd only come to the town relatively recently.

One of the main problems that we have had is in terms of funding, in spite of cohesion, at least initially, being high on the agenda. We had a white paper from the government that stressed the importance of interfaith forums in towns where there are community-cohesion issues, and the importance of working with young people, and even though that's there in the white paper, our funding went down from seventy-four thousand pounds annually to thirty-five thousand pounds. We had two and a half workers; now we've just got one and a half workers, unless I can get more funding.

This is only partially a sign of waning enthusiasm and urgency. The riots are gone, but addressing extremism is still a government priority. Extremism is seen to be linked, unfortunately, all too much with Islam, and every time this is brought up, the right-wing fascist groups start harping on about it. Even to use the words *extremism* and *Islam* together is not always very helpful.

The lessons and tools we used in Oldham can probably be applied across much broader contexts. A few years ago, I was invited to speak in Barcelona at a UNESCO conference and the following year in Brazil at a world conference on the development of cities. In Barcelona, my speech was picked up by the Catalonian and Spanish television networks because of the similar problems being faced there.

Clearly, the same applies in Northern Ireland, and also right across Europe. There's such a movement of people at the moment. I would suggest that many of the things I've been talking about in terms of identity, engagement, and equality apply everywhere.

8

Listening, Accountability, and Self-Determination

Malik Yakini's Practice Story

Editor's Preface

Malik Yakini was deeply involved in Detroit justice struggles, and as a result of his earlier efforts to create the Detroit Food Policy Council, he was drafted to be its leader. He had worked in Detroit schools for many years, and he had witnessed swings of Detroit's politics that involved the rise and fall of Black elected politicians, the exodus of significant parts of the automobile industry, white flight to the suburbs, housing abandonment in Detroit neighborhoods, and more, even as Detroit was world renowned for its music and cultural resources.

The Detroit Black Community Food Security Network represented not simply a few neighborhood people growing vegetables but a grassroots community-building effort devoted to local autonomy, community development, and political self-determination. Yakini's story chronicles that history and speaks clearly and directly to the presumptions of "helpers"—often white—coming from outside the community to "share their knowledge and expertise," often without so much as asking about local aspirations, capacities, and needs. Here we see how place-making efforts depend as much on the clear-eyed views of communities' political, cultural, and racial histories that make respectful collaborations possible, as they do on the accountability—though not the autonomy—of outside expertise.

Organizing for Food Security and Empowerment

For about twenty-two years, I was principal of an African-centered school in Detroit. It started as a private school in 1989 and evolved in

1997 to a charter school. In 2000, we developed a food security curriculum and started seriously teaching the students organic gardening. After about two years, that effort morphed into a larger effort, still centered at the school, with people who were part of the school community.

We created something called the Shamba Organic Garden Collective. There were about twenty parents and staff members who wanted to do gardens in either their backyards or vacant lots near their houses. So we created this collective to try to till the gardens for them and provide the things that they needed to make this happen. It provided a support network that continued to evolve into a citywide organization that was formed in February 2006, which we now call the Detroit Black Community Food Security Network [DBCFSN].

As principal of the school, in 2005 I attended a conference of the national Community Food Security Coalition in Atlanta, and I copresented in a workshop with Anan Lololi. He was my mentor, and he runs a program in Toronto called the Afri-Can Food Basket, which is servicing largely immigrants from the Caribbean and from Africa and other places within the former British Empire. He asked me to copresent at this conference, and at the conference, there was a lot of discussion on race in the food system and specifically on nonprofit groups that are predominantly led by whites doing food security work in either African American or Latinx communities. Upon returning to Detroit, I realized that what we were facing in Detroit was essentially the same thing that was happening throughout the country.

So within a kind of structure where whites dominate and hold the majority of resources and power, the way that people who get marginalized can gain greater voice and greater access is by banding together and galvanizing so they are operating from a position of strength. We created the Detroit Black Community Food Security Network for that purpose.

That organization, when we started, had a few objectives. One of them was to develop policy in the city of Detroit that supported food justice and food security. In June of 2006, we spoke before the Detroit City Council, and we were critical of the city for not having a comprehensive food security policy. We spoke specifically to the Neighborhood and Community Services Committee. The chair of the standing committee, Joanne Watson, appointed us, on the spot, to head a task force to create a food security policy for the city. Over the next eighteen months, we worked and researched and wrote and revised various drafts of the document, had public listening sessions, and finally, by March of 2008, we were able to get the city council to approve this policy unanimously.

The policy called for the creation of the Detroit Food Policy Council, and shortly after that, we started a convening committee that was responsible for drafting bylaws and kind of vetting candidates for the Food Policy Council based on the various sectors within the food system that are represented by the seats on the council; for example, we have a seat for sustainable agriculture. We made an exhaustive list of all of the people who were involved in sustainable agriculture in Detroit, and we sent them letters and said, "Are you interested in serving on the Detroit Food Policy Council? If so, please respond and submit your résumé."

Of course, many people weren't interested, largely because of their time commitments; people are already busy and aren't typically looking for another thing to do. That narrowed down the list. Then, of those who responded in the affirmative, we had another round of looking at those candidates and what their qualifications were. We were also conscious of creating diversity within the council.

The convening committee met for about a year and presented a list to the city council of the candidates that we were recommending for the eighteen appointed seats on the Detroit Food Policy Council. They approved our recommendations unanimously in October 2009. In November 2009, the Food Policy Council held its first meeting, and those members who had been approved were seated.

There were initially twelve seats on the Food Policy Council that are sector seats, and there are three that represent the government: the mayor's office, the city council, and the department of health all have seats. There are six seats that represent the grassroots community—or "the eaters" as we call them—so we have a total of twenty-one seats.

The Food Policy Council was birthed as a result of the Detroit City Council passing the city of Detroit's food security policy. The drafting of that policy began with the convening of an ad hoc policy committee within the Detroit Black Community Food Security Network. On that committee were a few people, including Katherine Underwood, who, in addition to being a member of our organization, works for the City Planning Commission of Detroit. She is currently the city council's representative on the Food Policy Council. Being a city planner, she had a great deal of insight into the food-related issues facing the city of Detroit. She, along with several others, helped to craft about eight topic areas that we thought would be important to be addressed in this Food Policy Council—such as economic injustice within the food system and looking at what happens with the money that's spent in the city of Detroit on food by "the eaters." Does that money really benefit the community, or is it simply a wealth-extraction strategy?

We did the same thing in each of these topic areas. We looked at what this large, broad area was that was impacting food security, and then we analyzed what the current situation was in Detroit, and we had some narrative about that. Then we made recommendations as to the types of things that can be done to impact the deficiencies in each of those areas.

Largely, that work was done by our ad hoc public policy committee, but we also realized that it wasn't the policy for just our organization. Although we were spearheading the work, it was going to be a policy for the people of the city of Detroit, so we wanted to make sure that we had input from others.

One of the persons that we solicited input from specifically was Kami Pothukuchi, a professor of urban planning at Wayne State University. She is considered nationally and internationally to be an expert on how food impacts urban planning. She has been one of the people at the forefront of putting food on the radar of urban planners so that it has the same level of importance as transportation or schools or green spaces. We are fortunate to have her in Detroit. We made sure that we got lots of feedback from her on the drafts as they were being developed.

We also had held a public listening session at the harvest festival that took place in 2007 at D-Town Farm. We announced it in advance and sent out emails to people doing food work in Detroit to tell them that we would be unveiling this policy. We asked people to be there to give input, and then also, for those who couldn't attend the session, we sent notices electronically and got significant public input through that process. We incorporated much of that public input into the final document that was approved by the city council.

Then we moved on to the Food Policy Council itself, which was the body that would be responsible for implementing the recommendations of the food security policy, for monitoring the degree to which those things were implemented and also for devising new policies as the need arose. So we shifted focus to the creation of the Food Policy Council.

We had another period of research where we contacted many Food Policy Councils in North America, and I think ultimately, we got responses from twelve that informed our work. We asked questions of them, such as how members were selected—if they had a council that represented sectors within the food system or just had members within the council.

We specifically were concerned with the relationship of Food Policy Councils to the municipal or county governments that they operated within. We were concerned about whether or not they were part of the city government, if they were totally independent of the city government, or if they played some adjunct role. We wanted to know about that relationship; that was particularly important in Detroit, because this was during the time when the mayor was under indictment for various felonies, and the city council was under investigation—so there was a real air of distrust of our city government. We didn't want to be perceived as being under the thumb of the city government, so we were particularly concerned about that.

Our questions to the other councils helped us to see how other cities were dealing with these issues. We found that there was a variety of models, from the Toronto Food Policy Council, where it is actually a part of the city's health department and the coordinator of the Food Policy Council is actually an employee of the city, to one in Ohio, working with Case-Western University, where it is more centered in the academy and doesn't have as much formal relationship with the government.

So after doing this research and sending questionnaires and calling the other Food Policy Councils and having conversations to further illuminate the points made in the questionnaires, we had extensive discussions with folks in several cities who had councils up and running. That informed the document that we created that recommended the relationships on the Food Policy Council, its relationship to the city government, and the number of members it should have. It spoke to our ideas about diversity, and it laid out the purpose and the main charges of the Food Policy Council.

So we had this document of recommendations on the establishment of the Food Policy Council, and then we had a second listening session at which we read through each section.

That second public listening session was held at Eastern Market. That was attended by more than seventy-five people representing most of the organizations doing urban agriculture work or some other food system reform type of work in the city. At that session, we had two students from Michigan State University who recorded and transcribed everything that was said. We had one of the city council members present to hear the input we were getting from the public, and essentially, we read through the recommendations on the establishment of the Detroit Food Policy Council. We were very careful not to give people feedback but just to listen. We read and just asked for comments versus defending ourselves. It was a difficult thing; we felt invested in what we had done, so we had to really detach ourselves and try to objectively listen without giving any feedback one way or another.

We captured every word that was said and reviewed all that. In some cases, views of the community members were conflicting, so we weren't able to incorporate all of the feedback. In some areas, there was pretty much consensus, so the things that had broad support we folded into the policy. The things that there might have been conflict about—which were only a few things—we tried to weigh which side of the argument made the most sense to us and incorporate that into the final document.

We revised the draft and presented it to the city council, and it was unanimously approved. That's what led the way for the convening committee to start and the members of the Food Policy Council to be seated. It was a pretty smooth process. Myself and several of the people in our organizations have been activists in Detroit for several years, prior even to getting into food work. So we had relationships with several people either on the city council or in the city government, and our previous relationships were useful in helping them move the ball down the field.

There were other groups in the field that had gotten funding for policy initiatives that had not done a quarter of what we had done, which we did with no funding. It was just our zeal and elbow grease and our sweat equity—so no funding at all. But because we had these preexisting relationships, people knew and trusted us, and we didn't have to go through the process of introducing ourselves and winning people over and developing rapport and all of that. That really helped the process to move smoothly.

Some of the challenges were more internal ones. For example, at one point, this public policy committee within our organization essentially broke down. Really, the way that I ended up being in the leadership of this effort was because I was chair of the organization, when the ball was dropped on moving forward on writing the policy and moving the whole Food Policy Council down the field. Rather than have the ball just be dropped and sit there, I picked it up as the leader of the organization. Charity Hicks (rest in peace), DBCFSN's secretary at the time, and I picked up the ball and made it progressively to the end zone.

It really wasn't my intention to be directly involved in policy work. Although I think that's important, that's not really the area that I'm most interested in. I am most interested in on-the-ground projects such as the farming project we manage and the development of a cooperatively owned grocery store that we are helping to lead. But out of necessity, I found myself in a position of leading this effort. Then, as a result of leading it, and leading the formation of it, and leading the convening committee, and being the chief spokesperson at the city council meetings, it was decided by the members of the Food Policy Council that I was uniquely positioned to be the chair of it. It wasn't a position I sought, but it was a responsibility that I somewhat reluctantly shouldered. So that was a challenge.

When it came to community involvement in the process of creating the food security policy and the Food Policy Council, because of our long time activism, we already had relationships with people who were actively involved in transforming Detroit and the food system. Our organization had a lot of trust and was seen as having a lot of integrity. It was more the groundwork that we had been laying prior to this effort that enabled us to have a smooth entrée to the community. People trusted the process because they were involved in it.

Of course, when we sent out the letters and the invitations to all of the food system organizations and invited them to come, we followed up with emails and flyers distributed throughout the community. We publicized it widely, but the combination of publicizing it widely and the people having faith and confidence in our integrity as an organization worked to get a number of people to give significant input.

I could only speculate on how the process could work in another city, but I can say that there were some factors in Detroit that I think made it ripe for the work that we were doing. First, the continuing economic decline had people looking for ways to foster community self-determination and to shape the city in a way that works in the best interest of the majority of the residents.

Second, the fact that in 2007, the last national grocery store in Detroit closed its doors—that began to open people's eyes to this concept of food access. Around that same time, Mari Gallagher, a researcher out of Chicago, released her report titled *Examining the Impact of Food Deserts on Public Health in Detroit*. That report got a lot of play and was picked up by the media, so people began to have conversations about this concept of food deserts. Many people were concerned about the issue of food access and the lack of food access in the city. That ripened people's consciousness.

Third, there are ongoing statistics that suggest that Detroit is having a severe health crisis and that there is a relationship between the lack of access to fresh, healthy food and the soaring rates of childhood and adult obesity, diabetes, high blood pressure, heart disease, and so on. Those three things—the declining economic situation, the closing of the last supermarket, and the unveiling of this report suggesting that Detroit was a food desert with ongoing health concerns—made people's consciousness ripe to support our work to create the food policy and the Food Policy Council.

Let me say a bit about who can be helpful here and how that might happen. Young white people coming to Detroit trying to work on this can have a rough time, to tell you the truth. There has been this long history of people coming to Detroit, and that, in recent years, is increasing by leaps and bounds. We have lots and lots and lots of people who have degrees, many from the University of Michigan, who want to come into Detroit to help.

While most of those people are well intentioned, often, because they have not divested themselves of their white privilege or have not really studied the system of white supremacy, they unconsciously come with an attitude of paternalism or with a missionary attitude. So after people here have seen this happen repeatedly, there is a defensiveness, like, "Here comes another outsider."

Even broader than that, for Detroiters, Black Detroiters—and what I'm about to say is not often understood when people study Detroit, and it's a dynamic that if you don't understand, you won't fully know why Detroiters function the way they function—there has been this long history of discord between the city itself and the mostly white suburbs surrounding the city. There has been this long struggle for fifty or sixty years for Black empowerment.

So on one hand, you have Detroit's majority African American population trying to galvanize the political strength to control the political structure. This resulted in the election of Coleman Young as mayor in 1973. This resulted in the fact that we now have a predominantly Black city council, and the school system is controlled by Black people. So Black people were able to galvanize the political will and strength in order to exert a great deal of control over the city government.

There's been this feeling for some time about the ring of mostly white suburbs, which were created largely by white flight beginning in the 1950s and accelerating tremendously after the 1967 rebellion. There's been this feeling for some time that white people in the suburbs want to come back and take Detroit.

I have heard this over the last thirty or forty years—"They're coming back, they're coming back"—and now there seems to be a lot of evidence to suggest that those fears were not unfounded. There is a great deal of gentrification going on, there are incentives being given to professionals—which doesn't necessarily equate to whites but often does in certain sectors of the economy—folks in the police department, or people who are employed by the Henry Ford Health System. Compuware also, and others, have offered incentives to their employees to move back into the city. So we have this movement of whites more into the center city, which is closer to the downtown area, where many of them are employed and which is closer to some of the resources.

This history of these two competing things—Black empowerment, and acrimony with the suburbs—has been manifested in a lot of ways. For example, there's the closing of the Recorder's Court, which was a Detroit-based court that was largely Black controlled, and now those issues are handled by county court. In the county, Black people are not in the majority, so now we have a court system that is not reflective of our own community.

Also, the closing of Highland Park Community College—which was not in Detroit but in Highland Park—was seen as another attack at the state level on this effort for Black empowerment. Also, there was the effort to make the city water department a regionally owned system, and efforts to make Cobo Hall [now TFC Center], the convention center, instead of being controlled by the city government, also part of a regional system. All of those moves are viewed as continuing efforts to disempower Detroit's African American community and to enable mostly white suburbs to regain control and power in the city of Detroit. So the question of young whites moving in—who might have good intentions—has to be seen against that background.

During the time I served as chair of the Food Policy Council, we worked with different levels of power. One of those levels is the grassroots community—the people themselves—and it's my view that what is most important is people being conscious and mobilized themselves, because the politicians are supposed to be servants of the people. So regardless of what the government does, what's most important is instilling this sense of consciousness in people and getting them mobilized and working on their own behalf.

The other level of power that we worked at is the elected and appointed political leadership of the city. We had multiple conversations with the city council as a whole and with individual members. We've had conversations with the mayor and some of his executives. We tried to create a dialogue and openness to hearing the suggestions that we are bringing forth, and we are trying to create greater legitimacy for the Food Policy Council so that as things were being considered in city government that were related to food in any way, the Food Policy Council would be consulted.

When we started the Food Policy Council—again, being aware of this history between Detroit and the suburbs—we were trying to create a balance between the empowerment of the citizens of Detroit and not isolating ourselves so that we were operating in a silo.

The reality is that there is no such thing as a Detroit food system. There is a food system, which impacts Detroit and also the region that we are a part of. We're not foolish enough to think that we should operate in isolation without a relationship to the rest of the food system of our bioregion. But we're also aware of the fact that there are many efforts where people from the suburbs come into Detroit to determine what's going to happen to Detroiters, and the voice of the Detroiters is not there. We didn't want to replicate that. We insisted that to be a member of the Food Policy Council, you had to be a Detroit resident or affiliated with a Detroit institution.

For example, Kami, whom I mentioned earlier, doesn't live in Detroit, but she is affiliated with Wayne State. There were some people who were disqualified because they lived in Southfield or Oak Park with no tangible relationship to Detroit. But we also realized that we needed to create liaisons between our group and other groups in the county, region, and state to work on specific issues as necessary.

One of the things that we've done was a presentation before the Michigan Food Policy Council so that they were aware of our work. At the time, I was a member of both the Michigan Food Policy Council and the Detroit Food Policy Council, so I was able to serve as a link. We worked at balancing those two competing interests—empowerment of Detroit citizens and working in cooperation with those who are around us—but not playing a subordinate role, not allowing that working cooperation to dilute our strength.

We received no funding for writing the city of Detroit's food security policy or leading the creation of the Detroit Food Policy Council. We were later approached by the W. K. Kellogg Foundation, who had been watching both the Detroit Black Community Food Security Network and the work of the Food Policy Council. I had extensive discussions with the program officers assigned to Detroit for the Kellogg Foundation. They offered to provide funding to both DBCFSN and the DFPC. There were conversations with Kellogg about creating openings to other funders as well.

When we started the Food Policy Council, we were concerned about having a diversity of funding structures. Just as we didn't want to be under the thumb of the city government, we also didn't want to be under the thumb of any particular foundation. Our intent was to have at least four funders with a quarter of the funding coming from the city government itself, three-quarters from other foundations.

In talking to members of the city council and people who were close to city government, it was decided that initially, we didn't want to derail the efforts to start the council by putting the money issues on the table at a time that Detroit was cash strapped. We didn't want to scare people away by saying we need you to put up seventy thousand dollars or forty-five thousand dollars or what have you, so we decided to hold off on the request for funding from the city. The result of that was that all of our initial funding came from Kellogg.

There were a few surprises. There is a situation that I don't want to go into in too much detail, but a lot of the surprises have been internal surprises. These were not so much ones that we ran up against in the city government when trying to do the work, but mostly just internal surprises in terms of human interaction. There was some friction and some disharmony within the council because one of the members applied for a job, was subsequently offered the job, and then the offer was withdrawn. That created some tension within the council.

We dealt with that by creating a committee consisting of two members of the Food Policy Council and one person who had been on the convening committee who is also well respected. She is a nun and an activist in the community.

That committee met, and their intention was to create a mediating dialogue between the two sides to try and help resolve the situation. The dialogue never occurred, but they were able to collect a narrative from each of the perspectives of what happened, and they made some recommendations to the Food Policy Council as to how we could better move forward in a way that will not result in these kinds of tensions.

Overall, I can't think of anything I would have done differently. I think the process worked well. You are always going to have glitches when you are dealing with human beings, and things are never going to go as planned. I think it was a sound process that has resulted in a Food Policy Council that is looked at by many people throughout the country as a model.

One of the most valuable lessons I've learned is that the people themselves can organize to impact the communities that they live in. This was a bottom-up effort. This is not a Food Policy Council that was started by a university. It wasn't started by a foundation. It wasn't started by big agriculture interests. This was truly a grassroots effort, and we are very concerned about making sure that it maintains that grassroots character and that it is not co-opted by any force. It reaffirmed the power that people have when they step up and they do the work and organize themselves. That would be the biggest lesson that I've learned.

There's still the issue of outsiders coming in and telling us where they see a problem. I respond to that by saying, "Why would you come in and tell us where you see a gap? Why wouldn't you ask us where *we* see a gap?" That gets at the type of approach that we are concerned about.

Often, what young whites do—and this is not out of any maliciousness or any kind of negative intent; it's cultural conditioning, particularly coming out of universities—is to bring the mindset, "I come in and see something that other people are not seeing."

A better approach, we feel, would be to come in and embed yourself in the community and find out what its assets already are, what's already going on. How are the people doing the work? Where do *they* perceive their gaps? For me, that's the difference between coming in and assisting and coming in and trying to direct.

Let's say that you said, "Malik, would you come over to my house and help me clean my house?" What if I would come over and say, "Sure, you need to move your shoes over there." That's not the approach I would take if I'm coming to assist you. I would say, "How can I help you? Where can you use my help the most?" That's what we're concerned about: people coming in with humility and recognizing what's already in place. There are strengths in places. It's a matter of not looking at it from the deficit model, but instead looking at what the history of building resistance has been and trying to see how you can complement that.

I think that the first thing is developing a rapport, relationships. You have to let people know who you are and what your intentions are. That doesn't happen in a week or two weeks. It happens from building with people, working with people, and talking to people. People getting to know you takes some time, and again, that's what we didn't have to do, because we had already been doing work prior to starting the food work.

But if you're coming in fresh, there's an automatic level of suspicion based on our history, and those suspicions aren't unfounded. So there needs to be training in how people enter communities, how they can do it in a way that is respectful and complements the work that is already going on, as opposed to coming in with a missionary attitude—someone who's coming to save the day.

The Food Policy Council has working groups, and there are some people who aren't Detroiters who participate, and that gives them the chance to learn more about the work. Then from there, they rise to a level where they can have more influence over the decisions that are being made. It's a process.

It's not that we need outsiders. We need resources. We can look at our situation to decide what we need to do. There are plenty of smart people in Detroit. Again, we use a strength model as opposed to a deficit model. Just because something isn't happening doesn't mean that people haven't thought about it deeply. It may be just that the resources aren't available.

I think that food is a good thread to pull in the tangled knot of Detroit, because in many ways, it's a great unifier. It works across race and class and religion and gender and sexual preference. Most everybody agrees that people having access to good, healthy food is a good thing. It's a good platform to get people working together to create these models of participatory democracy.

In the process of putting all of this together, the reasons that we had the listening sessions and got the public feedback was because we were very conscious that we were creating a public participatory democracy that we hope will be modeled not just by other people in the food systems but by people in other sectors of society who are looking to make social change.

People, especially young people, might be reluctant at first, but once they plant something, even if it's a radish, they see the relationship between their input and the final product, and a lot of times, that's what it takes to convince people. Most people are not won over because of an abstract idea or a philosophical concept—except perhaps in the case of religion. People tend to be won over by things that bring some tangible benefit to their day-to-day lives. To be effective, this is what the food movement must be able to do.

Art, Imagination, and Value Creation

Introduction to Part Three

Part 3 explores how place makers treat the unique and special attributes of the places and spaces at hand as opportunities. We see that local officials have often been driving in the rearview mirror, managing what has always been there rather than asking what creative purposes might transform our taken-for-granted parts of cities and neighborhoods into newly vibrant places.

City engineers devoted to efficient transportation and public works have established routines, and we've seen that they're not always thrilled by the sometimes out-of-the-box ideas of local residents. But in Rochester, New York, no less than in Paris, France, the engineers found that residents wanted to talk to them about new possibilities. Through those conversations—at times with the blessings of local elected leaders—they came to work with residents to allow, encourage, monitor, and approve a range of innovative land uses. In Providence, Rhode Island, no less than in New York Mills, Minnesota, and Eagleby, Australia, local residents found themselves delighted and enchanted by artists-turned-place makers.

At stake in these cases are the contributions of public participation, the appreciation of varying sources of expertise, and the always careful leveraging of the unique qualities of specific locations for public benefit. Not least of all, here, we see the work of integrating, instead of separating, art and politics, design and public welfare, connecting practically and financially the worlds of art and those of city planning and public administration (Markusen and Gadwa 2010; Nicodemus 2013; Zitcer 2020). In these cases, too, we see that place making is not done by solitary heroes but by many talented neighbors who worked together with equally talented designers and planners. They involved politicians, city officials, journalists, storefront greeters, and agency staff, all overcoming together traditionally fragmented clusters of expertise, while nevertheless coming together to create surprising new places (Hester 2010; Nowak 2007).

In the very different and yet stunning examples related by Barnaby Evans and Wendy Sarkissian, public ritual plays an important role: drawing public attention to possibilities not previously considered, uniting participants as members of communities as they had not previously felt themselves connected. In every instance in the following cases, we see new public benefits emerge as the work of place making reconsiders what is possible and what can be actual in a new arts center, a new ARTWalk, a new community-gardens initiative, and so on. Imagination trumps precedent, expertise reaches across traditional boundaries to collaborate, and broad publics benefit (Jackson 2012; Markusen 2014).

The cases in part 3 all have quite ordinary beginnings and quite extraordinary endings. Barnaby Evans recounts the humble origins of the WaterFire festival in Providence, Rhode Island. Wendy Sarkissian describes how recognizing the sense of stigma felt by residents of Eagleby, Queensland, led to a community's reclaiming of both their park and their own agency. On the other side of the globe, we see Laurence Baudelet bringing community gardening as an actual practice to Paris, France, where the traditions of large city gardens seemed to have little room for do-it-yourself neighborhood initiatives. Then Doug Rice provides an urban neighborhood experience from Rochester, New York, even as he struggled with city staff and experts, just as Baudelet had found it necessary to do. John Davis, finally, begins in rural Minnesota and belies stereotypes to show how local residents supported and rallied behind creating vibrant places for the arts in New York Mills, Minnesota.

9

Public Art, Economic Development, and the Origins of WaterFire

Barnaby Evans's Practice Story

Editor's Preface

Barnaby Evans was a contented enough, if conflicted, victim of his own success. Curious about the aesthetic possibilities of water and fire, Evans turned his attention to the river flowing through central Providence, Rhode Island. Nobody seemed to pay it much attention; maybe something else was possible.

One evening's experiment linking water and fire led to people asking, "When are you going to do it again?" And though no second effort had been planned, a few years of annual events later, WaterFire would be integrating a downtown waterside passeggiata, small cradles of wood burning every forty yards or so in the midst of the river, music playing, and vendors selling their wares in an early-summer festival worth a small fortune in economic development monies to the city of Providence. Here Evans tells us the beginning of this remarkable story.

What the Community Needed Was What Art Tends to Address

I came to Providence from Hawai'i to attend Brown University. I arrived here in 1971 and graduated from Brown in 1975 with a degree in biology and ecology. Having finished my degree, I decided, before going on to graduate school, to spend some time exploring architectural things. Because I did sort of a double computer/ecology major, I didn't have time to take many arts classes. So I decided to take some time exploring my other interests, which were more urban, architectural, and aesthetic. One of my big interests was photography, so I got a job working in a photography lab so I could learn color-printing techniques, which at the time was a somewhat complicated process, using a lot of organic chemicals. I found that my interest in photography exceeded my interest in ecology, so I never went back to graduate school, and I started doing a lot of photographs, documenting urban landscapes. Gradually, I got interested in the psychology and social ecology of those landscapes, and I began to do site-specific installation pieces to influence the social behavior that I was seeing being exhibited in those landscapes. This was based primarily in Providence.

First Fire

There were other site-specific pieces, but I first did WaterFire in 1994. I wanted to figure out how one could talk about the fragility of life by putting fire and water close together. I'd been thinking about fire and water from an earlier project having to do with a memorial for the Holocaust. It was a project that I wanted to do in Berlin that I modified to try in Providence.

About three months prior to December 31, 1994, First Night Providence made it known to the arts community that they'd like to come up with something to celebrate their tenth anniversary. The executive director of First Night at that point was a woman named Doris Stephens. First Night is all about the arts community. It's always been engaged; everything they do is getting the arts community involved and celebrating New Year's Eve. First Night has always had all kinds of artists doing lots and lots of things—ice sculptures, performances, installation pieces. But they were looking for something celebratory.

What I'd been looking at is this river park that I would go to. The moving of the river had been a long-time project, consisting of many, many phases. By 1990, the rivers were in their new locations, and much of the walkway had been done. The details of Waterplace Park were still being constructed, and it was not formally dedicated until July of 1994. The Basin [Waterplace Basin] had been formally dedicated by then in 1994. This had been around for about a year and a half.

I kept being struck by what a change it was for the city and by how absolutely nobody was there. It was completely deserted. Even at lunchtime, there was nobody there. The Foundry was near the depart-ment of environmental management's [DEM] office. They wouldn't walk one block to be in this park. It was astonishing to me.

When I went to get the permits from DEM for WaterFire, no one there had walked across the street to be in the park across the street. Not one person in the office had seen the park. When I went in with photo-graphs of what I wanted to do, they said, "Oh, yeah, this is what it looks like. That's interesting. Yeah, I heard they were doing something down there." People were, "Eh, whatever."

I was just dumbfounded, particularly about the regulatory people. Clearly, to do all this work, you need permits. So they had seen it on plan. They knew about it; they were overseeing it. But none of them had been to the finished park, and it had been there for a year and a half!

So I felt this intense need to create something that would spark inter-est in the pretty astonishing thing that was accomplished here. I mean, not only did we move a river—two rivers—but we moved two highway systems and the entire northeast railroad corridor. It was a huge project. So the idea was to celebrate this section of the new park.

Remember—this is an important thing to remember—I was doing this as a one-time, one-night installation on a very temporary basis on temporary permits to happen once only, on December 31, 1994.[1] Even though, I had to talk to lots of permitting organizations.[2] The strategic advantage of doing this with First Night—which is why I welcomed the opportunity and I went to them with a proposal—was that we had an existing nonprofit as an umbrella that already had liability insurance and already had all kinds of general permits to do all sorts of mayhem down here anyway—they were doing explosives, fireworks. They had crowds. They had bands. They had a police presence. So a lot of the organiza-tional infrastructure and legal liability and legal authority was in place with them being the sponsoring organization.

I don't think WaterFire would have happened if it hadn't been for First Night. Not so much that I don't think the city would have said yes to it, as much as I don't think I would have felt comfortable trying to negotiate that many things; it would have been too daunting for me to consider doing. There were three valuable watch words for us. One was, it's an art project; second, we're doing it for a nonprofit, First Night, that had enthusiastic support; and third, it's temporary—it's only going to happen one night, and then it's gone. So those three things allowed us to do the first installation.

Now, the first installation was very well received by the public. I thought it was an utter failure, but I did recognize in it that it had the spark of something that could work very well. The failure that I made here—which was a failure both of imagination and conception but primarily a failure of funding—was that the fires were too small and there weren't enough of them for the size of the space that we were attempting to animate. There were only eleven braziers. Right now, there are about forty braziers in that same area from the Basin to Steeple Street, so initially, we only had one-quarter of the density we have today. It didn't have the necessary visual presence to command that large of a space. So I felt that it was too small and too inconsequential in the landscape. That was mainly driven by finances. But it did prove to me that my initial concept that fire, in opposition to water—in very close proximity to water—the poetry of that, people would understand.

There was music at the first WaterFire, though you could make a lot of money by placing bar bets on that fact. There was music near the Basin, and at Exchange Street. It was forty-five minutes with music and forty-five minutes without music, so it alternated all evening. So you have people who walked through the whole thing who absolutely swear there was no music, and you have people who walked through the whole thing who absolutely swear there was music and who could tell you what music they heard.[3] You can win the bet either way.

That was the initial installation. First Night gave me a check for about two thousand dollars. It cost about twenty-four thousand dollars. I got a contribution from a few individuals in town who said, "Yeah, I'd help with that." One of them was Buff Chase.[4] At that point, we weren't a nonprofit; he was just writing a check for an artist to do this. It was a very gracious thing to do. The rest of it I just fronted. A lot of it I borrowed—the boats, the outboard motors, the trucks. I worked with scrap steel. I did a lot of the welding myself. In fact, a local ironworks helped make a lot of the stuff at very reasonable cost. So that's how we did the first one, a sort of proof of concept.

SecondFire

WaterFire returned a year and a half later. This was in June of 1996. It was for the International Sculpture Conference, which Providence hosted, and for the Convergence Arts Festival, which was a continuing project that Bob Rizzo did. Bob and the parks department said, "We really liked the first installation," so I agreed to create Second-Fire. You see, we weren't thinking of this being ongoing. The second fire we did at Bob's request, and Convergence gave us, I think, a thousand dollars.

And again, we were not a nonprofit—just me as an individual. For Convergence, we expanded. We did this larger installation for four nights, continuously—every night of the conference, with lots of volunteers. Some of the volunteers came from the conference, most of them were my friends, but there were other people who just pitched in. The material used to build it was consumed by the end because most of the material was built out of wood. So the fires were not only burning their fuel, but they were also burning the infrastructure that supported the piece. It barely lasted the four nights. Much of it self-destructed. We also had a higher density of braziers for SecondFire.

We wanted to make an urban site for the conference that would be an alternative to the convention center. So the sculpture people tended to migrate to the river, and there was just this magical expectation and transformation. It was relatively sparse with people on the river because we didn't announce it. No one knew it was coming; it was a surprise. So the first night, a few people from the conference came, and a few people from the city came, and they said, "Whoa! What's this?"

Of course, the *Providence Journal* wrote about it the next morning, saying, "Whoa! What's this?" And so the public came the second night. Then they talked to people for the third night, and by the fourth night, there were a lot of people there. We did it Wednesday, Thursday, Friday, and Saturday. By Saturday night, there were a tremendous number of people there. There was this viral marketing phenomenon of people talking to each other by word of mouth, saying, "Have you seen this?" Then a very interesting social phenomenon happened. We started to get phone calls from people asking, "When's the next one?"

I explained to them that there wasn't another one, this was a one-time thing, and yeah, we did it a second time, but that was it. People were disappointed, but we kept getting these phone calls, from all sorts of people.

Creating WaterFire

Two people in particular—Joan Slafsky and Jeannie Sturim—called me and said that we really ought to do this on an ongoing basis. Joan Slafsky is a woman involved with the arts, who was the public relations person for the Rhode Island School of Design Museum. She was no longer working for the museum at the time, and she was struck by how it had transformed Providence, and she felt that the city really needed something like that. I didn't disagree with her at all, but I did question how one would do this on an ongoing basis because it was such an effort of hundreds of volunteers who were willing to donate boats, and trucks, and people to do it once.

But suddenly, if you're going to do it on an ongoing basis, you can't borrow a truck, or a boat, or an outboard motor, or a dock. It's one thing to get permission to tie your boat up for free for three nights, but to suddenly have it all year long, that's a different story. I told her that it would be possible to do that, but it would require a million dollars. She said, "Well, let's raise it!" I hadn't really considered that it would be possible to raise the funds to do that. She organized some people to come to her house, and we talked through how we might do it.

Joan and Jeannie were pushing for an ongoing piece, and I was in favor of it on several conditions: one, that it would remain an art piece and not become a carnival; two, that it always remain free, because I felt that it was a celebration of the urban identity of the city and it was in a public space, so you couldn't charge admission; third, I didn't want it to become too commercial; fourth, I didn't want to have to be too involved with fundraising.

It was at this point that we talked to the mayor and the business community, when we first considered establishing a structure to do it on an ongoing basis. Remember, this project had not been engaged in by the city in any way, or the urban planning department, or the business community. They discovered it. An early conversation that Joan and I had was with the publisher of the *Providence Journal*, Howard Sutton, who pledged support. We also went and talked to the Chamber of Commerce, and Dick Oster, the businessman who took over the old Union Station. He also pledged support.

Mayor Cianci saw it for the first time at New Year's.[5] He immediately understood its potential value to the community as a symbol of renaissance, as a gathering of social space, as an activator of urban environments. But he didn't know about it prior to that. One of his aides had called him and said, "You've got to come look at this," and we actually put him on the boat. He toured it from the water, and everyone waved, but he didn't know anything about it prior to First Night. For Convergence, he probably knew about it at that point, because Convergence was a parks department event.

This was a contemplative piece that was engaged with the music and with this idea of fire and water as representative of life, but also being representative of destruction. I had this sense that life was an ephemeral, fragile entity that needed to be celebrated with the religious overtones of fire as a symbol. So what I was entirely opposed to was taking that and converting it into a beer-drinking festival with rock music, and fireworks, and clowns, and stuff like that.

What was interesting about WaterFire, and what the community needed, was what art tends to address—something a little quieter. You can always get a crowd for anything if you give them free food and cheap alcohol and loud music. That's easy. It's done all over the world. You've got jazz festivals, Mardi Gras, you've got all kinds of things that do that. You don't need an artist to do that. All you need to do is have a budget for a festival series and have Budweiser sponsor it, and you can do that. And I didn't see any social need for that. We already had festivals like that in Providence. I felt that the response to WaterFire was in part because it was none of those things. It was a much more spiritual, quasi-religious experience for those who wished it to be, but it was still entirely free of any sort of dogma or religion, so that people could also just enjoy it.

It also promoted two things. One, it promoted conversation. At a concert, you can't talk. It's quite telling that the most popular thing to do for a date is to go to a movie, because you don't have to talk to the other person, which is awkward. It's difficult to have conversation. So I wanted an event where people could talk, where you could sit by the fires and choose to listen to the music, or you could choose to talk quietly. Or you could, ideally, cycle back and forth between the two.

Number two, I wanted a piece that was about paseo and passeggiata and about walking. I didn't want everyone sitting in their seats, watching a performer on the stage entertain them, which was to just occupy their time and make them feel that all they had to do was to sit and look. The point was to make a socially viable urban space. You have to participate in its urbanity, and you have to walk through it and be engaged with it and interact with strangers and talk to strangers and have social interactions with people.

You needed wild diversity. If you have a rock concert, you get—depending on the band—a Latino crowd, or a white crowd, or a Black crowd, and they'll tend to be sixteen to twenty-four. Well, that's not the city. If you have an opera performance, you're going to get a totally different circle. It's going to be mostly white, it's going to be mostly older, and it's going to be mostly wealthy. If you have a jazz concert, you're going to get a different constituency. There are very few things that are going to bring everyone together.

But everyone comes to WaterFire. Almost all arts events are under-represented by lower-income people, including minorities. We actually have a higher minority participation rate than any other arts activity in the state. But it's still not what it should be. We only want people to come because they want to come. If people don't want to come, we're not going to bend their arms and say they have to come. But it is a celebration of the community.

Waterplace Park started as a state park. It should have remained a state park because the state has deeper resources to maintain things; the city doesn't. It became a city park for political reasons. That's an important point. It was moved from the state to the city so it would be possible for Bella Vista to have a liquor license. It's the restaurant that used to be called the Boat House, overlooking Waterplace Park.

That building was never built as a restaurant; it was built as a visitor's center. It's a really awkward site. And the reason why it's there at all is that it meets the ADA [Americans with Disabilities Act] requirement for handicapped accessibility because it has the elevator. That visitor's center solved the handicapped access problem so visitors could take the elevator down to Waterplace Basin. For a while, it was left as a visitor's center. But since no one was there, it was left utterly unvisited.

The city wanted to convert it to a restaurant because they wanted it to be an urban activator for the space. But if it was owned by the state and leased from the state to a restaurant, it's illegal by state law for it to serve alcohol. Everyone interested in bidding on it as a restaurant said they couldn't make a restaurant work without a liquor license. So in order to accommodate the visitor's center being converted to a restaurant that could serve alcohol, the park was transferred from the state to the city.

The consequences of that are both positive and negative. On the one hand, I think people are right—it was smart to turn it into a restaurant—though it should've been built to be a restaurant originally. For the restaurant to be successful, it probably did require a liquor license. But on the downside, the city parks maintenance department, which already doesn't have enough funds and has too much to do, suddenly inherited a very large park that they had not budgeted for and a very difficult park to maintain because it involves water, and rivers, and tides.[6] So there was a big tradeoff.

It was transferred too early to really have a comparison between the state and the city maintenance. Right now, maintenance is an interesting patchwork quilt. There is a program, run by the state with prisoners, that takes care of Waterplace Basin. They do a very good job. They do the Basin down to Steeple Street. There is some shared maintenance—the city does some, the state does some. The problem with the state program is that all they have is labor. They don't have any money for paint, or parts, or for contractors to fix things. If prisoners can do it, it gets done. So they'll pick up the litter and stuff like that. But if you need to buy something like paint brushes or paint, there's no money for it. It's a park that had been planned for under the state budget, and its transfer over to the city has raised lots of problems, which they're working through.

It's a perennial problem with all projects done with federal dollars. Federal dollars will give you a large infusion of cash that you have to match with a certain percentage of local dollars to do the capital infrastructure construction, but maintenance thereafter is the city's responsibility. You have a great big new wonderful project, and the city is eager to have the project and the federal dollars, but the larger project of ongoing maintenance always, somehow, is not budgeted for. This is a problem all across the US, and you've seen that problem here. The newest efforts to resolve that problem—and the park department's been quite forward thinking and engaged on this—is to establish a business improvement district, a BID for the area. The current BID is just for the downtown and does not include the park. But the next phase that's anticipated by the Providence Foundation and the parks department is that the BID should be expanded to include GTECH and Citizens and the new Intercontinental project and probably the mall. And then all of them can participate in the BID, and that can provide a source of money for maintenance to the park.

The Cost of Success

I'm very pleased with the collaboration with SoundSession; Providence SoundSession is a multi-day, multi-genre concert series organized by the Providence Black Repertory Company. That's a very different WaterFire than what we normally do because it's a live band on the stage. But that's alright; we can have variation. I think SoundSession is a great project, in its third year now and growing. The problem for both SoundSession and us is that many people come to WaterFire expecting WaterFire. Suddenly, when there's a jazz concert there, that's not what they came to see, but then we have some people coming to see SoundSession, and they're wondering who all these other people are. That's okay. They can all get to know each other; that's a good thing.

The difficulty for scheduling things at the same time is usually traffic. We've tried usually not to do WaterFire on the same weekend as Gay Pride only because they've got to close so many streets for the nighttime parade that it makes downtown really complicated. Plus, it's a fun thing to go to, and now I have to work. That's an interaction that we'll have to explore this year. I think you want to have lots of things happening downtown all the time, so why have both sets of crowds descend on the restaurants on the same night?

The problem for SoundSession is that Waterplace Basin is too small a site for a program as successful as that is. The stage at Waterplace Basin is very, very nice as long as you don't get more than three hundred people. Once you get more than that, then it becomes an awkward site. It's very difficult to get a piano down there, for example, and even more difficult now that building construction is going on.

The bigger difficulty when we combine SoundSession or any live event on the stage with WaterFire is that there is a strong tradition of paseo and passeggiata, where people want to walk. So now you've got twenty to thirty thousand people who want to walk around the Basin, but to walk around the Basin requires entirely blocking the view of the stage. Because of the way it's designed, you completely block the view of the stage when you walk across the path. To avoid that, you've got to tell people that they've got to go up six flights of stairs and then down six flights of stairs to go around the stage and viewing area. Well, people don't want to do that. So it's a very awkward site to try to balance things. And we've had issues with people who say, "I can't walk up six flights of stairs." So it's a hard problem to solve.

We've got a proposed solution for this, which we'll explore further with the parks department, that would involve building a stage that's six feet higher so you can divert the crowd under the stage, or in front, so people can see the stage. That has problems of its own, too. We do a range of things on the stage, and we'd do more of them if we could solve that pedestrian flow problem.

The other problem with SoundSession is that the event is too damn good! You can't fit more people in Waterplace Basin, because it's only got so much seating capacity, and only 180 people can get in Black Rep. So if you get a great event, and you get twenty thousand people coming, you're disappointing nineteen thousand of them who can't get in. It's a real Catch-22. So the better they make the event, the larger they make the venue, but the larger they make the venue, the less intimate it is.

One of the best things I went to was at Black Rep. It was a concert by BB King for a hundred fifty of us. That was fantastic. It would have been totally different for twenty thousand of us at the convention center. It's hard to balance those things.

Structurally, the park was very thoughtfully designed, but no one imagined sixty thousand people would be coming to an event there. So the popularity of WaterFire has caught all of us entirely by surprise, and the park facilities were never built with that in mind. There is a bathroom, but it only has two stalls, so the parks department is scared to open it. It's under the stairs that lead up to the mall. They open it for smaller crowds, but they won't let us open it for WaterFire because of the capacity issue. I don't completely understand what the issue is, but it's a plumbing problem. I believe in order for it to be at grade with the park, it's below the sewer system, so every flush has to be pumped up to Francis Street, and the pump capacity can't keep up with the number of flushes that would happen; I think that's the problem. Again, the whole thing was never built with crowds this size in mind. I would love to get those bathrooms large enough and installed and working as a support for the park, but it involves a lot of money, and it should have been done, just like the visitor's center should have been built originally as a restaurant. So the physical infrastructure of the park was not planned for seeing the success of the events like SoundSession or WaterFire.

We enjoy astonishingly good support from the city, the state, and the business community. There are downsides that are real. One of the biggest headaches for the city is that suddenly, their park budget is completely wrenched because there are twenty-two events that WaterFire does that require park crews to pick up litter. We've offered to pick up the litter, but we can't do that under city union contracts. There's no solution other than the parks budget takes a hit.

There's the same problem with the city for police. Suddenly, you need all sorts of police directing traffic down there. It costs the city about thirty-eight thousand dollars a year just to handle it. We hire some police in the park for certain sites, like where we have alcohol. But the police who are handling basic vehicle traffic through the city—that's a real expense to the city of Providence that they've absorbed as part of their contribution to WaterFire. But that's a challenge for them.

From the economic development point of view, the more fires the better. From an urbanism, excitement point of view, the more events in general, the better. You want to have SoundSession, Black Heritage festival, AS220's Festival, the Women's Playwright festival, Shakespeare in the Park. There's stuff going on all the time. But that means more costs for the city and for police. Now, the economic benefits of that more than outweigh it. But that doesn't necessarily mean that new taxes paid on the meal tax essentially filter all the way down to the parks department budget. I mean, the city makes money off WaterFire, but it's a challenge for the individual departments to figure out how they're going to cover those costs.

We're always short of funds. We've been severely underfunded ever since our inception, with a staff that works way too many hours. Our paid staff numbers about fourteen right now; it varies from winter to summer. More than half are just in management and fundraising. Our proposed budget for next year is 1.7 million dollars, so we've got to be audited, and there's bookkeeping and filing, just like any million-dollar business. There are payroll people, insurance, and all that kind of stuff. There are thirteen workstations just in this office that are just covering the invoices, getting the insurance liability for the bands, figuring out who's going to supply the porta-johns, doing the audits, writing grants, negotiating sponsor benefits.

It certainly doesn't just happen. That's an important point, because the impression you want to give to the visitor is that the sunset goes down and the fires just start, and it's beautiful and wonderful. You don't want the process or the mechanism or the worry about things like insurance, or "Who pays for those outboard engines?," or "I wonder how much it costs to dock those," or "Who sandblasts the bottom of the boat?"—all those expenses are deliberately meant to be not shown. It's supposed to just happen; we want it to be that ephemeral, light. But that presents us with a perceptual problem: because all the background's hidden, people don't understand why it's so expensive.

We could go into all the technical details, which just aren't very interesting—for example, what the liability insurance requires us to do. We have to insure the city for four million dollars of liability insurance, so we spend probably about a hundred and twenty thousand dollars each year just on insurance. That's almost ten percent of my budget. First Night and Convergence already had liability insurance in place. They already had the police committed to be there that night. They already had the parks department committed to cleaning up the debris. So a lot of that was in place. Now that we've expanded it, there's a real series of tradeoffs there.

Most of our funding comes from corporate sponsorship. We get about forty-five percent of our funding from sponsorships, and then we get about twenty percent from the public and about twenty-five percent from the state. We get three hundred thousand dollars from the state and have for the last six years, and we got seventy thousand dollars from the city this last year. In addition to the seventy thousand dollars, we get a lot of in-kind support, probably another fifty-five thousand dollars to pay for police, street sweepers, parks department.

From the public, we get checks mailed in, sometimes large gifts; we got a check of fifty thousand dollars last year from an individual. A large number of our donations are from the arts community, but also the business community—and we also do collaborative enterprises for corporate sponsorships. I think this year, we're doing something with Volvo. But we always try to do these things creatively.

Volvo's new campaign is called "Volvo for Life." So instead of just displaying the car, we want to do live tableaus, so I'd like to do some sort of living sculpture of models doing something. It might be a fashion or film shoot so people will be wondering why there will be lights and fans. But it will actually be something that people walking by will encounter and so be invited to be part of it. Or it might be a Victorian picnic, with gentlemen in nineteenth-century garb and a butler. But people aren't expecting it.

University students make up many of the people who come to WaterFire. RISD [Rhode Island School of Design] has been a very cooperative partner with us, not financially, though they are a sponsor, too, but with providing us access to facilities, restrooms, auditoriums, parking lots, roofs of their buildings for wiring and lighting and different positioning of equipment. We have rewired some of their buildings to provide power for us. We've had to pay for that, but they didn't have to give us access, and they don't charge us for the power. They give us an area where we set up a jazz stage, where we take over the executive parking lot. So RISD's been very cooperative. Brown University has been cooperative as well, but Brown's a little further away, so Brown's connection is slightly more distanced. But this year, Brown is going to build it in as part of their graduation exercises and also their reunion activities.

Also, there's a study to remind everyone that it's well worth it. The economic impact study, which we commissioned from Acadia Consulting and the University of Rhode Island's Tourism Economics group, estimated that 1.1 million people came to WaterFire in the 2004 season, and it generated 40.5 million dollars in spending.[7]

For economic impact, they're looking at the out-of-state visitors.[8] So the state income from the 2004 season was 2.32 million dollars. So for a three-hundred-thousand-dollar investment from the state, they're getting in direct state taxes back almost seven or eight times their investment. That's with the narrow definition. So economically, it's well worth it for the city, but the intangibles are actually far more valuable to the city in terms of the media coverage, the change in expectation of what the city was, the branding of the city. That's what this report is talking about.

* * *

I have the copyright on the event. This event preceded the nonprofit's engagement by three years, so I had the copyright and the trademark before I lit it for First Night. It's owned by the artist that created it; particularly in this case, where the artist created the event two or three years before we even thought of having a nonprofit involved. The nonprofit is an organization that decided that this piece that the individual artist, Barnaby Evans, did was interesting, and that we ought to figure out how to allow Barnaby to keep doing it. So it has a license allowing it to produce WaterFire in Providence. The license doesn't say that they can produce it anywhere else, and it doesn't say that I can't produce it anywhere else.[9]

Houston, Texas, and Tacoma, Washington, were one-time licenses. Houston was done under a nonprofit, which was the Downtown Improvement District. Tacoma was done under the nonprofit of the Museum of Contemporary Art and Glass.

There is concern in Providence about losing an event that's unique to Providence. But it's not Providence's event to lose. I mean, it's my event, and it's licensed. Remember, I said it was from a Holocaust project, an idea for Berlin. So if WaterFire is a piece about building community, you can build that community all across the world, and I think that's a really interesting prospect. There are mixed feelings in Providence about that. We've already done Houston and Tacoma. The third one we did was Columbus, Ohio, and we've been talking to a lot of other cities.

We want to do it where there's true social engagement with the entire community on a large scale and really make it an interesting civic experiment. So in Kansas City, Missouri, we're trying to do it on Brush

Creek. Brush Creek goes from east to west across Kansas City, so it goes from the wealthiest part of town to the poorest part of town, right down the middle, divided by Troost Avenue. The poor part of town's east of Troost and the wealthy part of town's west of Troost. This river cuts right across that. They've now developed a park along it. But people from *this* community don't go to people from *that* community. So we're very interested in using WaterFire to link those two. It's a much larger social experiment in building urban community. That's an interesting project. We've been talking to Kansas City for five years, and they are slowly building the momentum to do what Columbus did.

So there's mixed feelings in Providence about how unique it ought to be. There are people who feel that this ought to be the only place in the world you see it. Indeed, if there were sufficient funds for us to be able to do it that way, that might make some sense. Providence is divided on that. There are members of the community who feel that it should be a unique event to Providence. And if they wish it that way, I guess we could negotiate a license for uniqueness, but they wouldn't be able to afford it anyway.

But there's also a substantial number of people in Providence who think it would be really cool to have Providence as the head of a cooperative arts exchange all around the world. So that if we had WaterFire in Rome, and Dublin, and Glasgow, and Seoul, and Berlin, that would be a really interesting thing. You've always got this phenomenon that some people don't really value what they've got when it's local. It would almost be better strategically to go after Rome, and Seoul, and Kyoto.

There are a lot of unauthorized knockoffs of WaterFire in Rhode Island itself—nine of them. When we tried to tell them that they shouldn't do it, Rhode Islanders got upset with us. They're really small, and they're kind of sad, and they're really dismal. But there's one in Jamestown, there's one in Westerly, there's one in Pawtucket, one in Woonsocket, and one in Pawcatuck, Connecticut. There was one in East Greenwich. Some of them are fairly naïve. They're all tributes, in a sense.

The one that bothered me the most was in South County. The sense I had from the South County people was, "Well, we want to have our own. We don't want to have to go up to Providence, where there are poor people." They didn't say that, but that was the impression I was getting, even though the whole idea of WaterFire was to celebrate the larger community and create an event where everybody is welcome and could come.

So if you then make little, teeny versions all over the place, you're doing exactly the opposite of what the intention of the piece was. So now the rich white folk in Wakefield have theirs, and we've got one for the blue collar people in Pawtucket. That's not what was intended by the piece at all. But a few years ago, when I told Pawtucket to knock it off, that they were in violation of copyright and trademark, the local Pawtucket people got upset, and so the state legislature more or less said, "Let them do their thing," in exchange for the state funding. They just said, "You need support from all the legislators from all over the state." So it wasn't an official quid pro quo, but it was a message that was delivered to us loud and clear.

What's interesting is that the people who are most parochial and think, "Gee, it ought to be just here, in Rhode Island," are also the people who said, "Hey, how come you're beating up on Pawtucket, telling them that they can't do it?" See, you can't have it both ways. So my policy is that we want to do it in places where it will work, where the site really is appropriate. The Pawtucket site's not appropriate.

More than Water and Fire

What WaterFire's trying for is a very tricky balance between intimacy— and it seems to work, although it's a tricky balance—between an individual looking at a fire twenty feet away and feeling a triangle of the fire, him or herself, and the one, two, three, or four persons they're with, so there's that intimate space. Yet at the same time, you're in the midst of a civic celebration with as many as sixty thousand people, but the two don't intrude on each other. So at a big concert in the civic center with twenty thousand people, you never have that sense of intimacy. That's not possible. But you can have that at WaterFire.

There's lots of other things we try to do to create that sense of intimacy, like the creatures, and the gargoyles, and the performances on the boats. There are a lot of performances on boats, and there are a lot of surprises where people don't know what's been orchestrated and what hasn't been, to try to get the intimacy working—and specifically to get people to question whether that was programmed or not.

If you put it on a stage with spotlights, that's programmed—"Oh yeah, they paid them to do that." But if someone comes up to you and does something really magical and wonderful, that's cool. Who's to say if it's programmed? That makes it more interesting as an urban experience. But our problem with those is when we get pressed for funds, we've got to shrink back down to cover the core event.

My favorite crowd interaction was something that we called Guerrilla Tango. On the soundtrack, we would play a lot of tangos anyway. We had stationed, throughout the park, maybe forty tango dancers who were dressed however they wanted to dress, probably somewhat fancy but not so much so that you knew they were performers. They knew by their watch that ten seconds after this song ends, a tango is going to start. So when that song ends, but before the tango starts, all across the park, we would have two of them start a really loud fight.

We discovered very quickly that the guy couldn't yell at the girl or people would intervene. But the girl could yell at the guy. This was all throughout the park, all over the place. Just two people. So if you were at Waterplace Basin, looking at the fires, suddenly you would hear this commotion and turn around—"What the hell's that?" Because people don't fight at WaterFire.

So, for example, she would say, very loudly, "I thought you weren't seeing her anymore! Jesus! You told me that you weren't going to see her anymore!"

Then the music starts. He puts his hand out to invite her to dance, and she tosses her head, and then comes in, and they do this *amazing* tango. Like, "Whoa! Did you see that?!"

When it's over, she just turns her back and says, "Basta!" And she leaves the guy standing there.

The crowd comes up to him and says, "Hey, it's gonna be okay. Can we buy you a drink?" Other people are saying, "Did you see that?! They were fighting, and the music started, and . . . and . . . it was amazing!"

So that's the kind of spontaneous thing we'll do in the crowd, but we haven't done that in years, because we haven't had the funds. It's that level of very intimate, very small thing, which maybe only twenty people will see around that particular couple. Now when we did it, I think we had a dozen couples in a dozen different places doing it simultaneously. We did that also with opera singers, where suddenly the instrumental part of an aria would be playing on the river, and you'd have sopranos in the crowd suddenly just step forward and sing the piece in unison all along the river. Those were students from Juilliard. We gave them the train fare to come up and do it.

We do stuff with local groups, too. We work with students from Berklee School of Music, but not much. We don't do a lot of live performance stuff, although the jazz stage and the ballroom are always live. Almost every year, we do something with the local mandolin orchestra. They're scheduled for July this year, I think.

So we do stuff like that. They're interesting. It's the more interesting area of trying to animate an urban space, which I think is more exciting and more influential. It's that sort of guerrilla event that we love to do, but it's that sort of event that's in the "frills" category of the budget. They're the sort of thing that we really would love to get back to.

WaterFire also does the Jazz Stage at RISD and the Ballroom at the Turk's Head Building on select WaterFire nights. I designed both of those events to solve a problem we had. Both of those events are decoy distraction events to draw the crowd away from WaterFire. We were way over the park's capacity. Both of those events were designed to create something a block away in a desperate attempt to get people to move away from WaterFire. So that was the first motivation.

The second motivation was that if WaterFire was being used as a vehicle to enliven and engage an urban space, we needed to figure out how to spread that energy beyond the river. People only walk one block. So the next site that we would propose for an off-river event would be on Westminster Street by the Arcade. Where SoundSession is being overly optimistic, in terms of crowd psychology, is in trying to get people to go from WaterFire all the way down to Black Rep. That's too long and poorly lit a passage. Now they did it with a parade, which was great. But once you miss the train, it's gone.

The bottom line is that this project was done entirely independently of the city planners, but it was made possible by the innovative planning and design of deciding to make the river a public urban park, and then by the city's being open to creative ideas from the community, such as myself, and then SoundSession from Don, and Bob Rizzo's Convergence festivals. Because we have an arts school here that's fairly active, the city's got a pretty good tolerance for wacky ideas, which is good. I think it's what's allowed WaterFire to get its foot in the door and then to prove its success.

10

Place, Identity, and Rituals of Turning Space into Place

Wendy Sarkissian's Practice Story

Editor's Preface

Wendy Sarkissian had a reputation for thinking outside the box. In Eagleby, Queensland, she mixed orthodox and unorthodox methods as community members reclaimed public space that appeared both poorly maintained and unsafe. Training local residents—who became the Flying Eagle Facilitators—as facilitators of SpeakOut booths at a local festival, Sarkissian not only built local capacity but ended up creating jobs. Working in the high school and doing community interviews, she learned that many in Eagleby seemed stigmatized by the surrounding wealthier communities.

Sarkissian recruited a community artist, Graeme Dunstan, to work with her, and what happened then was quite extraordinary, involving the local community in a moving and powerful way. Together with local youth and residents, they designed, built, and then—with lanterns and fire, with a march to collectively overcome stigma and disappointments—ritually burned a papier-mâché mock-up of the "Eagleby stigma" in the form of an eagle under a thumb that symbolized the stigma suffered by the local community. Wendy's account merges youth organizing, community engagement, learning, and reclaiming by residents of the local park they had come to fear and to avoid, as her place-making efforts produced new senses of community ownership, safety, respect, and, arguably, empowerment.

Reclaiming Place via Arts and Community Development

I want to talk to you about Stories in a Park, a project we did for Queensland Health in a suburb, Eagleby, that's about thirty-five kilometers, or a bit more, down the road from Brisbane, on the way to the Gold Coast. So it's midway between the Brisbane CBD [central business district] and Southport CBD, which is the center of the Gold Coast—a bit like Miami, a surfing tourist mecca—in a small estate that was about sixty percent low-density public housing established in the late 1990s, with a population of about eighty-five hundred people and virtually no jobs.

It's a small residential suburb. In the state government's listing of disadvantaged places, it's in the top thirteen for the whole of Queensland. So it has high levels of unemployment, single parents, public tenants, high turnovers in the school system, and crime involving young people. But the major thing seemed to be that it had been forgotten. Its values were not consistent with the values of the Gold Coast City Council. So they and their predecessor council kind of forgot about Eagleby. In 1999, two state government agencies, Health and Housing, started working in Eagleby in a big way, and I had a most bizarre experience of being the consultant for two state government departments at the same time in the same place.

The housing department was implementing the Community Renewal Program: upgrading of the physical and social infrastructure in low-income public housing estates. Community renewal was seen as being about what was beyond the front fence. So it was not the "urban renewal" of dwellings and their yards, but the public spaces, streets, and social infrastructure facilities. There was a parallel urban renewal program, where the government would fix houses and often sell them to richer people, but that's a somewhat separate matter.

Queensland Health took an entirely different approach to their project, which was very unformed and not bureaucratized, whereas the Housing one was quite formal because it was operating in thirteen housing estates, suburban housing developments with a high proportion of public housing, that had been targeted.

Queensland Health had an entirely different agenda. They were influenced by a Heart Foundation program called SEPA [Supportive Environments for Physical Activity]. It was about getting people out and about, walking to the postbox rather than driving in their cars.

The Housing bureaucrats thought they knew exactly what they wanted. They were going to assess needs and develop recommendations in a participatory way. Health had no idea of what they would find.

So after winning a competitive tender for Housing with lots of other consultants, I was managing the consultation for what became the Community Action Plan and the Local Area Plan and all the planning bits and pieces to guide expenditure of public funds to upgrade this housing estate. I just did my part, and the engineer did his part, and the landscape architect did his part of it.

So maybe there was a cast of ten or twelve people ferreting around in Eagleby, but in a very prescribed sort of structure of deliverables, which would ultimately be managed by the council. On the Housing side, it was quite formal: the same geographical area and a whole lot of consultants working on it, and they did exactly the same stuff in all the other housing estates.

But the health department, under the SEPA project, wanted to know what we thought might work, how we might encourage people in this low-income place to get out and about in their neighborhood. We had, rather than a tightly constrained budget, budgets related to the end of the financial year. Danny O'Hare, an urban designer, was involved in this project, and we tried to imagine what would be necessary to help local people reclaim a relationship with their public spaces. It wasn't reclaiming them from anything except fear and stigma. But it was an entirely different assignment, and new pots of money appeared, so there was actually a lot of money, and we kept managing to get more. It was hugely enhanced, and it went on for a year, whereas the other Housing project took a few months. The Health project went on for a whole year, and my relationship with the community has gone on until now. I was down there just last week.

The Health project was enormously enhanced by the fact that the young Queensland Health project manager was having a passionate love affair with the young council planner for the Gold Coast. That helped a huge amount. Their love affair enriched the whole thing. Actually, it was very wonderful having a couple of lovebirds working with you, but also we joked about it. Without question, the partnership was made much easier with the council, because Rebecca could make it happen with Thor.

Rebecca was working for Health, and Thor was working for the council, and that was very significant. So if we had a problem with the council, we could talk to Rebecca, who would do the pillow-talk stuff with

Thor, and a lot of things were smoothed over because of that. Now I know that sexual politics can often cause problems, but here it was the opposite. It was very good.

We had been approached by Health on the recommendation, I think, of Danny O'Hare, who teaches urban design here at Queensland University of Technology. So it wasn't a tender. I had been living in Brisbane for only a few months, and this job fell out of the sky. The other one was tendered for, against everybody, and this one we were given.

Furthermore, we invented it. We were just opportunistic—which has its disadvantages— but mainly we moved from one opportunity to another, kind of backfilling it with a program as it began to emerge. We discovered our process as we went on. In the beginning, actually, we didn't know what we were going to do.

We started in August 1999, and there was to be the first festival, the Spirit of Eagleby festival. They'd never had one before, and the community center was organizing it, a fête.

Because this was happening, even though we were only a few weeks into our project, we changed what would have been our direction: to scope the project by means of a search conference with professional stakeholders. We would have asked them to codesign the process with us—and share the blame if it went wrong, I guess—and then we would have developed a methodology based on their advice. We would have set up what I call an "accountability group"—a really feisty working party to work with us, and then together we'd figure out what to do. But because we had this festival approaching in a few weeks, we decided to use a different approach, and that was where our opportunism began. We set up a marquee [tent] at the festival, and we did a model that we now use a lot here, which I coinvented, called a SpeakOut. It's a bit like an open house, but more intensively facilitated. We had a core of issues about the public realm that had been presented to the council by the multicultural group in Eagleby—a small group of residents led by a Maori woman from New Zealand—and this was really just a list of complaints, a list of concerns.

On that list of issues were cracked footpaths, bad sightlines, overhanging trees, damaged lighting—things that just impeded pedestrian movement, really—and a lot of issues around safety. Those were not really "We're just scared to go there" but rather "We just can't get there. I can't push my pram on this footpath because it's so cracked and broken" or "The footpath ends, and I've got to walk on the road, and I'm afraid I am going to be hit by a car."

The multicultural group decided that was their agenda. That was all we had, about a page of concerns. So this was before the festival. I mean, we were only convened as a team of consultants a couple of weeks before the festival. We met with these people, the community development worker in the community center, our client, and whoever else they could gather initially, and we worked up this list into a bit more than bullet points. So we had a few examples and points below that. We gave the members of this group disposable cameras, and they went off and took photos of the public realm in the community for us.

The group at that point was the multicultural group and a few others we'd gathered together. Their representativeness was not an issue then—we were desperate. So we prepared SpeakOut with seven issue stalls in this marquee, each dealing with a major issue that concerned them. For example, there was no public access to the river, even though this suburb is bounded on three sides by rivers. The land was all in private ownership, or it was the public land you couldn't get through. There were issues of crime, issues of things for kids to do. We presented each with a few points and a few photos underneath at the SpeakOut stalls, and that was all we had to display.

From this group and some others who had been involved in the community center, a group was formed—all women but two, I think. I trained them in basic facilitation and recording practices, and they staffed the seven stalls, so we had fifteen workers there, two for each stall, a listener and a recorder for each stall at the SpeakOut, with our client helping a lot, Queensland Health, with Rebecca and Kate, her boss.

We were very successful. Lots of people came to the festival. We wanted to provoke comment. We tried to make it as much like a meeting even when it wasn't a meeting because it was a drop-in. So as you came, and you were complaining about the fact that you couldn't fish in the river, even though the river was there, everything you said was recorded by the recorder, while the listener paid close attention to you and drew out your comments.

When someone else came an hour later and saw all this stuff that you had said, they thought, "Ohhh, and I've got more!" So some of the synergy that you get in a meeting, we managed to replicate with the vertical recording on the butcher's paper at the SpeakOut. This generated a huge amount of information, which we sorted.

What it also generated—which is the good-news story, really—were the foundations of what became a successful local enterprise, the Flying Eagle Facilitators. We've established a community enterprise of facilitators in Eagleby, and they work all around the state, facilitating in public workshops and meetings. So these women and men who had been trained to do listening and recording are now doing it all around the state as a business.

This was the first experience of these people who had been trained. They were very scared, very relieved, very happy, very affirmed. Initially, they were scared—absolutely shitless—and then delighted. We put a lot of effort into the training. We role-played it, we videoed it, so that they weren't manipulated or embarrassed or anything. Embarrassment is a huge issue here in low-income communities.

I think manipulation, humiliation, and embarrassment are the stock-in-trade of many of my colleagues, and I'm very concerned about that. From a purely pragmatic point of view, if I want to do business with you, and you're an Eagleby resident, I'd like you to be feeling good about yourself in this process, even if your life is going to hell in a hand basket. But if the process makes you feel incomplete or incompetent, or silly, or just uneasy, then aside from the ethics of it—which are really important to me—I'm not going to get any good stuff out of you, because you're going to be sitting there thinking that you're wearing the wrong shoes or whatever.

Other planning processes often get into those problems. They're elitist and formal, and people speak in a secret language. The suits are sitting on the stage. It's a cold, drafty hall. The people are sitting in rows on the floor. You can't hear properly. There's no roving mic. You feel like you're being toyed with, even when the planners are trying to get information or sell something to people in a so-called participatory process. So the planners can get in their own way. Sometimes it's just plain ineptitude. I don't even think it's bad intentions. That explains the subtitle of my firm: we call it Planning with Care—that's our motto. We think it's important that the seats are comfortable.

We were talking about the stalls and the training of the listeners and the recorders as an alternative to some ways that planners too often embarrass and humiliate people. Planners sometimes use language to make people feel "other," not always intentionally, but to confuse.

Sometimes I feel that people are trying to make decisions where no time has been spent raising their levels of literacy or knowledgeability about the topic. I mean, I'll be in a place where people have told me there is no global warming: "We don't have global warming in our community, so it doesn't matter that the methane's coming out of the rubbish buried under our park." You have to put some effort into helping people understand global warming if you're going to have an informed conversation. You've got to do it in a way that doesn't make somebody feel like a schmuck—and that's just a job of work. But humiliation and embarrassment are major issues in the way people are treated by planners in this country—absolutely.

Then after the festival, we held the stakeholders meeting that we would have normally had at the beginning of such a process. We got together representatives of the schools, and community organizations, and the professional stakeholders, and we had a meeting at which the residents presented the results of their SpeakOut at the festival. We did it kind of backward—so then the stakeholders worked with the residents in facilitated sessions at tables—facilitated by the now emerging Flying Eagle Facilitators to work out the research process for discovering how people might get out and about safely and comfortably in Eagleby.

From the data they generated, we tried to identify stakeholders; they were easy to identify in a small place. I mean, they were the usual suspects, really, plus others whom the information yielded. It was easy to get them together. But the question of stakeholders is interesting. We had private owners of some of the land through which you might get direct access to the river. They popped up because of all the discussion about the alienation of the riverfront. That was an issue. It was a pretty standard search-conference model, except that we introduced this nice little element in the middle of the workshop where the residents took the professionals on a bus tour of the suburb.

By this time, I had gathered together a core group of residents who were advising us on the planning. We had a bit of money to pay them, so we tried to be fair about that. They said, "We get professional people coming down here all the time, and they got no idea where we are. This is a very diverse place, Eagleby. It's got a lot of rural land, and we've got a lovely river that we can't get to. We want to show them. We'll take them on the bus. We'll give them a guided tour, and they can eat their lunches on the bus."

That was fantastic. I actually didn't go on the bus, but it was very good for them.

By the time we'd done the SpeakOut at the festival, we had a core of ten people who were hot to continue this process and who wanted to be further involved, but they were residents—except for the community development worker who was helping—and they said, "When we get the professionals, they see a very strong distinction: that's the Others, the guys from the police, from the local cop shop, the principals of the schools . . ."

Plus there were all those people in suits who were then coming in to work in some kind of partnership with the community around this more formal process; they were all going to come, too, and be educated about the community renewal aspects. The residents said, "We have to educate these outsiders, including the local professionals, about what's really going on here and also about what's important to us."

What was interesting was that there was this nasty rumor going around that I was a "river obsessee," that I was obsessed with the river and that I'd created this discourse about the river for some reason of my own—but I'm not. I'm lots of other things, but the Gold Coast City Council was very nervous, because when you open up the conversation with the river, they were going to have to get their plans out and show that there was public land that had never been opened up.

But the Eagleby people saw all these as the Others, and they were determined to educate them. So the bus tour was their idea, and the community leader, who had been the local Christian minister for years, led the bus tour, essentially, and worked out the trip and spoke on the microphone.

It was great. They were very happy. They stacked the bus so they had one resident for every Other, one to one. They sat beside them and explained things to them as they went. I think we had a sixty-seater, a big bus, a great big bus. There were heaps of residents who went. Everybody went from the whole search conference, and it was about a one-to-one relationship.

Afterward, people were shocked that you were surrounded by rivers on three sides and you couldn't even go there to fish. The professionals were shocked and saw things more through local eyes. I think that was very transformative for them. I think they were impressed by how articulate Eagleby people were. We'd been helping them along in giving voice to things, really teaching them to talk about it. How did we do that? Just listening. We went there a lot, we hung out with them a lot, we went to meetings, we sat with people. When we typed up the results of the SpeakOut at the festival, we brought it back and asked them what it meant. We were constantly handing this stuff back and asking, "So what does this mean?"

We socialized with them, so we went down and had lunch. The young project manager was very warm and open, a lovely young woman. We were around the community center a lot. And after a while, the residents started getting this feeling that we were their friends and that somehow, we were between them and those Others. We were different from the Others.

So this search conference was pretty formal, but it did have one nice touch when the current Christian minister, a local woman, from a local evangelical church down there, got up—after some priming by me—at the beginning and gave a speech about language. She said that she would prefer it if the professionals would speak in plain words.

This problem—language—is one of my things, and I primed her a bit, but it had an interesting effect on people, because it gave the facilitators, the nascent Flying Eagles, permission to stop people if they were talking jargon in the discussions at the separate tables. So we must have had about eighty people at that search conference, and I guess we had eight tables of ten or something on that order. They felt quite empowered to say in the sessions, "I'm sorry, I don't understand what you're talking about," or, "You're speaking too fast, and we can't write it down."

As I said, this bit about language is one of my things. My first two degrees are in English literature, and it has influenced my attitude toward planning a lot. Language is a great means of obfuscating or a great tool for reform. I think it's really mean to say a big word when you can make ordinary sense to people without dumbing it down. I mean, we can say "T-junction"—it doesn't have to be "axis termination," you know? It can just be a T-junction. Everybody understands what a T-junction is. This does have a connection to humiliation, I think; it's about not being embarrassed in public processes.

It's interesting. I want people to feel that they are received and accepted and comfortable, and then I don't mind provoking them terribly about the content and arguing back and getting very feisty. But I like them to be sitting down and comfortable and feeling like they are secure when we get into the hard stuff—because sometimes it gets pretty hard.

But we haven't gotten to the juicy stuff yet; this was all business as usual. So we held a search conference, and that was fine; it generated a lot of information. On the basis of the information that was there, the planning consultants who attended went off and started doing their formal studies—of economics, and landscape, and traffic, and all that.

By that time, it was November, and we went off in another direction. We had concluded—and by this I mean me and the one person who was working with me, my husband, Karl—that we had the opportunity to do something really radical, that these people liked us, they trusted us, and we'd been fair with them, and they were ready to do something.

They had started out depressed, disappointed, with very cool energy, not a lot of rage or anything, just flat and dispirited. We knew that a lot of money was coming from the state government; 2.6 million dollars was coming for social and physical upgrading, completely separate from money for fixing up houses. Health had money of their own, and they had also found a bit of unallocated money.

So we decided to see how deep we could go into just the topic of the public realm and parks with the SEPA program. The other Housing work, the formal plan, continued in a very conventional way, and it doesn't bear talking about. They did it. It was nothing very special.

So with Health's approval and a lot of money—I mean, maybe a hundred thousand dollars; like, serious money—we hired a community artist, and we developed this process, which we started in March 2000. It took us between December and February—which is also our Christmas close-down time, so nothing much happened—to get the budget together and to figure out what we were going to do.

I hired a community artist to work with me—a hippy artist who is about my age, a very flamboyant character, heavily into drug reform, which became quite a topic, working for Queensland Health when he was into cannabis law reform; that was an interesting side-story! His name is Graeme Dunstan, and we developed this project, which we called Stories in a Park, nested within this more straight and conventional park planning process. By this time, we had a formally established community body, the Eagleby Residents Action Group, or ERAG. They were formed out of the search conference in November 1999, and they were formally constituted in February 2000.

We'd dreamed up this model, Stories in a Park, and we pitched it to ERAG. They didn't dream it up. They'd have never dreamed this up in a fit. As their consultants, we dreamed it up, we pitched it to them, and we pitched it to the client, Health, and the client agreed, and we did it.

Really, we just asked two big questions. We said we want to know what the deeper story is here about why people feel the way they do about Eagleby's parks and public spaces. We think it's not about the physical. We think—because people were telling us this—that it's about some elusive thing called "stigma." We think people aren't going out because the whole place has got a bad rep. We think it's about that.

I had just finished a PhD in environmental philosophy and ethics, so I was also interested in asking the question, "If we're asking how we can make Eagleby's parks"—it boiled down to parks—"more conducive to human use and enjoyment, what about what nature thinks about this in its own right?" This was the environmental ethics question from an ecocentric perspective. What if you asked, in terms of their inherent worth and intrinsic value, "What do the *parks* want?" This question is asked a lot in environmental philosophy, and Graeme and I decided, since we're both deep ecologists, that we'd see whether the Eagleby people could wrap their minds around that as well, as part of the Stories in a Park.

The third thing that we wanted to do with Stories in a Park was to tackle the issue about how we felt that local people didn't know enough about basic concepts of human behavior in parks: the play needs of children at different ages in childhood, the fundamentals of social design—I've taught this stuff in universities—to raise their levels of literacy so we would all have a better and more informed conversation.

So we were pitching this to the Eagleby Residents Action Group and the client to get the money. It was hard to pitch the green ecological stuff. They saw it as really airy-fairy, the deep-ecology stuff. It took a lot of chutzpah, but we managed it. We just barely did it, and then when we got started, the whole thing lasted only three and a half months. It was like we were on a speeding train.

They said yes easily to the stuff that we did in the high school, teaching the high school kids about social behavior in public open spaces. It was difficult to implement in the high school because our timing was terrible; the academic year was well underway. But the client and the residents all thought that was a great idea. And the model was fine, but our relationships with the schools were too rushed. Graeme and I were both trained high school teachers. We had learned a lot about life in the modern Australian high school.

We were teaching environment and behavior stuff, but what it ended up being was about stigma, because that's what the kids knew about Eagleby. We ran training courses in the high school for year-ten students, gifted and talented students, who were supposed to be from Eagleby. But they turned out mostly to be from neighboring suburbs, so that affected the shape of it. But we taught them everything from basic research methods—how to interview, how to video interview—to all kinds of child development stuff about how little kids have different play needs from big kids, and if you don't take care of them, then big kids will trash the little kids' play areas, and so on—urban sociology 101 in a few weeks, really, I guess.

The main pitch to ERAG was that we were going to work in the high schools and that the adults would come and help and be involved. So that was a feature for them, and for the schools it was a "get all this free teaching from these two people who were both qualified teachers," and so we did that, both as high school teachers.

We were a bit too smart for our own good, though. A teacher said, "They weren't very cooperative," and they said that we didn't know how to teach high school kids. We thought that our problem was that we were too bright and sparkly and fun and interesting, and we worked with an actor trainer and it was just too juicy—and so maybe they sabotaged us a bit. That was a problem. That was an interesting lesson about how to work in high schools.

How did stigma come up? Everybody had been talking about stigma from day one. From the very beginning, people were saying, "Eagleby's a nice place, and it's a nice place to live, but our biggest problem is that other people look down on us." There was the classic stuff: "You have to give a different address when you are applying for a job," and, "You don't admit that you live here." So the second strand of this was Graeme working directly with the residents, and that meant whoever showed up. It was a widening circle. But overall, probably, only thirty-odd people were involved at this stage. We were asking them what this stigma looked like, and finally someone said, "It's an eagle that's lying down, and the thumb of other people's judgment is holding it down so it can't fly." So they built *The Stigma* out of cardboard, and it was as big as five meters long and two and a half meters tall and two meters wide. They built it out of cardboard: an eagle with the thumb of judgment holding it down. It's cardboard art. It took four men to carry it on bamboo poles integrated into it. We had asked for months, "What is this bloody stigma?" and they finally said, "Well, this is what it is."

So then Graeme designed it and made it. But this was no cup of tea— this was absolutely right at the edge. It's not common in this country to mix community arts and cultural development and planning, which is what we were doing, and I was really battling with my client for them to understand that when we needed fifteen bales of fencing wire or all these bamboo poles or all this bizarre gear, that this was about Supportive Environments for Physical Activity! This is cardiovascular disease prevention. We were actually doing the job here.

The making of *The Stigma* went on for weeks. Graeme camped in the most defiled Eagleby park in his van. We rented two shipping containers and set up electricity there, and local people and classes of primary school kids came and made lanterns for the community celebration and were involved in the building of *The Stigma*. I've got some great photos, some fantastic photos. The eagle with the thumb holding it down was called *The Stigma*; that was its name.

My husband, Karl, slept in his car for a whole week down there. And what was so interesting was the occupation of the so-called dangerous park. Karl and I were helping Graeme so he wouldn't have a breakdown from overwork. Karl helped Graeme build things, and he was working with me.

But it was also very symbolic. This was absolutely thrilling, absolutely amazing, because *The Stigma* was so big. Everybody could get it, the bigness of it: it was a big stigma that they talked about all the time, and we made a bloody big thing that was so big, we really felt that we got it.

This was difficult because Graeme is also a bit of a mad hippy. How did we pull this off? Well, I stayed very present with the residents. It was important to me that they didn't feel we were studying them or using them. I was down there a lot, and then I spent a lot of time explaining things to the client.

The client had their own larger steering committee for the whole thing, so I'd go in and do slide shows or make speeches to their advisory body—I had to be "Dr. Wendy" a lot. I had to be quite credible and in my good clothes and so on, because it was pretty dangerous stuff, really, pretty much at the edge. Either it was going to be seen as off on a tangent or it would fall over for some reason, and we wouldn't actually be able to finish, to get an outcome.

What we had in mind was that we were purging, or cleansing, Eagleby's negative perceptions of itself, and we were healing some ancient problem in Eagleby that we also felt. One of the women who was working with us was a Wiccan, a witch, and I think the three of us felt that there might have been some terrible massacres in Eagleby, that Aboriginal people had been massacred there. We felt that we were healing something about Eagleby that we didn't even understand by giving voice to all this stuff about stigma. And then we burned it in a huge fire ceremony. We burned *The Stigma*.

This was all pretty complicated. I could barely wrap my mind around it. On the day of the Winter Solstice, the longest day of the year, which is traditionally Children's Day, when the light begins to return to the world, we held this day of community celebration in this bad park—it was the seventeenth of June, 2000.

We had a day-long celebration where we showcased all the local dancers and singers, ballet classes, and musicians, and all the community organizations had stalls and sold food. It was a really big production, and for the last few weeks, local elementary school kids had been making paper lanterns that they carried on long bamboo poles. We had a number of large bamboo standards with six lanterns hanging off them, which could only be carried by a man, that had also been constructed. At sunset, the children collected their lanterns, which they had also spent the whole day at the celebration painting. They'd made them in the school groups, but they painted them during the day, and then we had four hundred of these lanterns. Each lantern had a candle in it, and there were some large lanterns that the high school kids had made, which represented different features that they wanted in the park, and they were big. One of them took thirty-nine candles. There were lanterns to represent ducks and rubbish bins. And *The Stigma* was in the middle of it—this huge, big, white thing.

During the day, I went around with a basket with preprinted paper in it, and we asked people to write their disappointments on the paper and then to put their disappointments in the belly of *The Stigma* so they could also be burned—their disappointments about Eagleby, all their dreams that hadn't been realized. We had planned to burn all this. The engineering of burning something like this in a public place, though, means you've got to be very careful—it required a big scaffold and guy-wires.

Where did the idea to burn it come from? Fire ceremonies are quite common in community cultural development. Graeme and I had been to ones down at Nimbin—the alternative center of Australia—and he's managed lots of them in other communities, and we knew already about the Burning Man festival, and I knew about this, but I only knew about it because of him. Planners don't know about this. But this enriches planning, because it's another discipline; we're cross-disciplinary here, we're across a dozen disciplines.

So how was this part of the park planning process, burning this sculpture? Where to begin? I guess our shared values are around myth, and using myth and archetype and story—we called it Stories in a Park. I mean, the whole time, people were telling stories about Eagleby and Eagleby's parks, and our belief is that cleansing is possible, that symbolic acts of healing can make differences to communities. I guess it's our shared community development philosophy and an interest in ritual.

Graeme and I believe that ritual can be reintroduced in ways that can be cathartic—I think we were after something cathartic here—so that people could feel they'd given voice to the bad stories and that there could be a new beginning marked by this event—not that it would take away their problems, but that it would be, symbolically, the return of the light, which is why we used lanterns.

We had worked in the schools with kids. The stories being told had identified stigma. The kids were interviewing their adult neighbors, they were interviewing other kids, and they were videotaping interviews with kids and neighbors about Eagleby and about the use of park spaces. We had worked with an actor who was also doing sort of socio-drama and tableau and using body movement to invoke, to give voice, to represent different bad stories about Eagleby, stories of muggings and crime.

So we were collecting stories the whole time. There was one big story, and that was the bad story that everything was caused by stigma. It was like somebody saying, "Well, you know, the day the house burned down, that's when everything started going to hell in a basket."

Everything came back to stigma. If we could get to this stigma, whatever the bloody hell it was, then we wouldn't be imbued by this depressing feeling that we were trapped in this place. That kept showing up in the kids' stories.

So this was a dominant theme, and there weren't many hopeful stories. It's interesting. We knew we would have a celebration of some kind, but we didn't know we'd have a "stigma." We didn't know what it would look like. We planned a lantern parade because that's quite a common thing to do in community cultural development, but *The Stigma* emerged on its own. Then we built it there for the celebration.

The ritual of making and burning *The Stigma* became the dominant story. It was the big daddy of the stories, the stigma story. Everybody said it. They wrote it down. When we evaluated this study from the residents' views, it was, "We loved all this stuff about the stigma," or, "We loved making it because it was men's business"—building *The Stigma* required a lot of men doing it, sort of an engineering job.

They loved it, but they said, when it got right down to it, that it was Graeme's idea to build this gigantic thing, and I wouldn't say that they said they didn't want to do it, but they felt that because it was rushed, they would have preferred on reflection to have codesigned it and then made it happen with him, rather than having him and me, Graeme and me, design the process, pitch it to them, and have them agree to it. And so it was, I think, that we were into cleansing, Graeme and I—that was our judgment. But I think it came more from us than from them, yes, and from hours of community development interviews, and so on.

So there was a lantern parade with the four hundred lanterns, and there was probably in the parade, we reckoned, for every kid, there were probably three adults, so there were maybe fifteen hundred people there. That's a lot in a suburb of eighty-five hundred people. And they wound through the park just after the sun went down, and I was standing with

Bob, the man who'd been the local Christian minister, on a hill looking down, and he was just crying, openly.

It was so poignant—this park had such a bad reputation, and here are these little kids walking through it with these beautiful painted lanterns, and everybody's laughing, and then we all gathered in a little kind of central area in the bowels of the park, in the more overgrown part, and Graeme told them fairy stories about loss and redemption. It was the most charming moment, with all these little kids are sitting around. It was winter, but it wasn't that cold, and they're sitting around on the ground with their little lanterns burning, and there he is standing there with his long white beard telling Grimms' tales, his version of a redemptive fairy story—it was really amazing.

Then we all walked back through the park. And then we took *The Stigma*, which by this time had already been erected on this giant scaffold, and we had protective fencing and so on, and then they torched it, to the chanting crowd. It was unbelievable. Really it was. I could feel all that disappointment going up in smoke. It was palpable.

Then the high school kids threw their large lanterns onto the bonfire. The people were yelling, "Burn, burn, burn, burn *The Stigma*," clapping and chanting.

A lot of people understood what it was and why it was there. During the entertainments during the day, we'd had people with a microphone telling stories, telling good stories, telling bad stories, telling hopeful stories, just telling stories about Eagleby.

We had this thing that we called the Tree of Stories, a large construction—it must have been about three meters high, and off of it we'd hung big cardboard messages which were summaries of some of the stories told, and we had a big board on the bottom with lots of butcher's paper, and somebody facilitating, and so people responded by telling more stories. By this time, we were story-mad, I think. That was very cathartic. That was very cathartic.

What did we hear from people that led us to think that this was important to do as part of community development? "I heard something change tonight" and "Something changed here tonight."

It was the whole thing. It had a rent-a crowd quality, there's no doubt about it. When you do something like this, the grandness of the scale is very important. The Eagleby Festival, the previous year, was really not a dramatic affair. People came, but it was subdued.

The grand gesture, which you get when you work with an artist, gives a loud voice to the softer voices, I guess, by its dramatic nature, and fire, obviously, is very powerful.

People said things like, "Well, standing there and seeing all those little kids, the primary school kids, walking through that park, I thought, 'We can be here, we can be in our parks, we can . . .'" This is what I heard, this isn't verbatim, but the sense of it was, "We can be in charge of our destiny in this community."

It's almost like the biggest thing that people said they learned from us was the distinction between perception and reality. "We had perceived this as a dangerous park. There's Graeme camping in his van for three weeks, with Karl sleeping in his car, and all the people coming, and they never had a single intruder." They were never ripped off, nothing was ever stolen, nobody let down the tires, they never saw a syringe, a junkie, nothing, and the police came around and sat around Graeme's bonfire, and people drank beer with him—that was about the most illicit behavior that occurred in the park in that time.

I guess our major thing about Eagleby was that the parks needed upgrading. The crime wasn't all that bad; it was mostly in people's heads, and we were trying really to change their perceptions so they could see what wasn't there, so that we could demonstrate in an embodied way, in an active "occupation" almost, that "We can occupy this park with legitimate activities, see! See that kid, three years old? You can have this, you know. And it's not us, you know, it's you. There are thousands of you, you know. This is possible."

We had thought about the ritual pieces of this earlier, in other work. Graeme and I had done a project together ten years before in Melbourne, just a community survey, but we ended up writing it up in a meta-poetic way, and there we recommended rituals of atonement for what had happened to this community. The client was quite befuddled by this, but the report was a great success with the local residents, and it went on to win a couple of national planning awards.

The hard-hitting stuff there was the issue of betrayal—that the community had been betrayed—and we wrote about it, and we did all the other straight things in the report, but chapter four had been written in a more mythic way.

I guess we remembered that project, both of us, and thought in that other community, what would an act of atonement have looked like? I guess there it was about being betrayed by government. Here it was, "What could an act of cleansing or healing be?" Because we chose the festival, this very important day; it was about re-enlightening, something about enlightening or lighting up, lighting their fires into the future. I don't know.

After this massive march with the lanterns and the kids and these comments about "We can do this," it was very hard for the client, and it was also a bit more expensive, with a bit more fencing wire than they counted on, I think. It was difficult. To be quite honest, I think we worked with powers that were stronger than we realized, because actually it was a bit of a love fest—we were all getting pretty much into it, the residents and us, and the young planner and the young project manager, but it was a bit like deep therapy without a reentry strategy. People were really opened up.

Graeme and I were adepts, so we were used to being opened up in spiritual processes and managing ourselves, and we were reasonably good with the residents as much as we had contact with them—but I think a couple of the residents were blown away, but then they were more let down that there weren't deliverables later and quickly. They're happening now, they're all happening now, but there was a timeline that was hard for them.

But our boss in Health, Kate, was blown away too. This was really big, and sometimes it was overwhelming. A dose of the stigmas can really blow you away—it was huge. And the community emotion was huge, and the insights!

I mean, I've had people say to me simple lines. For example, one woman, Heather, just said, "Wendy, I will never look at a park the same way again." Just nested in that sentence is everything, you know, and she went the night before, she didn't even go to the ceremony, but she sat in on the Research Methods 101, and Planning for Kids 101, and Lantern Making, and all these conversations about crime and perceptions of crime—and she just had her head rewired about local parks, which is not particularly her topic at all. So just all of a sudden, Heather is park-aware!

It's like in environmental ethics, we talk about an ecocentric sensibility, and deep ecologists say that it's not achieved through rational means; it's achieved in what the philosophers call self-realization, and that's not the Maslovian notion; rather, it's that instant when you get it—a moment in the wilderness, or whatever. Heather just got it.

So a lot of people got it, but the client was blown away, and not always in a positive way. That cost me thirty thousand dollars to handle it—that's what it cost. When the budget ran out, I had to write the "cover-your-ass report" to ex post facto rationalize and explain every single step using every bit of community cultural development theory I could find, matching things to people's objectives. I had to do a big survey of the participants. I had to hold a debriefing meeting, all with no funding, hiring people to help me write my report.

I had to do that because it bothered me that there was a story in Health that was apparently going around that the budget had blown out and that there had been no concrete deliverables—and that's a bad rep for a consultant, and I didn't believe that that was true, actually.

All of the budget had been approved; it's just that the young planner, the young health department person, just kept saying yes. Every time I asked, she said yes, and so we bought whatever it was that we needed for the process. More than that, I just felt this was cutting-edge stuff, and I didn't want it to be discredited, and so I thought I had to write it up, and then we won an award for it from the Australian Planning Institute, which was good and helpful, and the residents came and collected the award from the minister for planning.

I thought I had to show that there were deliverables, that some of them were incommensurable but they were still deliverables. I was able to match outcomes—where there were outcomes—to their quite bureaucratic objectives, which they'd written after we'd started. I mean, some of it was crap; I couldn't show that cardiovascular disease had been reduced, obviously, but they didn't quite want that. I spent a lot of time in a kind of interpretive qualitative research mode with the residents, asking them to tell us what had happened to them, what had changed for them, what they saw were the benefits and the problems and so on.

We also had a meeting with the local people whom we had worked with so that they could hear each other and build on what they said. They helped us understand what went wrong in the school—we were too late, too fast, and so on. They said they were very touched, that it was a very emotional time for them, that they were very provoked. Sometimes they were a bit scared because it was moving fast, and they didn't always know what was happening.

They felt competent—they were able to make a lot of things happen and organize a lot of things. Organizing the big celebration—that made them feel very competent, because obviously, we had to have a cast of hundreds helping, and they learned a lot about what was involved. I guess as consultants, we were very open about all our problems, so they learned a lot about managing a complex project and also managing a community celebration, about everything that had to be done, all the dramas and the permissions and so on.

But more than anything, they understood this stuff about the difference between perception and reality, and they seemed to learn, they said, ways of speaking back. We did some barefoot mapping exercises with the high school kids which really affected the adults, where we drew a huge, big map, and the kids stood on the map, and the non-Eagleby kids spoke the stigmatizing stories to the Eagleby students who stood there on their own, where their house was, and then the students spoke back, with Graeme and the teacher supporting them.

They'd say, "Yeah, so that's your opinion of Eagleby, and that's what you think, but I live here, and let me tell you what happened on Saturday. When somebody got into trouble down the street, all the neighbors came out and helped them. What you're saying isn't true. It's just your opinion, and I live here, and my views count." So they practiced with that.

Our facilitating the voicing of non-stigmatizing views, I think, was very empowering for them, but scary, too. They also learned how to talk, through the whole process, not just through the Stories in a Park, but through the things that started with the first SpeakOut; they learned how to talk to bureaucrats, how to manage the bureaucrats.

A lot of our work was also about forming this residents' group and teaching them how to run meetings. We had to do all of that sort of thing, and all that was part of the process as well. So they learned how the bureaucracy worked. They learned a lot about consultants, most of which they didn't like—the other consultants!.

Did this help us with the client? Not really. I think it seemed too much, too big, too expensive, too fast, too provocative. Would I have done it again very differently? Graeme's nude yoga in the community center was a bit of a problem—and we needed to manage a few negative responses to Graeme's activism around drug reform. As amazing as he is, managing Graeme was one of my major challenges in the whole thing. You don't work at this depth in such a kind of passionate way without there being some collateral damage. But to sum up what I think the community development work yielded: *The Stigma* yielded a speaking of the unspeakable. We gave it voice, and it was huge, we made a big one for them: "You wanted to talk about stigma. Well, this is the biggest goddamned stigma you'll ever see!" Speaking the unspeakable is something we've encountered a lot, and we often try to write it down or say it out loud or whatever, because people are too scared often to say anything themselves.

We were working to create a safe environment where conversation about these unspeakable, weird things—that's not the common discourse of low-income people—will be possible. I remember Graeme using the term *alienating judgment*, and he explained to people what *alienating judgment* was, and that was actually a good term: it was other people's negative perceptions that made you feel like you weren't OK.

So opening up the conversation about things that people hadn't spoken about—that was very important. Helping people see that their problems, their park problems, were never going to get sorted out until they came to grips with this, and then they would feel that Eagleby was worth spending money on.

Now, I've just been there. All the parks are fixed up. There's public access to the river. There's a new pontoon. There's a new wharf. I just gave a speech at a crime conference last week on this, and people were just delighted because I was able to show what happened as a result of all this.

At the end of the whole thing, we produced their recommendations. Their stories yielded things they wanted changed. If this park was dark and scary, then they wanted it animated and lit, with clear sightlines on the path, and programs in it, and the toilets fixed up. We produced a set of recommendations. They went to everybody, but it took a long time for them to get acted on, and I guess the lesson for us was that the actual manifestations on the ground of the things that people repeatedly called for—it's only just happening now, two years down the track, and the response didn't match the energetic, great, passionate "Ta dah!" Instead, there was what felt like a deafening silence for eighteen months or maybe a year. But within a year, things were really happening. We were pretty much, then, out of the picture. I've kept informally in touch, but there's been no new consulting work since then, down there.

11

Giving Paris a Green Hand

Laurence Baudelet's Practice Story

Editor's Preface

Laurence Baudelet did not think of herself as a revolutionary or an anarchist, but the official landscape architects who traditionally oversaw the Parisian gardens seemed to treat her that way. What would come of the world, they seemed to wonder, if ordinary citizens started to design their own community gardens!

Drawing upon models, ideas, and experiences from as far afield as San Francisco and New York, Baudelet found herself meeting gardeners in networks reaching all across France and soon advising and educating newly elected political officials in Paris. Baudelet was not only present but encouraging and committed to developing an idea of community gardens whose time had clearly come. Here she shares her practical early experiences as she worked to develop and implement Paris's novel Green Hand program (Programme Main Verte) in 2003.

Community Gardens and Community Development in Paris[1]

In 2001, I cofounded an association called Graines de Jardins, "garden seeds." This association represents the Île-de-France region, so it's larger than Paris, in a national network called Le Jardin dans Tous Ses Etats, which has been the pioneer network on shared gardens in France.[2] It's a network that got created in 1996–97.

Then, in 2001, Bertrand Delanoë was elected mayor of Paris, and with him, a Socialist, Green Party, and Communist Party coalition was elected. Yves Contassot, a member of the Green Party, took the budget for the department of parks and gardens of Paris. He quickly saw many demands coming from associations who had the desire to create gardens. To tell the story quickly: he didn't really know how to answer this request or what these gardens were that people wanted, this form of collective gardens.

Because Graine de Jardins had just been created, we were a part of a network that had experience with community gardens. I was a consultant at the time, and I found myself sought out by the Paris Town Hall to produce a document of studies on community gardens, of what shared gardens were. That was the initial demand.

Very quickly, I realized that there were many projects happening in Paris and that each answer to the desire of having shared gardens varied according to the arrondissement, because there are twenty arrondissements in Paris. I quickly told the town hall to change the mission on which I was working and to transform it into conceiving a municipal program. As a consultant between 2002 and 2003—for a year and a half, then—I worked with the City of Paris Town Hall on the creation of a public policy, which is called Programme Main Verte, the Green Hand program, which was adopted by the Council of Paris in 2003.

I was already a member of Le Jardin dans Tous Ses Etats, and I was also an original member of this network. I was more interested in what was happening in other regions that were more advanced than the Île-de-France region on this issue of new forms of community gardens. In 2001, between 1996 and 2001, I didn't really worry about what was happening in Île-de-France. I lived in Paris, but I felt that it would be very hard to unlock land in Paris to build community gardens, that politically, we didn't necessarily have the right town hall partners. There were other regions in France where it was much easier to work on community gardens. So I was wandering all about France on projects that weren't happening in Île-de-France.

In 2001, we thought, with other people, that we were really sorry that we didn't have a representation of the network in Île-de-France and that we weren't trying to start something, a dynamic. And as it just so happened—and we hadn't banked on it—it was a coincidence, because we really didn't know what was going to come out from the polling stations when we laid the groundwork for our association. But the conditions changed then in Paris, and there was political interest from the team elected in 2001, and thus we worked together.

First, we were two co-contractors. One was let go, so I found my-self alone in this mission, which is why it took so much time; it was an enormous job. The luck I had was that in Yves Contassot's team, the responsible member of the project was my partner, Alice Le Roy, a French American. She was born and raised in New York. She arrived in France when she was around ten, so she knew very well the reality of community gardens, and that was a stroke of luck for me, because in the team of the elected members, I had a partner for community gardens who actually knew what community gardens were. She played a really important role to convince Yves Contassot, who was the elected member for the parks and gardens department of Paris, who started the program and took care of it.

Yves Contassot had a huge mission; he had all the environment, the cleanliness, and parks and gardens. And when he started his term, he was much more focused on environmental questions than on parks and gardens. And Paris was late in terms of the recycling of waste; we didn't have separate bins in Paris. The first thing he concentrated on was this question of recycling. This is really where he started to work, very hard, with his team. The idea of community gardens appeared *very* secondary to him.

Very quickly, with meetings with the elected member—which were huge meetings—there were also engineers from the parks and gardens department, and you must know that the culture of parks and gardens in Paris is very patrimonial. These are people who feel they are completely inheritors of Napoléon III and [Adolphe] Alphand, who was his engineer and who established all the stylistic vocabulary of the Paris gardens—the colors, the fences, the music kiosks, everything. Everything in gardens is part of historical patrimony in Paris, so there is this very strong inheritance, this patrimonial dimension that is very strong.

The other thing: the engineers of parks and gardens are people who come much more from the culture of the civil engineering, much more than they are landscape architects or horticulturalists. So that, too, was a challenge for me, because these people are much more accustomed to taking care of large urban projects.

So the conflicts I had were mostly, on one hand, cultural conflicts with these engineers with this civil-engineering culture, who weren't interested in working on these small projects of two hundred or three hundred square meters with city residents. On the other hand, I had conflicts with Yves Contassot, mostly because he didn't really know what community gardens were. So I tried to explain the model, I projected diaporamas of pictures I had taken when I was in the United States, and I explained how it worked, and so on.

But at first, in fact, Yves Contassot understood this as a privatization of public space, the fact of planning a plot and making it only available to residents of the neighborhood, because he had in mind the model of allotment gardens. So he was thinking, "The community is going to spend money for fifteen or twenty people who will benefit from this planning, but can I, as an elected person, justify that I spent so much money, and justify the use of land that could have become a day care center or a neighborhood library, to make a garden when, in total, only twenty people will take advantage of it?"

So I tried to move beyond this worry by saying, "But no! With community gardens, what is interesting is that we have both public and private uses." In some cases, we are on private land, because it is only the members of the association who can be in the gardens, but there are rules that say that when they are in the garden, they must open it up for visitors, so there's the public dimension, too.

This is where the model of community gardens was interesting, and he started to see how it could function. What convinced him was, first, the fact that he went to see a community garden called Papilles et Papillons, which works on the New York model, that had just opened in September 2001. He also went to Lille, where I had recommended his team go, because there were gardens there that functioned like American gardens. There was also the internal work done by Alice Le Roy through her director, Sylvie Laurent Bégin, who also knew the gardens of the United States and of Canada and was convinced of the importance of the project. There were also the meetings where I presented slideshows that I assembled, and I answered his questions. Little by little, it took some time, but we managed to overcome the objections of Contassot.

But internally, there were still the engineers from the parks and gardens department to address. What they criticized about the project was that it enabled the inhabitants to think and propose things in terms of planning. The Green Hand program had proposed that on independent plots—that is, plots that aren't in public gardens but are on barren land—on these plots, the associations had the possibility—and they were even asked—to think of what they wanted for their gardens. We would put the inhabitants in a position of participatory urban planning; we were allowing the inhabitants to be in a situation where they could carry out projects and to reflect on the planning they wanted.

I myself helped design many projects, but because the residents are the users, they know what they want, so it's important for them to think about that. So that was also a problem. We were hearing stories like, "But we did long studies. We are engineers. We are architects. We are landscape architects, etc., and residents—they are residents! They don't have competence! We are in Paris! There is a long and strong tradition of patrimony. It's absurd to allow residents to create the city."

There were many projects being done, and because many associations wanted to start—or had already started before the arrival of Delanoë, when Jean Tiberi, the preceding mayor, was here—the parks and gardens department already had some projects to take care of. These projects were pioneer projects that allowed us to test the process.

I'm especially thinking about a garden called Jardin Nomade, which was the first community garden that came out of the process. We had gathered around the table. There was the association Quartier Saint-Bernard, which carried out the project, the concerned engineers, those who were responsible from the arrondissement, the Contassot team, and me, not as consultant working for the town, but from Garden Seeds— Graine de Jardins—giving out advice for the associations, because I gave out advice at the same time for associations and for the elected members, and also for affordable housing organizations.

It was interesting because we saw how the deliberation process worked in vivo, directly. It was interesting because afterward, we organized a day on community gardens, in which some engineers from parks and gardens participated. I remember the testimony of one engineer who said, "Community gardens are very interesting, but they take time. It's a lot of meetings, and it takes time." But on the other hand, he was also honest, and he said, "As an engineer, it also taught me things, and it was the first time I was directly working with the residents on the conception of a public space, I mean a garden. And at the same time, I took pleasure in it, it was exciting."

So we were also exploring new methods with these engineers. I don't guarantee to you that today they are all fans, but at least it's definitely moved something in terms of public policy.

* * *

I had done a study—I was trained in urban ethnology—and did a master's research project on a Parisian square in the 17th arrondissement in 1994. I did a terrain study during several months in this square, which was actually celebrating its hundredth anniversary. It had been conceived under Napoléon III. My research question was, "Do these squares, these urban objects, which were built hundreds of years ago, still have meaning one hundred years later in a city that has completely changed?"

So I undertook many interviews, and what mainly came out from these interviews was that these squares still played a very important role in Paris in many ways. But people were telling me they were frustrated because they couldn't garden, and because they were only spectators in this story. This also goes back to the philosophy of Napoléon III and [Georges-Eugène] Haussmann. We are offered a very beautiful theatrical setting with an ornamental nature—and it's all about the technical knowledge of the gardeners, their knowledge of how to marry color, to know how to make the garden beautiful in all seasons. But the residents, they are spectators; that's the role they've been assigned. So the people were telling me, "We really like these gardens, but we really miss the chance—we'd really like—to garden, to plant." I was hearing them very clearly.

When Contassot called on me, I had lived a few months in San Francisco. I had seen community gardens there for the first time; I had participated in a garden and interviewed some associations of the Bay Area, so I had seen what could be done. I knew this model, which didn't exist in the French culture, and I had seen how it had worked in the US. I had done many interviews in San Francisco. Then I joined this national network in France when it was created.

So I had this background. I knew where I was going, and I had the experience of what was happening in other regions of France because I had followed them in the preceding years. I had participated in two international forums on community gardens, and we had invited people from the US, Canada, England, Belgium. So my ideas were very clear. I knew the Parisian context, its history, its culture in terms of parks and gardens, and I had my ideas clear about what community gardens were and how they worked. So I was really a good kingpin, in fact, for them at that moment.

But you can't force things. You must do them when they are ripe. You also have to listen to what people want. I didn't come in and impose something on people that was completely strange to the history of Paris only because I was convinced of this whole thing. What I did was that I facilitated things—I was just a facilitator. The Contassot team gave me the files that were coming into his office from associations. When I read those files, it was more than clear that what these people wanted were gardens, community gardens. I at once read, at once understood their demands. This is what helped me explain to Contassot's office what exactly was expressing itself here.

What is interesting is that in big French cities—be it Lyon, be it Nantes, be it Lille, now Paris; it's starting in Toulouse; there were experiments in Marseille—you always end up finding similar demands from urbanites. At least in France, there's a kind of feeling of angst, I would say, regarding all the environmental catastrophes and sanitary catastrophes that occurred in these years. In France, we had a big food crisis, with mad cow disease, the dioxin issue with chicken, the illnesses with pigs. People suddenly became very conscious that what was on their plates could make them sick. Suddenly, there was a movement—like that, very strong—toward gardening, good vegetables, etc. Another tendency was that gardening became the first leisure in France these last twenty years. There's been a very big development of nurseries and garden centers. Now, gardening has culturally become something very strong in France.

So these urbanites—whom I was describing, who have totally lost horticultural knowledge, who don't know at all how to garden today—they want to eat good vegetables. They want their children to know how to garden, at a minimum. They want their children to see how strawberries grow, or let's say sunflowers. They're also sensitive to environmental questions and to questions about pollution. So they want to better their environment. They see gardens as a tool to see cities as a more pleasant place, greener, less polluted, and so they know what they are eating.

The other demand is a demand for conviviality in the big cities in France in these last years, and people have complained about solitude. Mobility has increased in France. Youngsters do their studies in another place from where they grew up. They are obliged to change regions for their work. They end up parachuted into cities where they know no one, in big cities, where they have neither family nor friends. Often, they stay there four or five years. They don't really have time to create networks for themselves. They leave, they continue without having had time to anchor themselves in this region or in this city.

In the demands of the associations that were coming to the town hall, there was also this demand of conviviality and social ties. There was also the idea that the garden would serve to animate the neighborhood. This is why it was so close to the idea of the community gardens that I knew that immediately I told myself, "We need to put in place a policy around that, because there's demand there." Otherwise, I wouldn't have done it. The files were flowing in, and it was ripe. This was an emerging social demand, emerging in Paris like it emerged in Lyon, like it emerged in other towns.

At first, the demands were spontaneous, and they were sent to the town hall. Very quickly, I made contact with all these associations, to see where they were heading with their projects, to see what they wanted exactly. So it was in this way that I found myself—at a time, at least, when I was under contract with the town hall—with a consultant hat for the city and an advisor hat for the associations, helping them build their projects. It allowed me to help them. These associations knew approximately where they were heading, but they didn't know how to make it work. I accompanied many in their projects, by trying to give them guidance to help them put things in place.

The first thing to do was to meet with the association, to talk about their desires, what they wanted to see become real. Then, I backed their ideas through the knowledge I got from the Jardin dans Tous Ses Etats, through this national network. I had best practices coming to me from Lyon and Lille, mainly, at that time, of gardens already functioning, according to what interested the associations. So it allowed me to speak to them, because they had so many very practical questions: Should we do collective parcels, should we do individual parcels? Is there some kind of model plan of these gardens? How do we function with the schools? There were all these questions, depending on the project—very practical things like that. What I did was to open up the horizon of possibility, to tell them, "Listen. Here, on the precise question that you asked me, I can tell you, in Lille, they did it like this; in Brest, they did it like this," and so on. It gave them very concrete examples from which they could learn. It gave credibility to what they had only imagined. It wasn't them anymore, alone, imagining things in their own corner. They suddenly found themselves connected to a much wider dynamic, to other urbanites who had the same desires as them, who had already moved into action, and who had organized in such and such a way. So what I would always say was, "It happened like that in this place. You don't need to do it like them, but at least it gives you ideas." So I nourished them in that way, at the project level.

It was very subtle. It really depended on their demand. I didn't like to intervene in their internal decisions. I always played a role, and continue to do so, of an external advisor. Associations call on Garden Seeds/ Graine de Jardins when they need it.

The principal message that I wanted to give to them was that there is no single model, there is no immediate three-page model of a garden. What I always told them, and continue to say, is, "What is interesting in these stories is that you do your own projects, from your desires, coming from the group of persons you are at the start and the ideas you have, enriched by the ideas that newcomers bring in. But it's no use reinventing the knife to cut the butter. Don't lose too much time either asking yourself thousands of questions when other associations already mounted similar projects. These can help you move beyond certain thresholds, because by seeing how they pulled through, you can gain time. But at the same time, I always told them that just recopying an interior regulation, or some statutes, or some project, to me, it makes no sense."

I am not alone doing this work. At the Île-de-France level, the experience capitalized at the national level, I was its spokesperson at the regional level. That's it. That's what I tried to do. Because we see each other in the national network every three or four months, we exchange ideas about what's being done in different regions, in different cities, and that allows me to be very aware of what is happening elsewhere. In the same way, some things happening in Île-de-France influenced other regions and other cities, because good ideas must be circulated and repeated. But my position was not dogmatic: "There's a model of community garden that I find compelling, so now everyone is going to do this thing, because I think it's the way to go!" My position was rather to say, "Ah! Here in Paris, I feel something is ripe, it looks a lot like a demand that I already saw elsewhere in another city in France, and we must now craft a public policy that is appropriate to Paris."

So this is why it took so much time. I really wanted to create a public policy appropriate to Paris, not pumping up something directly copied from elsewhere. So the Green Hand program is, for example, inspired greatly by New York's program, Montreal's program, Lyon in part, and Lausanne in part. So it's a mix. I took everything that could interest Paris in these different programs. And I also wanted to conceive it not only with the elected members from the town hall, but with staff from the technical service. We agreed on this idea with Contassot's cabinet. We really built, step by step together, the project methodology.

We voluntarily scheduled meetings with the other city services so that they could address this question and also to be closest to their way of functioning, to create a program that would be a wheel that could be adapted to the machine, and the wheel would function, not as a UFO. Because Paris is an enormous administrative machine; it's forty thousand public workers. The parks and gardens department has four thousand people. So one needed to build a public policy able to fit into this enormous machine.

The director of parks and gardens was a graduate of the School of Administration. So I also worked with these people, who knew very well the functioning of internal administration and who could help me, too, because I'm not a specialist in the functioning of administration—in detail, anyway. By working with them, I also understood how it was necessary to articulate the Green Hand program with what already exists. So the program is led by the city, by a piloting team that groups all directions concerned with the program: parks and gardens, but also the housing and habitat department, schools, the direction of finance, and the direction of roads. So it seemed to me very important to have a transversal approach, to create links with these other teams, so that this program could function at its best, without being a very small thing alone in its corner, not working very well.

For example, take the Nomade garden in the 11th arrondissement in the Bastille quarter. When I began to work with the project, along the way, there were several interested people in the association, called Quartier Saint-Bernard.[3] That is a big neighborhood association in the 11th arrondissement that does many different things. It takes care of neighborhood activities like flea markets, but also with school assistance and many other things. So it was a big neighborhood association. A few people within it, among them Claudine Raillard Clément, had wanted to do a collective garden and had sent a request to the city.

They had already thought a lot about their project; it was already very elaborate. What I did for them was assist with arrondissement meetings, the town hall of the 11th arrondissement, the parks and gardens engineers who were concerned, and the Paris City Hall to consider both questions of planning and the uses of the gardens. During the meetings, I was able to answer some questions of the association or of the town hall of the arrondissement, or the city hall, or the engineers of the parks and gardens department, because I knew other gardens, which were already functioning, and I could explain how they worked. It allowed the project to move on quicker, because I was providing precise answers, and from the different options I presented them with, it allowed them to determine their project, be it for the association or the arrondissement town hall or the City of Paris Town Hall. I would tell them, "You could do it like this. According to my knowledge, you can do it like this, like this, or like that, regarding this question. This is what I know on this matter." From this, they could determine their solutions themselves. I followed this project during at least the first year.

That association was the first to sign the Green Hand charter, agreeing with the city for the disposal of their land. What was interesting for me was that it was the first association with which we tested the program. The charter of the program indicates the values that the city of Paris supports across the program. It's the document that the association signs. It makes them commit to using less polluting products, opening their garden each time a member of the association is present in the garden, to allow entry for the public for two half days per week in the garden, and also to organize at least one public event a month in the garden. That's what the charter says. There's also a convention, a kind of lease, which is a judicial document voted by the arrondissement town hall, voted by the Council of Paris, which puts the land at the disposal of the association for six years, for free, in exchange for the opening of the terrain under the conditions cited in the charter.

So the Nomade garden was the first garden that signed the Green Hand charter, which signed the convention the city gave them. It allowed us this experience. It allowed me to see if the program functioned or not. And it did work, the clockwork worked. The dialogue between the arrondissement's town hall and the central City of Paris Town Hall, the suggestions of the technical services of parks and gardens, the association Quartier Saint-Bernard and Graine de Jardins as support—that all worked well. From there, we adapted the scheme for other projects.

We had meetings along the way. In the case of this project, of the Nomade garden, the association had both done a project concerning the functioning of the garden: "Why are we asking the city to give us land?" So in its project, it explained what it wanted to do with this garden. In this case, it was to welcome schools, which was the case, to create conviviality, which is also the case, because they organize public soups that work really well; there were exhibits, I mean, there are many things in this garden. So that was an element of their project.

The other element was the planning of the garden itself. The association had done a pre-plan—which wasn't exactly implemented in the end, but they were already in that dynamic, and that was what was interesting in this project. The land was virgin; it was bare. We had constraints because the garden was built on a concrete slab. So I remember the meetings we had at the arrondissement town hall, with one or two engineers who would come. There was one person from the 11th arrondissement mayor's cabinet who was in charge of mission, an assistant from the 11th arrondissement's town hall, and one or two engineers from the department of parks and gardens who followed the project. There were representatives of the Association du Quartier Saint-Bernard, Claudine Raillard Clément and Claire Deffontaines. There was Alice Le Roy, who was there for Yves Contassot's cabinet, and then me, who played a role of the expert on these questions, and to advise. For example, the meetings were about, "Will the association have individual or collective parcels? And how are we going to plan the garden regarding that issue? And because we are building a garden on a concrete slab, which technical choices should we consider?" The association wanted mostly individual parcels, which were two square meters, and some collective parcels for the schools.

This is the role I would play. This whole story was incredible. For example, for the engineers of parks and gardens, having parcels of two square meters made no sense to them. In France, they knew allotment gardens, and the parcels were of eighty, or even one hundred and fifty square meters. Until you've been to the USA or Canada, you've never seen parcels of two square meters. They would say, "It will never work. People will never want parcels of two square meters."

These were things on which I could bring credibility. I would say, "But yes, of course, for urbanites today, two square meters is enough. People don't have enough time. They don't know how to garden. It's basically leisure gardening. They'll plant a few aromatics. They'll come mostly to meet their neighbors—not to do large surface cultivation." So they answered, "OK, we'll see."

The fact that we can have a mix of collective and individual plots also seemed really strange to them. The association had contacted students in architecture to construct a house made of red earth. So there, too, their jaw would drop. I described before the patrimonial stake surrounding green space, public gardens in Paris. They said, "An earth house! In the Bastille neighborhood!" Everything seemed crazy in their eyes. In this case, Yves Contassot agreed to this project. Bricks in red earth were pressed on-site, with architecture from sub-Saharan Africa, with students who had worked in Mali and Niger. Not at all the vocabulary of Haussmann and Napoléon III! So we had this kind of thing to consider!

Also, because we were on a concrete slab and below there was a parking, the city had to inject concrete underneath. At one point, we had a problem: a third of the garden collapsed, because there was an air bubble. The compacting of the soil had not been done properly. The enterprise had to break and redo. There was all this to follow all along, all these meetings that are normally technical meetings, where associations and inhabitants are not usually invited. But here, everything was done with the association. We all followed the whole evolution of the construction; we validated the construction, we validated the planning with the thought of the future use that the association wanted to have on this land, knowing that they were told that the use was temporary. Indeed, the city had planned to build a public library on this piece of land.[4] This obliged the association to ask themselves the question, "How are we going to function?" "Yes, we are going to function with individual parcels and collective parcels. If we have collective parcels, we have to start contacting the schools." All this was done. "If we have individual parcels, we also have to start public meetings with the inhabitants." I also helped them regarding that. I intervened in neighborhood meetings to explain what community gardens were, how they functioned.

This association already had experience in dealing with these kinds of public meetings, because as I said, this is a big neighborhood association that has maybe two hundred or three hundred members, so they were used to meetings with many people. I still had in front of me key members from the associations who already knew how to deal with communication, information, in the neighborhood. They also had the capacity of finding rooms to accommodate a hundred people, or fifty people. But I also worked with residents who started from scratch. There, you had to give suggestions, you had to direct, at least for the first time, so that they could put together these kind of logistics.

The Association du Quartier Saint-Bernard started the meeting by explaining the project of a neighborhood garden. They explained what they wanted to do. Then I would, in general, have ten minutes or so to explain what these gardens were, to explain that this idea was not crazy, didn't come out of the head of the representatives or members of this association, but this idea was also implemented elsewhere, and it works like this and like that, and this is what you can do with these gardens, especially neighborhood activation—because it wasn't at all a reflex in France. I explained that it wasn't only gardening, but that the garden could become the support to organize neighborhood dinners, organize exhibits or concerts, do many things. I was here to support the association.

There was always a debate. The idea was that people could also ask questions, and also that they could become members of the association. The idea was not to get money from them, but the idea was that they could be part of the project, that they could become gardeners. The objective of these meetings was not only to inform them of a new project in the neighborhood, but also to tell people that the project is open to them. It's a project for everyone.

Were there objections? Almost everywhere. In the first meetings, there were always—it's normal, I think—people who weren't supportive, who thought it wouldn't work, that two square meters was not enough. I would tell people that community gardens are a new form of collective gardens in France. And precisely in France, we have the luck to have a whole typology of collective gardens, because we have a whole tradition of the allotment gardens, that we now call familial gardens; we have insertion gardens, pedagogical gardens.

What did I say to those people who thought that two square meters was not enough? I told them in that case that it is better for them to speak to associations of familial gardens in Île-de-France, because we have a fair number of those in this region. Those would be more appropriate to their wishes, and they'll be able to provide for surfaces of eighty or a hundred square meters. So I would try to respond to the concerns of people, to orient them toward such and such a path that responded better to their wishes.

These people might not come to the following meeting, because they understood that this was not a project that would interest them but that there were other things that would interest them in Île-de-France. Then the problem of familial gardens was that they are all in the periphery, they are peri-urban. You have to take public transit, or you have to have a car. What we explained is that we don't have the surfaces in Paris to create a hundred square meters per person. The Nomade garden is three hundred square meters. If you do one hundred square meters, that's three gardeners, but today, they are forty-five gardeners! People understand that well.

Today, I get my salary from Graine de Jardins. I am not in the administrative council of the association any more. I became salaried in 2006. I continue to accompany projects for associations that are in Paris or elsewhere, in the other departments of Île-de-France. That's quite a large part of my work. Also, I work on all the networking of these associations, networking even with already existing networks. I work a lot on internetworking, on associative platforms, trying to create links between different associations or different networks that work on social ties and nature, on citizenship and the environment. That's a large part of my work. It's fifty-fifty.

To give you a concrete example, Garden Seeds/Graine de Jardins was a member of a regional network called the Collective of Insertion Gardens of Île-de-France.[5] Within that, we work with three other networks, called Réseau Cocagne, Chantier Ecole Île-de-France, and La FNARS Île-de-France, which are networks specializing in social insertion and gardens. What we do together is that we, for example, have organized two days of study on this question of gardens and insertion with elected members of the Île-de-France region and the associations. We have asked for funding to film a documentary on insertion gardens in Île-de-France, which would be fifty minutes long and broadcasted. We have also found funding for a big study on diagnosis and advising of insertion gardens in Île-de-France. What interests me is to create links between community gardens and insertion gardens. That's why Garden Seeds/Graine de Jardins is a member of that associative platform, because in truth, if you start to create even smaller gardens than the insertion gardens, you're splitting hairs.

We are also, of course, members of the Jardin dans Tous Ses Etats, the national network. As a result, every three months, we have seminars, two days of seminars in a French city. It so happens that the next one, this month, is in Paris, but the preceding was in Nantes, the one before that, we went to Toulouse. That allows us to continue internetworking, because within the Jardin dans Tous Ses Etats, we find big national networks, such as Réseau Ecole et Nature, which is a big network of environmental education in France; like Réseau Cocagne, which is a gardening and insertion network. Associations like Garden Seeds/Graine de Jardins work at a regional level.

What else do we do? We have put in place a regional internet website to give visibility to these associations of community gardens and insertion gardens in Île-de-France so they can find themselves on the map, so that they create links between themselves, and also so that the public can discover them. That's another tool of networking.

In May/June 2011, we've organized the first regional day of community gardens of Île-de-France, to start gathering associations and making them work together. We got the funding that year to recruit a few more people, because we were only two salaried in the structure.[6] I hope we'll be a bit more this year, so that we may participate in many more networks. Garden Seeds/Graine de Jardins is very sought out to internetwork, because it's our culture.

It has changed, hopefully! Our position is that we must share information. We think we are stronger by sharing information, by reinforcing the associative tissue, carefully making sure that there are not ten thousand associations each working in its own corner, but rather one hundred associations which are well funded, well organized, with tools that use the internet, which are well coordinated, which can be spokespersons regarding politics and the elected body, so that they may be able to carry a voice. We did this for the insertion in Île-de-France. The elected body was so happy to see an internetwork shaping up. They were so happy to have real interlocutors, and advancing with us with the politics needed. We are more of this culture.

We also work on mediation, on issues of conflict. This year, we are trying to work on these issues within associations, to see how we can create a tool to prevent conflicts in associations. There are small things, some very simple, which will allow associations, we hope, to avoid certain conflicts.

At the time of this interview [March 2008], we have two salaried employees. I'm full time, and the webmaster of the website works half time. Otherwise, there are about ten persons working in the administrative council of the association. The president is now Valérie de Lescure, a social activist and a journalist specializing in wine. Otherwise, there are many people who share my profile: educated in human sciences who are researchers, as the sociologist Françoise Dubost for a long time, teachers such as Catherine Wolff and Christine Monatte, and other people who work on the question of landscape, such as Jacky Libaud, a tour guide. It's quite varied in the administrative council. There's also Frédérique Basset, a journalist who writes on environmental issues. For now, we have around fifty formal members, associations and individuals, but our network is much wider.

What was it like to see this work actually implemented? I admit that I remember the first time that I saw a great big poster at the Paris Town Hall, with the Green Hand charter on it, which I had in part written. It's a curious feeling. You think, "It's done!" but at the same time, "I'm so happy, because it doesn't belong to me anymore. It's become a public policy." There's the difference between a study you do as a consultant—the document stays in a drawer; your name is on it, but it stays in a drawer—and a document that is incorporated in public policy—it won't have your name on it, but the logo of the city. Then it completely over-whelms you.

Today, it completely overwhelms me. There have been about eight community gardens created each year, recently. So now, we're near one hundred forty community gardens created since 2003. Of course, it has validated the program for the elected body, it has legitimized the creation of the program in their eyes, because they couldn't ignore the fact that it truly corresponded to a real demand in reality. There's also the fact that Yves Contassot was completely convinced. The opposite had happened; he decided to put one community garden in each new public garden. So that increased the number, but there are also many projects sent in by associations. From the fifty, I accompanied around fifteen—not even half. It went so quickly that Garden Seeds/Graine de Jardins couldn't respond to all the demands and answer all the solicitations.

Some gardens got built on their own. I also wanted the program to work by itself. I'm relieved in that way. For projects for which there is no problem, the program is sufficient to allow them to come through alone. And that's what happened for many projects. They didn't need Garden Seeds/Graines de Jardins. They got by with the city's services, with the arrondissement's town hall, and the Paris Town Hall. They did that very well, and the garden came out of the ground. And that's great. If we had stayed at how it was before the creation of the Green Hand program, today, there would just be fifteen community gardens in Paris, because I couldn't accompany more. But with a public policy put in place, with the fact that an interlocutor was designated within the department of parks and gardens to take care of administrative questions, this whole mechanism was thought out, so that in 2011, we already had fifty. I didn't accompany even half of them. Some gardens I don't even know, because I don't have time even to go see them. And I'm so glad, so glad. Because it's beyond everything I could have hoped for. The program functions by itself. That was my great fear: that it's so fragile when it only relies on one person's shoulders. But, today, it's a policy assumed by the city of Paris. That's compelling! Garden Seeds/Graine de Jardins is here to give advice on some projects that demand a specific assistance, but globally, it happens without us, and I think it's the best.

In terms of urban landscapes, I think that these gardens are really interesting, because it's a new form of urban landscape in Paris. They resemble nothing else. They don't look like public gardens, they don't look like private gardens. It's exactly something else, both private and public, like we said. It's a surprise. Between two buildings, at the corner of a street, poof!—there's a gardened space. You're surprised. It's vegetal, it's color, it's smell. There are many people from whom I've had many happy comments—many people are so happy to have these small gardens down their apartment blocks.

They have this informal quality because, like we said, it is their users who have thought about their planning, especially for those on autonomous parcels, who belong to the city of Paris but also belong to other owners. That's what's interesting. They don't have this slick aspect of a space conceived by a landscape architect.

It was also fascinating at times to work with landscape architects. You work with different cultures in these projects. I think that the voice of the future users—which I don't think should be idealized, however; it's not the alpha and omega of planning—generates other forms of planning of spaces, because they have not been formatted by schools. And I think that's interesting.

I'm one of the persons who promotes a participatory urbanism in France. There's this whole movement, since a long time ago. Globally, it's becoming integrated to our culture. On many projects, people are not at all happy with the fact that the elected body makes the decision. There's a demand from the inhabitants, a demand that becomes important.

And people will come to these meetings. We can see this in Paris, on the great Halles projects, there are crazy crowds in the consultation meetings. And I saw it in many projects. People come. You start realizing that they want to ask questions, they want to know what we're doing, they want to take care for their neighborhood. I think it's a good thing. It's a kind of democracy, which is very important. I get the impression landscapes architects, architects, and public works engineers do not have this culture in their courses; they learn it by practice. Some of them like this idea to design through participatory processes, and hopefully, there are more and more among the young ones, but to others, it's really a challenge.

To give you an example, I was a member of a jury for the giving of a landscape architect diploma at Ecole du Paysage de Versailles. One of the members of the jury, who was a landscape architect, when he heard the student who was taking his diploma say that he wanted to work with users, that he wanted to let users appropriate the space by themselves, that he wanted to create a minimal structure, the answer of this landscape architect was, "It's the death of the profession." He said that exactly.

That is still the culture of many planners in France. The idea that inhabitants can create projects, they see that as a kind of competition with their own competency. There's this idea that when one is a landscape architect, or an architect, or an urban planner, one has a certain knowhow, a certain culture. Even if the users who will use the space that we are conceiving are not happy, well, tough, because in a way, we had pleasure. Some, at least, think like that. We did the project we wanted to do! Tough, if some people think it's not practical, that you can't walk with your pram, your baby stroller. At the same time, I see other planning professionals in France seek out Garden Seeds/Graine de Jardins because they want to work in a different way. I see also an evolution within the professionals.

I see today two tendencies: those who position themselves on dialogue, who say that we really can't conceive space without the users anymore, without working with the users; and those who form the school that says, "Ah, but they're going to make us lose time, they're annoying, we won't be able to do what we want, they're going to prevent us from doing the project we want to do." It's evolving in France in that regard.

I've worked on a project lead by John Thompson, a British architect who works in London.[7] He's a specialist in creating dialogue with users. He works in the whole of Europe. He does community planning. I worked with his team on a project in Paris in 2002, with the hands-on planning method. It was super interesting to experiment with different types of dialogue creation. I was sought out as an urban ethnologist. My role was to work with the inhabitants in the uses that they could project on the Périphérique, near the Porte de Vanves, which is in the process of being covered; the concrete slab has been inserted, actually. There was a space like four hundred linear meters, and several hectares suddenly became a space of meeting between Paris and peripheral suburbs.

How it happened was that they joined this whole team of landscape architects and architects, and I was there as an urban ethnologist, and there were also urban planners and elected officials. So you make groups. There's a phase where the inhabitants tell the story of their neighborhood, and identify what works and what doesn't. They project the neighborhood they would like to have. From that, you constitute subgroups for each theme. From each subgroup, with an architect, a landscape architect, and people from the town hall who can answer all the questions, we created plans. It's interesting to see the techniques that exist on these questions.

One last thing you should know; it's important to note. In France, since 1998, we have a law called Democracy of Proximity. This has created neighborhood committees, neighborhood councils. These are instances of local democracy. It's compulsory in all towns of more than ten thousands inhabitants, but that's to be verified on the internet. It's consultative, these neighborhood committees or councils. These are places where, for example, architects or landscape architects come to present their projects to the inhabitants. For example, there are projects of community gardeners that have been initiated by neighborhood councils in Paris, or the project has been presented during a neighborhood council. It's important to note that. In Lyon also, they got shouldered by neighborhood committees. They have a consultative role. They give their opinion on what is done at the scale of their neighborhood. They give their opinion, but they can also propose things, make suggestions to elected members.

12

Creating ARTWalk—Organizing, Inventing, and Creating Value

Doug Rice's Practice Story

Editor's Preface

Doug Rice didn't think of himself as a city planner, but he did care about his neighborhood. Within walking distance to his home were rich artistic, historical, and cultural resources—a museum, a planetarium, an art institute—but the street maze surrounding them made getting to them difficult. Pedestrians had to be careful as traffic sped along. Signage called attention to traffic patterns, speeds, and directions, but not to the city's resources; one would have been hard pressed even to know these resources were there.

Without any clear long-range plans to set their sights, neighborhood residents found themselves transforming their neighborhood and dealing with the city's traffic engineers and planners, facing one another in a less adversarial way than any of them had expected. Here's one of the key organizers' story of how they did it.

"Hearing All the Voices Allows Progress to Be Made."

I live here. I grew up in Rochester, partly in the city and partly in the suburbs, moved back to the city when I was on my own. As far as a professional background, after a high school education, I always worked for myself. Sound engineer/sound designer is my profession, meaning working at concerts. I got into real estate, lived in New York City for ten years, so I picked up a lot of sensibilities living in New York in an artsy neighborhood. I moved back to Rochester in 1992. I live over on Beacon Street. The street plays into the beginning of ARTWalk because there

I got involved with my neighborhood. The impetus for ARTWalk was neighborhood discussions about a street construction project scheduled for University Avenue in 1998.

But first we have to go back a few years before I arrived. The neighborhood association president, Doug Dempster, had done several years of hard work laying the groundwork to define and brand this area as a Neighborhood of the Arts. At the time he began, it was quite a distressed area, and the neighborhood was looking to find an identity that could help stabilize it. Neighbors valued the assets that were there, and they wanted to preserve and add to them.

Richard Margolis, a photographer and neighbor, had been instrumental in convincing the George Eastman House not to sell a large part of its collection to the Smithsonian, and he helped raise the money to create better archival conditions and keep the collection. Richard was integral as cofounder of ARTWalk, largely organizing and inspiring area artists and arts/cultural organizations and providing expertise on the arts component, while I focused more on the community component. He has an equally impressive story to tell here.

Another development early on was that the developer of Village Gate, a factory converted to retail and office space, supported nonprofit gallery spaces.

The School of the Arts, a public high school, had recently moved into the old Eastman School of Music dorms, a big boost after that building had been replaced with a downtown dorm by the university. But at the same time, the city was looking to evict a small nonprofit, Writers & Books, that was renting a decommissioned police station right on the main commercial triangle of the neighborhood. The city could not afford to renovate the 1903 building for ADA [Americans with Disabilities Act] accessibility, so they wanted to sell it onto the tax rolls. At that point, the commercial potential of that block had not really started to be realized. The neighborhood association argued that an arts nonprofit with a lot of traffic would be an anchor for development.

At some point, someone said, "This is a neighborhood of the arts," and the name struck a chord. The neighborhood association really ran with the idea, and it caught on. Eventually, art studios and lofts were developed in various old buildings, and as icing on the cake, the Arts and Cultural Council headquarters moved in from downtown.

Even though few of us had thought of it at the time, all the assets were already here: warehouses along the railroad tracks that artists were working out of, as well as the Memorial Arts Gallery, the Museum and Science Center. No one had really put together as a rallying point that there was a high arts concentration here until that initial work that identified the concept. The Neighborhood of the Arts concept was there to capitalize on when opportunity struck.

By the time 1998 came around and the University Avenue road-reconstruction project was proposed, we saw it as an opportunity: while the bulldozers were out there, we could create something, because they only redo a road every fifty years. So we thought, "Now is the chance to do something. What is it that we want?" That was coupled with a concern we had about the roadway to begin with. It was already dividing the neighborhood. People didn't cross University Avenue at that time, and we felt strongly that it should be crossable.

So the beginning of this was a double issue. The first involved the design of the public realm for safety and accessibility of all users. We often referred to the question, Would you send your eight year old son across the street to the corner store? And if not, why not—and is that reasonable? Concerns like that were driving it, and simultaneously, second, along with those functional aspects, we asked, "What kind of enhancements might we be able to make that would improve the neighborhood?" That is where the ARTWalk part came in, and so they were both shepherded at the same time by a group that called itself CURB, Citizens for University Avenue ReBuild.

The street project crossed over; there were a lot of little block clubs around, and they hadn't really had a common issue for a while. With the University Avenue project passing many blocks, these block clubs formed a coalition for this single issue, and from the time of the redesign, we met for two years on a weekly basis.

I wouldn't say that I had a mentor, but my father was a community activist, and I think that rubbed off, not because we worked on projects together, but because the importance of community was instilled as a value, because he was always doing something of this nature.

I had a couple of key concerns during my first years in the neighborhood. Motor vehicle accidents on University Avenue created a fear of crossing the street in any way. I had a neighbor who would drive to the corner store rather than walk, because it was unsafe to cross—things like that. We wanted to get it to be walkable, and there was probably a crack house on just about every block. They were starting to go away by then, because people were buying and investing, but there were still absentee landlords. By the 1990s, crack wasn't sold on the streets anymore, but it was prevalent in the houses. It was sketchy when I moved and bought my house here in 1992. People thought I was crazy to buy in this neighborhood. So what you're seeing now is a very different place. I mean, it's the same place, but very different, and a lot of it came through the community organizing.

But I didn't pull people together at first. I was one of the people who were pulled together by a common project, and I had no leadership experience at the time. I was just one of the throng. However, one of the things I've picked up was that if you want something done, you step up and do it yourself, and that's part of my life: don't complain about something if you don't plan on doing anything about it.

At that time, I was an independent contractor for doing sound. I had had a six-week contract cancelled, so I suddenly had six weeks free right at the beginning of this, and this happenstance caused me to have time to jump in: "Oh great, I have six weeks to spend with this and be done with it." In those six weeks, I had a pretty clear idea of what things would be appropriate out there, and so I started doing research. I found out what people wanted; not so much ramming an idea through, but more starting out with a concept of what I thought, while really just trying to get a list of what would get support. For example, you can get a lot done by just walking around and talking with people.

So I started by walking around and talking to a few key people that I would regularly see, then reaching out and finding who was a key person. In a sense, it came down to who were key people on each block, and that's who ended up forming CURB. It was essentially block leaders, and they would speak with their blocks, and we would meet once a week and see how each block felt about each idea. So it was a kind of pyramid that was set up.

The first year of this, we were more in a reactive mode rather than a proactive mode, although once the idea of ART Walk was articulated, we had city support right away, not necessarily financially but certainly conceptually and a little bit financially. They had some money set aside for improvements, but I envisioned it on a far deeper scale. Our main concern was the traffic behavior on University Avenue and ARTWalk.

We had very strong disagreements with the city engineers at the time because there are formulas of how to build roads, and we felt that the formulas didn't fit our road. The engineers were kind of locked in. They don't look at every project, because they do hundreds of projects, and they do studies. We found that these are people who do care about it and want it to work, but their priorities may get clouded by their situation, just as our priorities get clouded by where we are coming from.

At the time, the city was encouraging citizen participation, and so that was giving us the opportunity to be heard. Really, we spent the better part of a year negotiating the concept of bump-outs with the concept of the street, with the concept of the crosswalks and the concept of twenty-four-hour on-street parking rather than having no parking during rush hour to allow two lanes. That really creates a whole different environment for the pedestrian experience.

The parking lane actually tended to be a passing lane in reality. The prudent driver would go in the middle lane, and hardly anyone was parked in the parking lane because everyone was getting sideswiped there because it was pretty high speed. Then people would pass on the right. So if you were standing at the curb, where the fifty-miles-per-hour traffic was, it wasn't conducive to hanging out.

More specifically, the inbound direction was restricted from parking during the morning rush hours, and the outbound direction was restricted during the evening rush hours. So consider that you were in an apartment. I forget if the restriction started at six or seven a.m., but a lot of people didn't want to wake up at seven a.m. to move their car. Then, with the restrictions on parking in the early evening, a lot a people don't want to get home and not be able to park until the end of rush hour. Now that was the driving force. Those restrictions cut the parking almost in half in terms of regular usage, but the ten a.m. to three p.m. users could come and go.

Drivers' behavior typically follows the street design. People don't usually follow the posted speed limit so much as they slow down if they have to go around a curve or over a bump or something. Then they'll slow down.

While the city wasn't proposing a widened road, the ramifications went there. I'm saying that deliberately because it came down to this. The city held public meetings, which they do by law with a certain percentage of designs, and they rolled it out as a no-brainer—a bad road will be made good, neighbors are going to love it, it'll be great. There was no red flag to think they were doing anything that would piss anyone off. But we pretty much universally got pissed off. We saw the road, with these traffic "enhancements" and these parking restrictions, as a needless barrier.

We viewed University Avenue as the main street of our village, and it was effectively acting as a divider. People didn't cross it; it divided. And so businesses weren't doing so well. I can't blame it all on the road, but businesses weren't doing so well compared to now.

Now people can cross the road, and now they have twice as many customers. Neighbors across the avenue didn't interact with neighbors on this side of the avenue. Even if they hadn't been afraid to cross because of cars, they felt a division in everything that went along with the two sides of the avenue—the quality of housing, quality of tenants; they didn't have crack houses over there [toward the prestigious East Avenue historic district] but we had crack houses over here.

So I got personally invested in the idea of trying to make the road work for pedestrians *and* cars. I personally had the idea that roads, which I felt were owned by the public at large, tended to be, at that point, in favor of motor vehicles rather than other users. I thought that I was going to live here the rest of my life, and I didn't want to have to drive to the corner store when I'm old.

So given the state of the road, the housing situation was run down. I bought my house for thirty thousand dollars. You saw the picture of the Flatiron Building in 1983 with no windows, and I can show you some more before-and-after pictures. It wasn't tough-tough because it was cheap housing. It turned the corner where there were owner-occupants buying and taking a stake, and I guess twenty years before, it had been all rental units by absentee landlords, so you didn't have the invested people. Enough people had been buying, though, so a lot of people were invested.

There were abandoned units; I mean, mine had been abandoned with the copper still on it. I bought the house across the street from me; it was a HUD house, it was vacant. And there were a lot of vacant houses. Squatters actually lived in mine, and there would be squatters, crackheads, and every night, they'd go out and rob the neighbors and come back and burn a piece of furniture on the fireplace. That was 1990; it wasn't too long ago.

Our first meetings were conducted by the city, and I think they were surprised, because a lot of people showed up. I hadn't organized anything yet, just a lot of people showed up, and that's where I met a lot of neighbors. We just shared this concern, and we got a lot of energy and commitment going to the idea that we really could change our environment for the better. We weren't going to take it just as it was. We weren't going to do something that we really thought was going to be worse.

At the same time, none of us had gone to college for this. Well, actually there was an architect who lived in the neighborhood who got involved and who was instrumental—Joni Monroe, who later founded the design center [Community Design Center Rochester]. So that was an important piece. We had a lot of important pieces that came together. It was about three months of negotiating back and forth with the city; I don't want to say in bad faith, but it was kind of negotiating back and forth but not really going where we wanted to go, not going where they wanted to go.

If you consider the community ideas and how it's configured now, at first, the city staff were very resistant. They didn't feel that according to their models, narrowing the road would work. Their concerns were based on their models.

We did a whole community charrette in Rochester. It was around this idea, and that began a bigger dialogue with the city. One of the commissioners, Ed Doherty, came to the charette, but we didn't actually know who he was. He had attended incognito, and actually, he saw the power of the commitment people had, and he started to see that there was merit to looking into this. He didn't necessarily agree, and he didn't have to agree, but he saw that it wasn't just crazy people. There are a lot of crazy people in the city, and a lot of people fight things, and they're nuts. It's more the exception to the rule to have an idea that is way off the beaten path that's well considered; that's just part of public life. And I think that's when we got sorted into the well-they-have-a-point pile, and that helped change the dynamic.

So then we started meeting on a weekly basis with city staff and our steering committee group—going through one point at a time—and it was interesting. They asked, "What was our agenda?" I had never heard the word *agenda* until about six months into this, and I was the convener, so it was really interesting and bizarre that they went along with it that long. We'd go to meetings at lunch, and we'd just sit there and talk. At that point, I'd never dealt with that world. So I had a big learning curve.

We started to realize, after the initial confrontation was over, that it was not that anyone had bad intent, it was that everyone had good intent but was coming from very different perspectives. We had to value each other beyond our differences and come to a resolution, but neither group had really properly valued the other's perspective.

First of all, as we negotiated, I think we were given a slightly long leash because of the numbers and passion we had behind us. At that point in city history, there was an interest in trying to build better partnerships. The city staff had just adopted the Neighbors Building Neighborhoods process and the whole formal adoption of "listening to the community," so we were a kind of test case.

Let me put it this way. At top levels of government, there was a strong commitment to citizen input, and at the citizen level, there was the same commitment, but the memo hadn't made it to the middle manager. And who do you deal with on an everyday project? So the concept was agreed on—but there had been no shift in the culture, so that provided pros and cons. It gave us a little extra time to get our stuff together, because they wanted to follow through with the concept, but it hadn't quite reached down to the people we were dealing with.

I want to point out a couple things about this. One thing that was an advantage, early on, was that we decided we didn't want to fight *against* something; we wanted to fight *for* something. So that required effort on our part, to figure out what we wanted. We can't just say, "Oh, you guys who just designed something, we don't like that. Go design something else that we do want!"

At the same time, we started doing some research to come up with a plan that was reasonable. I didn't just say, "Oh, let's stick this here, and that here, and there are puppies everywhere." We had to call it better than that. So some of us in the core group had knowledge or did research and looked around at what was happening in other cities, and what really could happen here. Although we did have the reputation of being activists for pedestrians and bicycles, that wasn't necessarily all we cared about, because we all lived here, too, and no one wanted to sit here in a parking lot stuck in traffic on their way home from work.

So the first breakthrough was this. We were all talking English, but we weren't speaking the same language, and this is a very common thing in community organizing. I still have those problems every minute of every day almost; it's a very different language. We started to pick up on their language: "Let's try to frame this in a way that communicates better."

So instead of saying, "It ought to be one lane in each direction because it's better for this and that," we started—mostly Paul Kramer and I, "the traffic study committee"—we'd go out there during rush hour and think of a design and park our cars with four way flashers on, and we began modeling traffic patterns. Our model showed that it did not fail. We started adopting some of that language and actually doing some of our own little studies that way. So we weren't just confident because we were cocky, we were confident because we had already seen it pass the first hurdle in our minds. And we weren't idiots; we were being pretty methodical about it. We'd put trash cans here—safely—and we'd put our four-ways on, and we found that in some cases, one lane worked better because it eliminated the people that would go in and out, in and out, which decreases the efficiency of flow, too, and so we got more and more confident about that. And we had better discussions, and we negotiated one thing at a time.

We were still on opposite sides of a table, but at one point, we became partners. So there was a period where the city would say, "How about this?" They would kind of be giving us something—which they saw as a concession but we didn't see as their giving us anything important—but it was as if we came to see, "Oh, they're seeing the light," they were giving us something, so maybe they weren't completely rigid.

Then we found a very effective tool when we didn't know what to say. We'd say, "Well, how about this? On next week's agenda, let's have you explain why we can't have this thing that we have been asking for." Next week would come, and they'd say, "Well, we're not going to do that anymore—we're going to do this." We realized they didn't have a firm stance. We would find that by just defending their positions, they would

244 | CREATING ARTWALK

go back and think it through, and then they would start seeing that their old model can work, but there are other things that can work too.

I'm sure there are direct examples from other cities, and I have some binders around here of traffic-calming types of study and propaganda that was out in the early 1990s. That would be the kind of thing we had. This is when the internet wasn't really around. But the research was really there, and we found people who collected information like that, and we borrowed ideas.

Rochester had actually installed the first bump-outs in the city on Monroe Avenue; this shows how Rochester's transportation department was already on the progressive end, just not as progressive as they thought. I personally have always noticed traffic. I don't know why. I can tell you what it was like sitting in the back of the car parking at Goodman when I was five years old, so I've always noticed these things. I noticed the behavior on Monroe Avenue change significantly when the bump-outs went in. It was four lanes, and they enforced it down to two, and they only did one bump-out or two over the course of the whole thing, and it did make an impact.

So assuming they had a big impact—which in our opinion, they clearly did—then also the problem of crossing the four-lane road was often just the distance. If you're not fit and in shape, four lanes versus two lanes is a big difference. With four lanes, you have to wait for two cars to be clear, but someone is always passing someone, whereas with one lane, it is a lot easier to find a break. With four lanes, it's double the crossing time and certainly more aggravating and scary, and so we said, "You're not supposed to park on a corner anyway, so who was it costing if you put a bump-out there? You shouldn't be parked there anyway, so it's not taking away a parking space. If parking is allowed all the time, that spot by the corner or the one by the fire hydrant is not allowed anyway, so let's put the bump-out there to facilitate the pedestrian traffic."

This enforces protective parking, which sounds more car friendly. What the parking point gets across is that a lot of people don't park on roads like that, because mirrors get taken off, because people are zooming by. Once the protected parking went in, the mirrors stopped getting clipped because no one was cowboying in and out. Then people started parking, and the parking creates a very important part of the public realm. It gives residents and business patrons the chance to come and go by car, and it's a buffer for the sidewalk.

During the process of this whole negotiation, when we were talking about safety, there was a collision at the corner of Merriman and University, where the playground is. The woman's vehicle was actually airborne for fifty feet, went over the fence to the playground, and landed on the playground equipment while children were playing on it. This is a problem. The speed limit's posted at 30 mph. But it doesn't matter who screwed up. How could it happen that the car was launched fifty feet? It took the jaws of life to get her out. Her car took part of the fence out; the wheel hit it, a four-foot wrought iron fence, and you can see the fence now.

People don't go 50 mph on Park Avenue; it's a couple blocks away. There are roads that people behave differently on, and it's not because there is a sign saying, "Behave differently," but because the average person drives to the environment. If you're on the state thruway and you see a sign that says, "Work Zone 40 mph," and there's no one working and no cones, you'll go fifty. I mean, forty miles per hour feels like you're almost in reverse because of your visual cues; you don't have what I call "visual friction."

That's very important. I think over the years with the interstate design, some things that may or may not be appropriate for the interstate were injected as appropriate for urban models, which I don't think is necessarily the case. I think a lot of road design was driven by considerations of efficient traffic flow, without taking into account unintended consequences, which always happen. For example, if you took University Avenue right now as it is, and traffic behaved the same way it does now, and you made it ten feet wider, it would be better for bicycles, but traffic won't behave the same. If the avenue were ten feet wider, and moving vehicles were five feet farther from the parked cars, they would be more likely to go fifty miles per hour instead of thirty miles per hour. So there's more room with it wider, but when they hit the biker, they kill him rather than injure him. So this tradeoff is seen every step of the way, and so one of the things we said when we were being a bit cocky was, "We're not telling you how to design the road. We're coming up with an idea. You're the professional—you build the self-enforcing thirty-miles-per-hour road!"

Well, on Park Avenue, you can't go over forty miles per hour because it's narrow and curvy. It has a lot of driveways, and all the egresses
and everything make a difference. But University Avenue is a straight
line, and out by Gleason Works and the Eastman House, there aren't
many driveways. There aren't many people coming and going, and that
changes people's behavior. It's almost like a highway—the secret fast way
out of town. If that was its intent, then fine, but we also felt, "Why would
you want to do that to a neighborhood?" It was taking on the role of a
highway instead of the role of a neighborhood road.

What happened was that the commissioner said afterward that
through this process, the city shifted its model. In that period, when they
were building arterials, they would take into account, "If there's a collision on I-490, we want to have the capacity to handle it." That was one
factor among many, and after our year together, they concluded, "Well,
if there's a collision on I-490, maybe they should just wait a bit longer,"
because what we all realized was that by over-building, we were building
to those rare occurrences.

It changes the behavior every day. If you build for the thirty-minute
rush hour twice a day, then during the other twenty-three and a half
hours, the traffic will behave in a way that prohibits safe pedestrian
crossing. There's really only a maximum of an hour or two a day when
there's a real conflict in traffic flow, if that's the priority.

But we still have to take cars into account. I guess if gas is ten dollars a
gallon, we won't think about it, but who knows—twenty years from now,
there might not even be cars. We don't know that. We don't know. Obviously, our society is built around cars now. We can say, "How about mass
transit?" but the houses were built in a way that doesn't cost-effectively
support that. You hear "mass transit, mass transit," but right now, we're
not quite there. It's, "How do you get there?"

It's hard to say what relationships were most important during
negotiations. Let me run through a few. Certainly there was Paul
Kramer, who was a developer in the neighborhood who had a very
vested interest in how things went and also had a progressive vision
of practice. People who were living here at the time wanted the best
neighborhood, but everyone was living here because we wanted to
live in the city. We could have moved to the suburbs, but instead, we
said, "We're going to stay and fight for the neighborhood we want to

live in, because a lot of families who live in the neighborhood can get away with having one car, because you can walk downtown in fifteen minutes."

Those are the kinds of people who live here. Not that everyone is super green or anything, but greener than your average person. Why not walk, save a health club membership and save a car? It's a lot of money; it's a lot of money. So Paul Kramer is my primary guy.

Joni Monroe has lived here for twenty to thirty years, and she is, as I mentioned, an architect by training who was active with a group called the Urban Design Committee. She had this very cutting-edge understanding of some of these principles that she would share with us. I would say that she probably—if she were in charge of the whole thing—it would have moved a little more militantly than it did with me, although we moved pretty militantly in a way.

We did not get to our fantasy result, but we really produced a paradigm shift in the city's thinking about neighborhood street design. This model of ours is now replicated all over the city, without anyone fighting it. Now it's the city's position that this is good for neighborhoods. If the neighborhood says, "No, we want straight lines," then the city explains, "Well, actually this reduces this, this improves this," and so it is just a matter of everyone stepping out of their safety zone long enough to look at it and say, "OK, maybe what our bosses left us isn't the right model anymore."

I would say there were things that we had wanted and things that we fought about that would have been cool, and at first, I was disappointed when we didn't get everything that we thought made sense. But then, after really understanding how hard it is to get anything done ever, anywhere, and seeing that in a matter of three years, the safety went up in the neighborhood, the property values stabilized, businesses started thriving—I mean, this exceeded everyone's expectations in every way as far as the result goes. I probably would have done a couple things differently, but I don't know if these outcomes would have been better. This was a very good outcome.

I do think the road should be narrower, because every foot of width translates to a certain amount of miles per hour, and it's one of those things where the old paradigm says, "Well, more room seems to make it safer," but by providing more room, cars will go faster, which makes it unsafe, and there's no clear answer. Yes, it is safer when someone avoids you going 50 mph, but the problem is when they hit you going fifty.

Most people may not know this, but the injury rate really increases exponentially after speeds exceed thirty miles per hour. From even thirty to forty, the difference jumps. If at thirty miles per hour you hit someone, then there's about a fifteen percent chance they'll die; at forty miles per hour, it's closer to a seventy-five percent chance they'll die. So it isn't linear. It doesn't make sense to our minds if there's only a ten mile per hour difference, but it makes a difference to someone who gets hit. That's not something a driver ever takes into consideration.

The average speed on University Avenue probably dropped closer to forty miles per hour now, but it's still posted thirty miles per hour, and I'd say it was closer to fifty miles per hour before. That makes a great difference in safety. But the bonus outcome is that the new design has allowed the community to come back, whereas before, the old, fast design was dividing it.

Interestingly, though, a lot of the sense of community was built by the organization that created the changes, by all that interaction and involvement among neighbors. Still, if every one of the people who took part either left or died, this community is better because this design facilitates community, whereas before, the design didn't facilitate that. The public realm is now a forethought rather than an afterthought, which can make a very big difference.

Early on, the main role I was playing was that I was going around talking to everyone and trying to meet everyone. I met a lot of people I didn't know. I would say, "Oh, I heard you're involved in this way. How do you feel about this? What thoughts does your constituency have?"

I was a kind of sponge. I was collecting information, and then from that, I would walk back and forth excessively along University Avenue because that way, I could be looking at it. I'd say, "Well what's wrong here? Something is wrong, but what is it? What is it? How do you say it? What is it? How do you see it?" I didn't know what it was; "I'll know it when I see it." No one was seeing it—and so actually, with me, there was one of those lightning-bolt moments. I was walking back and forth— we'd do things where we'd park our cars, and we'd count how many cars would go through an intersection. We'd keep track of how many signal changes there were, and we had all of this data assembled. I walked back and forth, thinking, "What's not right here?"—and not even not right, but, "What could be better?"

I was actually down at the Eastman House fence, and I turned around and saw the Cutler Union spire of Memorial Art Gallery, and that was when it hit me, because I hadn't realized how close everything with the art museums was here. It sounds stupid now, but no one walked up there. It's only a few blocks up, but no one walked there, even among us activists. People thought about the Eastman House being on East Avenue. You'd have to go out, drive down East Avenue, turn to drive down Goodman, and turn onto University Avenue, and it just wasn't a natural thing to think, "Well, of course. The entrance to the Eastman House is here on University." It's only four blocks away; that's how entrenched we were.

Even those of us who think we're generally progressive, we were still entrenched in a car mentality because we all had cars. You get in the car and say, "Oh, where was I going? Oh, that's right: next door. Well, I might as well drive." It's kind of robot-like in a way, even those of us who think we're really cool about it: "Oh well, I'll just drive to the corner store." But now, we try not to.

That's the idea that came with ARTWalk. The neighbors had claimed the name Neighborhood of the Arts because of the organizations, but there was no art you could see from the sidewalk. So I said, "Well, let's start claiming Neighborhood of the Arts and have art on the sidewalk, have it be part of everyday life. Art doesn't need to be a gourmet meal. It can be a breath of air." And it can be both, there are different kinds of art for different uses. We saw it as our duty as Neighborhood of the Arts, that we have to show it off—and that's where the ARTWalk concept came in.

If we have a bread crumb trail of art, sooner or later they'll get to the Eastman House, and maybe one more person will go in, or maybe one more person won't be scared or discouraged to walk out of their comfort zone or to the coffee shop. At that time, the perception of crime, the run-down houses, and the possibility of getting hit by a car all made it scary to walk from the Eastman House to the coffee shop.

So what else is going on? If we leave behind any kind of road considerations—we say the road is built; that's no longer on anyone's agenda anymore—what does ARTWalk, the organization that raises money for and administers open art, work on? What's the process?

It brings the two sides together. I was just having this discussion the other day with someone and trying to break down this concept of civic engagement. What is it that helps and creates or just makes close community building? We had all of these things where we said, "How can we improve *this*? How can we improve *this*?"

I ended up thinking about it a little differently. I'm not sure if I agree with this, but right now, this is today's thought. Rather than thinking of any specifics, I want to think of the fact that we have active civic-engagement building, passive social-capital building, and problem solving. It's one of them. Under active community building, I would put things like our organization meeting weekly to discuss things and come up with designs. *Active* means you're actually getting people to come together; you're setting up a meeting, setting up a party, going to a protest, whatever it is—it's active, you have to move to do it.

Passive social-capital building is a little different. For example, this was one of the important concepts that was behind ARTWalk—the idea that the closer you build it, the more they will come. If you build an environment that people naturally gravitate to, even if they don't know why, more connections will be made. The purpose of the art, among other things, was this, and I noticed along this one beautiful river trail, once—I was walking along it—and I noticed a beautiful nineteenth-century stone bridge. When the bridge was in sight, everyone looked me in the eye and said, "Wow, isn't that a beautiful bridge?" When the bridge wasn't in sight, everyone averted their eyes and walked by. I'm on the same trail, I'm in the same city, they're the same people, and the only difference was the stupid freaking bridge. But the bridge gave the neutral opening for the non-confrontational "Hello," and that's one of the hardest things to get.

All it took was a stupid bridge—a brilliant bridge, really—and so it was like, "Well, if we put art out there, and if people are walking along like this, their eyes are going to look at the art, their eyes are going to meet each other, and they're going to say, 'Great,' or they're going to say, 'Wow, it sucks.'" It doesn't matter what they say: "What a waste of money!" or, "Wow, that's the best thing we've ever had." Either way, it's building community, and people are interacting.

That was an important passive component of ART Walk. We had to actively build something so that even if we all dropped dead, anyone else who lives here will be benefiting from the design. And then on top of that, the way we go about things actively helps building different types of community in different ways, depending on what the project is.

It's not so much that we came to those conclusions—to use artistic bus shelters and benches and light posts—as that it was a much more organic process than that. We started with a concept that everything along the sidewalk should be custom made—fire hydrants, traffic signals, no-parking signs. Well, none of them are. What might we be able to pull off to customize and get permission for? Well, it's got to be easier to customize a bench than a fire hydrant, because the fire hydrant has to work in a fire. So start with an easier thing.

Then we said, "Can we fund it?" and, "What has a use?" Benches were partially funded with transportation dollars, and so the city was saying, "We have a little money toward that. ART Walk can raise the difference to make them artistic and not have to fund the whole thing." That's how the benches went up.

With the bus shelters, when the road project was happening, the bus company took down some old shelters to put up new ones. It was time; they were old and crummy shelters. So I went over to the bus company and said, "How about you don't just replace them, and figure out a way to give us the money for them, and we'll raise the difference to do artistic ones?"

So they're getting a shelter, and the neighbors are getting something that's consistent with what we're trying to do. They agreed to it. But had the new shelter already been installed, they wouldn't have given us forty-five thousand dollars. It was money they'd saved. So we leveraged that, and that took a long time, but that's how that came about. It's just a matter of happenstance. This is just a matter of what partners stepped up, what partners had money or ability—it was not just a matter of ideas; it was a matter of time and money.

We're committed to what we call an "open process," and the definition of *open* is open— as long as it's open. For example, with the bus shelter and things like that, we used an RFP, a request for proposal process, where we requested the artists to submit a complete proposal that they would deliver as a contract, start to finish. So even if they weren't about to do everything, they presented us with a package: "OK, I'll do the design. I'll have that company do the welds, that company do the glass."

They presented us a package, a well-thought-out package and even a model. They had to build models, and from those, the jury selected the top three—and that had its pros and cons. All the processes we've used have some good points and some bad points. But a good point of this is that we know that the artists have thought it through, we know they can think in three dimensions. On the other hand, that's a lot of time to invest for not knowing you're going to get a commission. So there are people that just don't apply. Our first attempt to mitigate that was by offering runners-up fees. We had three selected artists and gave nine a five-hundred-dollar drawing fee. So if you entered, at least you had a chance at getting money back for the time you put into the model. It may not be what the artist wanted, but it'll be more than just giving up. That attracts a higher level of artists because the better the artist, the more likely it is that they're busy. The busier they are, the less likely they are to do something on spec.

There are other ways of attracting a broader spectrum of artists without becoming closed off in an ivory tower of solely selecting previously ratified art. With our auction, this time one of the ways we did it was that we had a community panel get together and invite people. With that method, the panel has to be truly diverse and encourage a broad discussion, not just the old established voices.

We hadn't used an RFQ yet, but that's one other way to do it—a "request for qualifications," which is essentially where you ask people, "Well, tell us who you are, and if we like you, we'll give you free rein to do this within certain confines."

So they don't have to spend so much time, and you're just identifying what you like and saying, "Here's the concept. We trust you to do it," because you know their past work. That's something that Albert Paley might be likely to get. I don't think he'll submit if he knows he has to do a model first and he's one of forty choices, since he's someone trusted and qualified. If we had a process where he was invited, that can work, but we can't just say, "Well, he's great. Let's just use him." That's favoritism, and we don't want favoritism. So instead, we could use an RFQ and make sure that he knows we hope he will apply.

I do see my contributions in part as successful. My own goal was just to have a cool place for me to live. It's really pretty selfish. But in pursuing that, it helps everyone else near you. And I don't want to do any harm in the process. I think that I also thought that the connection between these organizations—Visual Studies Workshop, the Memorial Art Gallery, the Rochester Museum and Science Center, Writers & Books, the George Eastman House—was such a no-brainer. But the nonprofits, with staff cuts and budget cuts, they don't have time to focus on connecting. They partner a lot, but there was no one at any of these organizations whose job it was to figure out how to partner better with someone else, because it's all they can do to get through their business. So in a way, it took an outside volunteer base to create the neutral ground where these organizations wanted to be at the table. We helped to facilitate that, but it's a very mucky thing to be able to do.

What skills does this work take? Some of my specific skills are ADD [attention deficit disorder] and workaholism, even if I laugh; honestly, ADD and workaholism. An inherent disrespect for authority as a child taught me limits that I respected by the time I got to this point. I don't have a job—I mean, I work for myself—I don't need much, but not many people have that free spirit. People say, "Oh, if I lose my job . . ." It's different for me. I don't have a wife, I don't have kids. It cuts both ways. It can be a detriment, but it can be an asset when you're trying to forge new ground.

I think, honestly, my experience as a sound engineer helps a lot, because one of the jobs of a sound engineer is that during a sound check, I have to satisfy nine people on stage while listening to a manager talk to me in one ear and the girlfriend of the guitarist in the other ear. I try to negotiate how to make it all sound right while shutting the eleven of them up—and that's really what community organizing is. Hearing all the voices, and then somehow placing them in a way that allows progress to be made. It's a difficult thing to do. So I think that's one thing that helps, and that's something no one would understand unless you were a sound engineer. You wouldn't know.

You want to hear everyone's voice, but if there's disagreement, you've got to move forward, and at some point, you have to pull the trigger. Someone has to do it, and a lot of groups fail when no one can get the ball rolling in a direction or when people have too big an ego to let something go. That's when you have internal stress. Often, you lose a great volunteer because of a disagreement like that. We go through it every year, one way or another. We've managed to keep a lot of strong personalities that work toward a common goal, but it's difficult.

I'm not sure about what I would have done differently. If I look at it from my knowledge base now, I'd do everything differently. If I look at it as what our tools were and how they were available at any moment, in the end, we ended up OK.

There are things I regret having done. We're all human. I pissed someone off when I didn't mean to. And you feel bad about it, and that just happens when there are people who are involved in a group because they're passionate about it. They're all working all day already, they're tired, they have their emotions on a hair trigger. They're working toward a goal, and when there's a disagreement for some reason, it's all very raw. It's not like we're sitting around theoretically talking about whether sliced bread is better than non-sliced bread. It's something you're passionate about, something that means something to you, something you're fighting for, and something you've invested a year of your life in. It's tough.

My goal is to stay on until the organization is sustainable. I am committed to the mission, but I've been doing way too much of the stuff I don't like, and I'm doing it because I want to launch this baby. It needs to be independent of individuals to be sustainable, and we're not there yet.

In the last few years, lots of things have changed. ARTWalk, Inc., the Neighborhood of the Arts, and regional artists have ended up being held at arm's length as city employees, and consultants hired from out of town have done an end run around ARTWalk on grants that were based on ARTWalk's success.

More recently, although no charges were brought in the end, through freedom of information laws we actually learned that there had been pervasive fraud on the part of city staff. That explains the hundreds of hours we spent trying to understand what was going on. It was simple all along: they were stealing our money and giving it to themselves and their friends' projects. Actually, three principals lost their jobs after we provided documents to the incoming mayor's administration. But we had a good run.

We learned several lessons the hard way. When community organizing is your method, the product is never precisely everything that any one person or organization starts out wanting. The organizer isn't just a visionary who walks in knowing what should be and who then coaxes people to accept their idea as if it were their own. People see through that.

An organizer can bring good research to the table, but he or she should still be surprised at some of the wonderful ideas that can result. It might come down to this: Do you believe in your community? The Rochester, New York, region, after all, has a population much larger than ancient Athens. If we nurture it, why shouldn't we have citizens supporting—and creating— public art of lasting quality?

A community project has to be the product of many people's ideas, tastes, and preferences, or else the discussion isn't honest, and participants will know they are being used as window dressing or a rubber stamp. Sometimes, the powers that be will ask for broad public input but then take nothing that doesn't fit their preestablished vision. In ARTWalk's case, some of the authorities and power brokers were not comfortable with an in-depth public process—they did not relish sharing power. They wanted world-class art, preapproved by the professional critics, curators, and other arbiters of the international art scene. Never mind that we had many artists in Rochester who knew the international scene and who could sift through regional and international options very capably. But to be good, the power brokers insisted, both the advice and the art had to be imported. This attitude hobbled local development.

It had been my goal to leave ARTWalk, Inc., as a self-sustaining community-based organization. But the shift in power away from that community organization led me to refocus my personal energies to developing a multiuse community cultural center [MuCCC, a blackbox theater] that would help to develop community with performing artists.

Our experience suggests that community organizers should consider a set of red flags that might alert them to potential pitfalls and ways to avoid them. This might help to keep the process of community collaboration with powerful institutions from jumping the tracks. Watch out if you see decisions made based on people, not based on purpose or policy. Watch out for people who say there's only one way to do something; that can be the sign of a control freak unsuited for community work. Many working people have standard procedures that work for them. But no community project is standardized. Therein lies an eternal tension. Even so, be careful not to profile or stereotype coworkers. Don't think you have somebody's position or motives pegged based on previous observations. Periodically reexamine your assumptions as to who supports what. Support can come from surprising quarters. You don't know everyone's interests and life histories, nor do you know all that moves them.

Although it seems obvious, a project can't move forward if it's static. Someone has to budge if there is an impasse. There is no dishonor in changing positions if it's well thought out. Never changing positions is a red flag, even if they're yours.

Some organizations or institutions, like government, will have safety-net authority to reject final choices at times, but they should not be given preemptive power to intervene early to prevent ideas from being floated at all. Safety-net power should not be used as micromanagement. A powerful agency representative can say they don't think something will work without issuing a veto ahead of time. Don't let the bureaucrats snow you. "No" can be a "yes" to a different question.

If you hear, "We don't have this phase ready for your input yet," you should still be invited. Point out that it is never too early to prevent future misunderstandings, and walk in unafraid to give input at any stage.

Relationships of trust and power can change with the reassignment of roles. That introduces new stakes, new authority, or potential access to new resources. If big money is on the table, people can rapidly shift from a common perspective to one that serves a smaller constituency—or even themselves personally.

Those who ignore the past are condemned to repeat it. You cannot change problems in a relationship that you don't acknowledge. Let someone admit that the past didn't work. That can happen, and misbehaving parties can still save face by helping make rules that work for the future, but beware of the person who will never say, "That was wrong and/or didn't work."

Generally speaking, the community organization is historically the least powerful group at the table. So even though the community organization won the grant based on its vision, there are systemic pressures that can enable the more established agencies and organizations to get their way while leaving the community organization with relatively little voice. This is especially true when community organization board members feel in awe of other powerful players, or when they see affiliating with these folk as a source of social status. Statements like "That's above/below my paygrade" and "Stay in your lane" are fun ways to establish dominance. The community organization always has the lowest paygrade, and institution-based staff have little real respect when it comes to dollars and cents.

Watch out for empowering institutionalized racism and old boys' networks. Demands like, "All artists must have an MFA or have been commissioned for similar work before" takes the burden of responsibility off of the organization or its project jury and puts it onto the history of "the machine," and the machine has serious problems.

You want as much creative input as possible, but not the May Day parade in Moscow. Bringing in masses of people to contribute ideas that will never be considered or to vote on pre-chosen options will frustrate people instead of allowing any real participation.

Be wary when someone is flattering but fundamentally wants to change something that is already successful as a community process. Recognize that changing one part of the organization can influence others. If you change from a process of community-selected art to one that relies on an out-of-state expert to make selections, how will that impact your volunteer base or the community's level of vestedness?

Watch out for Trojan horses, anyone who might be put on the board or project to circumvent due process and push an agenda surreptitiously.

Watch for someone getting overly emotional and using that to get their way.

Trust is good, but trust and verify is better. If someone appeals to trust too often, ask for evidence or something in writing. Be careful about hearsay. Check the primary documents and sources that allow you to come to your own conclusions.

These years have been an interesting ride. In the end, I'm still the optimist. When community benefits are at stake, I hear naysaying as asking for more creative thinking. But when things settle down and the big money is all spent, we are back to addressing the questions that we started with: What makes a place worth living in? Why do you feel like a community member and not just someone who pays rent or taxes to live somewhere? What builds community rather than tearing it apart?

13

Cultivating the Arts in New York Mills

John Davis's Practice Story

Editor's Preface

When John Davis was painting houses in New York Mills, Minnesota, few people thought he might one day become a local arts impresario. Davis didn't think so either, but he was committed to encouraging local arts and culture. Why should art exhibits and the benefits of the arts be limited to the big cities? In this largely agricultural community, tourists were few, farms abounded, and the arts were not so well developed.

Where others might have seen gaps, lacks, deficits, and not much happening, John Davis saw opportunities. Soon, his artist-in-residence program had attracted a landscape painter from France followed by an illustrator who proposed that she could use the nearby grain elevators as her subject matter. The arts in New York Mills had a new foothold, and Davis went on from there.

On Hearing, "The Arts Can't Be Good Anywhere but in the Big City."

In terms of art and economic development, my approach is that the two are connected and need to be connected. Art can be an economic engine for a community. My philosophy is that in a small town, the audience is everyone. So my work revolves around integrating art into all aspects of a community. To do that, there's integrating into the political side, the community side, and the downtown business side as well—the sort of mainstream America side.

At the Lanesboro Arts Center in Lanesboro, Minnesota, my position is executive director. I am also the director of the Kids Philosophy Slam program, a national K–12 philosophy program for kids. The past several years, I've worked on developing Lanesboro as an arts campus, and I spent two years working on the arts commission that helped plan and develop the new Commonweal Theater that opened last year. That was a three-million-dollar theater project.

Now I'm working on the residency center for the Art Center and working on a music and literary series project with another arts organization. I'm also working to renovate another theater in the community.

As for the New York Mills Regional Cultural Center, there's not really a short version of this story. I went to art school. I attended the Minneapolis College of Art and Design, and after graduating, I just wanted to move to the country and work as an artist, without having a real grand plan or doing a project like New York Mills. I started a house-painting business to try and make some money and save up some dollars to try and buy a place out in the country somewhere.

There was a farm that was for sale that was ten thousand bucks, and that was all the money I had. So that brought me to New York Mills. Once I was there, the project really developed as I looked at what the community didn't have. The community didn't have an arts center. It didn't have a cultural scene. It didn't have musical performances. And I thought it didn't seem fair that a small town didn't have the same sorts of cultural and artistic opportunities as a larger community like Minneapolis or St. Paul.

When I started renovating the abandoned farmhouse that I bought, I would have friends come to help me work on it who were artists. They would tell me, "This is a great place for artists. You should really do something with this." So I started thinking about how to incorporate artists into the community.

For the first couple of years that I lived in New York Mills, I made extra money by painting houses and barns. People viewed me as someone who painted houses or barns, not as someone who wanted to change the community. So their view of me was different than my background. So I was accepted as a community member and as someone who worked hard to make a living.

The idea really took off when a friend of mine gave me a toy plastic tractor. When I'd looked at the tractor, I said, "Oh, this could be the logo for an organization that represents the arts." The tractor would symbolize cultivating the arts. That's when the idea of having a residency center for artists first gelled. It could be something that the community could use as well.

That's when I started researching art colonies—just seeing how art colonies were formed and how other art organizations were formed—and I realized that a lot of art colonies had many people stay at one time and were more communal. I wanted to create something that was more unique and individualized. Why reinvent the wheel? In addition, there still wasn't a large wealthy donor to donate a lot of money to help start a project like this, and one of the results of the research that I'd conducted was that most art colonies were founded by very wealthy patrons who donated land, money, or both.

So starting on a small scale, I thought you could still have a big idea and have a lot of impact, and it could be a good fit for the community, because what I wanted to do with the program was to host artists from around the country and around the world. They would have a chance to be out in the country and work on their artwork or ideas, but not just do it in isolation.

I thought that artists would have an opportunity to engage in the community and share what they know so that a community that doesn't have normal art experiences could be exposed to artists in different disciplines, cultures, and backgrounds. The community can win, and the artist can win as well, often gaining experience doing lectures and teaching that they might not have an opportunity to do otherwise.

But there was a lot of skepticism from virtually every person I talked to. I would go to organizations like the Minneapolis Institute of Arts and the Walker Art Center, and I would talk with people from those organizations about what I wanted to do—including the state arts board—and their response was, first of all, that they thought it was essentially a bad idea and a waste of time. They were essentially saying, "Who cares about one small town? Why would you want to do something for people in a rural area? What difference does it make?"

This surprised me, how much the arts were very focused around the Twin Cities in Minnesota. It was as if for everything else outside of it, well, the arts can't be good anywhere but in the big city. That bias and prejudice really was upsetting, as well as motivating. If anything, it reinforced my idea that having high-quality art experiences was necessary in spite of the bias against it. So that was one obstacle right there—people saying that it wasn't a good idea and that it wouldn't work, including people on the state arts board. They had a very successful but set way of doing artist residencies as a model. When I was in casual conversation proposing a different type of artist residence, they said, "Well, that's *not* how you do it." I said, "What do you mean, that's not how to do it? There's more than one way to facilitate an artists' residency."

So the challenge was figuring out how to do it anyway. I mean, I think that when people face opposition, they often just either take it too seriously or they recoil and say, "I've got to go in a different direction."

Just in terms of my basic approach to things, I would call myself a strategist. You can go through a brick wall or around it, and we tend to want to go around obstacles instead of trying to go directly through them. Most military strategy is based on the same premise. It's not to ignore people's opinions about whether something can or can't be done. It's just not giving those negative opinions too much importance if you run into a good idea.

Overcoming obstacles involves a series of turning points. In this case, I think just deciding to go ahead and do it was the biggest turning point if there was one, just saying, "This is going to happen, so *how* do we make it happen?"

The first turning point was forming a nonprofit organization and forming a board of directors that had some pretty key community members involved with the board. We had senior citizens and farmers, people who represented the fabric of the community. Once the idea was started, the organization started out as the New York Mills Arts Retreat. That was its official name. But once it started, there wasn't funding for it. We just put together a brochure and did basic research on how to do marketing, and we marketed it. Almost immediately, we started getting interest from all over the world from artists who wanted to do a residency.

When the program first started, we didn't have a stipend for artists; we just had the space, which was that farmhouse, and artists applied for the program. As part of their proposal, they would have to develop a plan for working creatively with the community. That would be a key part of their residency. So the more creative the plan and how they integrated with the community, the better chance they would have of receiving a residency.

Actually, the very first artist was a painter from France, and she did workshops with the community with kids and adults on watercolor painting. A more dynamic residency was an artist who was an illustrator, and her proposal—her big inspiration—involved grain elevators. Her proposal was to volunteer at a grain elevator for a month just working—answering phones, sweeping, and doing anything she could to work at a grain elevator—and then do illustrations of the grain elevator. Then her residency would culminate with a joint reception featuring her artwork of grain elevators at the grain elevator and at the art center involving farmers and community members.

When I approached the owner of the grain elevator to ask about this, I said, "Well, we've got an artist, and they just want to work for you for free for a month. What do you think?" His response was, "Well, is her artwork any good?" At that point, I knew the residency program had pretty much been accepted in the community. I said, "Her work's really good!" He said, "That sounds great. Let's do it." That's an example of an artist really engaging the community in a non-traditional way.

The program was well accepted by the community. A key part of that was how it was presented. We didn't charge the schools anything to have the artists come in, so we presented it as, "Here, your school has an option of having an artist come in for free," and the school was really excited.

It was great—very exciting. That was a big plus. The fact that it didn't cost the community money at first was a definite plus to the program. Of course, later on, we did get money from schools and donations from individuals and foundations, but it started in a very non-threatening way to introduce artists to the community.

The very first artist that we had was Beatrice Linarres, and she was from Montpellier, France; she had a very beautiful, rich accent. We were downtown just walking one time, and she noticed that I was looking at this particular building. She said to me, "You know, I see how you look at this building. You should ask for donation, no?" I said, "Actually, I *have* been looking at it."

I had heard through the rumor mill that the owner might be willing to sell it or even donate it, because it was in pretty poor condition. So that's when I thought, "OK, this could be a real opportunity to have the arts directly involved in the community. This historic 1885 building, even though it was almost falling down, if revitalized and renovated could serve as a sort of redevelopment tool. It could be a model for what else could be done in the community, to really help jumpstart the downtown. Other people could utilize that model for redoing their buildings and really help energize and revitalize the town."

The point of having a presence downtown was really when the economic development part came in. I think that starting the arts retreat was really more community development—and they're two sides of the same coin.

But getting the arts introduced within the community early on, I think, opened up the conversation for how it could help economically as well. So having the school and the school board members behind the arts project to begin with really helped with the downtown portion of it as well.

Looking at a building that was vacant and falling down and saying, "OK, we could have a real jewel here in the community if this were renovated" made for a better argument, community-wise, for people to get involved with it, because there really wasn't anything happening in the community culturally or artistically to bring people into the town. New York Mills really wasn't even vaguely a tourist town. So I think people were at least open to the suggestion of something new happening.

Getting people on board was a little bit slower process that happened over a few months. Having the right board of directors helped. Putting people in the community on the board who had leadership positions in town helped. I knew that one of the city councilmen would be a key player in the project, and his father was on our board of directors.

There was a level of political awareness for how things work that you really need to have. I had it with the board of directors—working with the senior citizen center and senior groups to make sure that that part of the community was being included in the project. We had the school and the education community's support, the seniors and the senior community's support. We had the farmers and their support. And since we were renovating a building on Main Street, we wanted the business community's support, too. That can all be a catalyst for community revitalization.

That was essentially the nuts and bolts of it; we went from individual to individual. It happened very gradually, but it culminated when the city council agreed to fund the project economically. That's really when the tipping point happened, when the city decided, "Yes, we're going to contribute thirty-five thousand dollars to the project."

The city has benefited from the center, absolutely. You can see this now, too, since they've probably had several different incarnations of a city council. Right after the arts center opened, people saw a very good return on an investment.

I had presented the proposition not as "You're contributing this money to an art center"—that wasn't how I pitched the concept at all. The pitch was, "You are investing money in your downtown, and this is economic development money. If you invest this money in your downtown, here's what the results will be. Here is the vision: this building will be an art and cultural center that will help revitalize the community through its creativity and its programming. So you can invest thirty-five thousand dollars in this building to help create this national model, or you can do nothing. But if you do nothing, the building has to get torn down. That's going to cost you forty thousand dollars, and then you're going to have a vacant lot. And where does that get you?"

So part of my pitch for the proposal to the city council was as a matter of risk, and I presented the risk as doing nothing. The lesser risk was actually taking action and being proactive and investing the money in the downtown. Part of what had alleviated the concerns from the city at that point was that the mayor had asked, "Well, what happens if it doesn't work?"

I said, "Well, here's the proposition. If this project does what it says it's going to do, and in five years it's a national model, give us the keys, and in the meantime, you can have the deed to the building. If it doesn't work, you're out nothing; you can resell the building, recoup your money, and you're good to go. If it does work, hand us over the keys, we'll own the building, and it's a win-win for everybody."

I'd had no formal training in the political process or in community development. But I will say this. I did gain valuable experience in high school. I had worked selling shoes in a shoe store, and so I did get to know how to make an argument and how to sell things. That's true with anything. If you've got a background in being able to communicate, that's very helpful.

I also have a soft-spoken personality, and again, I consider myself a strategist. So looking at how strategy works is fascinating, because a lot of times, when people move to a small town, they're too anxious. They're too anxious to change things, and as a result, their ideas are rejected.

I think one of the important things for me moving there was that in the very first few years, I didn't do anything but work and volunteer. I volunteered at the local senior center, and I just painted people's barns, so I got to know farmers and had conversations about art, and I said, "Well, what do you think if we had a music and film festival?" They would say, "Oh, I think it's a great idea." So my preconceived notions about rural life and rural America were totally thrown out of the window, because people in rural America really just want to have access to high-quality art and high-quality arts programming like anyone else.

How did I do this? When it came to navigating obstacles and chasing big dreams, one of my biggest supporters in New York Mills was also my mentor, Jim Buchan. He had worked in Washington, DC, as the press secretary for the surgeon general, C. Everett Koop. He was happily retired until he read in his local newspaper about a cultural center being built in his hometown. He only had one question for me: "Why New York Mills?" I had answered, "Why not?" and Jim moved back to help support this new arts vision. He was a valuable mentor to me about how publicity could be used as a tool to achieve our goals and how the challenges of small towns could be navigated.

I think the best thing to do, sometimes, is just to start doing it. I read books on marketing and on fundraising, but the political work, that's just a dynamic that came intuitively. Before I asked the city council for money, I attended the city council meetings for a year so that I could get a feel for their personalities and for how they thought. I had wondered if they would be able to contribute money to the project, because there were people on the city council who were against the project and against giving money to it. In fact, the economic developer who worked for the city was against the project. Actually, after the city had decided that they would give us money, he added a question as part of a city survey. His question was, "Do you think it's a good idea for the city of New York Mills to financially support the cultural center?" The response came back, and sixty-five percent of people thought it was a bad idea.

My board of directors said, "Oh my goodness, people think it's a bad idea, what are we going to do?" I said, "You know, this would have been a bad thing a year ago, but it doesn't matter now because the city has already committed to it." The board realized that this issue wasn't really a problem but was only a perceived problem by a select few people. A few of the naysayers in the community wanted to have another council meeting and reverse the decision. So I just made sure that our board of directors contacted different families so that we could fill the council chamber with supporters forty-five minutes before the meeting even started. And before it even started, people couldn't even get to the door. So there was no room for people who opposed it to even get in the doors. In reality, there were only two people who were grumbling about it. They showed up, saw that they couldn't get in, and then they just grumbled and left, and the city just moved on from there.

What happened later was that the city said, "This is actually a great opportunity. Let's keep this question on the survey for next year so that once the center is open, we can get a response from the community. This would be a good tracking tool, too, because it looks at how many jobs were created in the community as well."

I thought, "OK, this could really be a tracking device to show how successful the center is going to be," and that annual survey actually turned out to be a very good economic tracker. It was extremely beneficial.

Some people then said, "We don't want the arts to be included in this survey." I simply replied, "No, no, let's include the arts in this survey so that when it *is* successful, we can show how successful it was." In fact, the very year after the center opened and people saw how beautiful it was and how impressive it was, the survey came back with almost the exact opposite results; I believe sixty-six percent of people in town said that it was a good idea for the city to financially support it.

There was a lot of opposition along the way, though. There were a couple of important obstacles at the beginning. When it was just starting and the board had just formed, we found out that another organization that was starting—about twenty miles away—had gotten a National Endowment for the Arts grant to do a feasibility study for a new arts center—a new three- hundred-thousand-dollar arts center.

One board member said, "Oh my goodness, they just got this feasibility study from the NEA for twenty-five thousand dollars for this three-hundred-thousand-dollar center. What are we going to do?"

They looked at it as a real threat, and I just said, "Well, I'll tell you what. I really don't think that their community is going to be behind it that much. Actually, I can do a feasibility study right now, right here, in thirty seconds: 'Yes, we *can* do it.' So now, I've just saved us twenty-five thousand dollars for a feasibility study that we don't need. Let's move on to the next step, to actually move toward building it."

That alleviated some fears on the board, and we just moved forward with raising money to actually build it, not worrying about whether it was possible or what the impact was going to be. Sure enough, a year later, we opened the center. By then, the feasibility study for the other community was done. They said that they could build a facility, but they never did. They never took it past that first step. So I think that a lot of how to do this is just the mindset you have, a planning mindset as opposed to a *doing* mindset.

Another obstacle was getting the building. When I convinced the owner to give us a donation for the first time, I asked him to donate the building, and he said, "Yes, I'll donate the building." But I turned him down. I said, "We have to have start-up capital to go with that." He said, "Well, I'm not going to give you money." I just waited a couple of months, and then he offered five thousand dollars to go with it, and again I said, "No, we really will need more to start a capital campaign."

It wasn't until the end of the year—it was getting to be November—when I met with his wife, who, I knew, was a big arts supporter. Not only did they give us the building, but they gave twelve thousand dollars. We were actually paid money to take the building—which doesn't get into the story sometimes, but it's true; we were paid money to take the building.

About two weeks after he agreed to that, one of the biggest obstacles was something that came up unexpectedly. Our organization wasn't officially a nonprofit—a 501(c)(3)—yet. We had incorporated but hadn't gotten our status yet. It was pending. The donor said that he could not donate the building if we was not a 501(c)(3), because then he would not get his tax deduction. So he called off the donation, and everyone was just in a really bad state of mind—including me, because he basically said, "I just can't make the donation if you're not a 501(c)(3). Sorry."

This was at the end of the year, and he had to do it before December 31. I was just racking my brain because I had called the IRS, and they said they couldn't rush something like that. It was going to take another six months to a year—absolutely no possible solution to 501(c)(3) status before the end of the year from their end of things.

So what I ended up doing was, again, going around the brick wall. Clearly, you can't change the Internal Revenue Service, but who do you need to convince? Well, we needed to convince the attorney who was working for the donor. So I ended up talking to my dad, who's an attorney, and said, "Well, is there any way that we can get around this?" He said, "Well, no, not really. The only way to get around it is to guarantee that this person gets their tax deduction." So I thought, "OK, well, we can do that. That's just putting something on a piece of paper."

So I had my dad draft up a letter that essentially guaranteed that this person would get their tax deduction, regardless of whether our center was now officially a 501(c)(3) or not. That simple letter satisfied both the donor and their attorney and the donation and eventual tax deduction went through, and the project moved forward.

I think, more generally, that fear and resistance to change can be huge obstacles. Fear is very powerful, and I think the arts can be portrayed as nonessential. I mean, people think, "How can that possibly help us?" Fear can definitely be used as a very negative tool for people not wanting to see something happen.

I would say negativity matters as much as fear. In reality, that fear of change, while there is some, is not a real tangible kind of fear. It's just more that people are resistant. I don't think they're really afraid; they're just more comfortable with where they are, and they can view something that may be different or a change as a bad thing. But by showing by example that something different can be good, you can take away people's reasons to be opposed to something or to be negative. So throughout the process of developing New York Mills as an arts community, part of our strategy was to take away reasons why people might say no, as any community might be resistant to change. This community's background was that of Finnish immigrants. Like most people, Finns can be skeptical—and very practical. So presenting concrete reasons why something is good, and why changing something will be good, was helpful.

I looked at publicity as a tool, like a hammer or saw that could be used to build something. I used publicity so the arts were then viewed as a positive within the community, and people had a lot of pride about the arts because they were related to this community.

The fact that the tractor was the logo—a non-threatening logo—engaged the community in a non-threatening way to make it more accessible. So as more and more publicity surrounded the community, the city council certainly felt much better about contributing financially to it. In fact, they gave, every year, ten thousand dollars to fifteen thousand dollars. All of that money went directly to publicity and to promote tourism. The center served as the official visitor center.

So they saw giving money as a good thing because it publicized their town. The town then received publicity from the national media. One of the most creative programs I introduced was called the Great American Think-Off, a philosophy competition for the everyday person. It brought regular folks from across the country to New York Mills to debate philosophical topics such as "What is the meaning of life?" For example, then, CNN, NPR, and *US News & World Report* all covered the Think-Off. C-SPAN even broadcast the event live.

The Northwest Area Foundation recognized the cultural center as a national model for rural arts and economic development in 1994, and the economic model for this tiny town of New York Mills giving money to an arts center was used by the Fergus Falls Center for the Arts. They asked their city government to contribute money. The same happened with St. Cloud and other larger communities. They started using that same model, because their arguments were, "Well, if this little, teeny town can do it, why can't we?"

In the end, I felt that I accomplished everything that I could do in New York Mills. The last project I really worked on was the sculpture park there. One of the reasons I started the sculpture park was that actually, in 1997, five years after the center opened, there were more jobs than people in New York Mills. Businesses had increased. According to the annual city survey, there were seventeen new businesses that had opened up in that five-year span. Jobs increased forty percent, to the point where there were more jobs than people.

But while I was working as an unofficial economic and community developer, the economic development staff person who was paid by the city was somewhat irritated. One of his ideas was to work on an industrial park. Now, industrial parks are generally a very positive economic development tool and a community staple. However, at the time, I was adamantly against having an industrial park in a town that size, because we didn't need it. We had more jobs than people. How many more jobs did we need, really?

But he pressed forward, and people thought it was a good idea—and on a tract of land outside of town along the highway, land that they had bought for an industrial park. He was actually trying to move main street businesses outside of downtown to the industrial park, which would have been just disastrous. So he would talk with the city council, and then I would talk with business owners and try to convince them not to do it. His plan was to move the whole town out to the industrial park along the highway.

I thought that was ridiculous. At a chamber of commerce meeting he said, "Hey, this will be great. We'll have this industrial business out there. Just imagine. People will drive by town, and people see this fast-food place"—because he wanted to bring in a Perkins—"and they'll pull off and have something to eat and be on their way."

People were nodding, "Oh yes. Progress."

I just said, "Wait a minute. Here's an alternative scenario. You're driving down the highway. You see this sculpture park with all of these amazing sculptures. You think, 'What is this about?' You pull off, and you see there's a sign, so you think, 'Oh, there's an art center in town.' You go into town, and you look at the art center. You stop by the local café downtown and have something to eat. Oh, you stay at the B&B that's in town. That's more money in town. You stay overnight, drive to the next town, and tell all of your friends about what a good time you had in the town. What sounds like a better idea to you?"

People in the chamber were like, "Well, we like the sculpture park idea."

So that spot where the fast-food place was going to be—which was a prime spot right on the corner—the city actually donated to use as a sculpture park. That's how the sculpture park started; it was taking a potential negative like this industrial park, realizing that the general idea couldn't be defeated and trying to make something positive out of it that engrains the arts into the community, while working side by side with business. The sculpture park went with this larger plan of having the arts as a physical presence in the community, and it integrated the arts into everyone's life, along with having the sculpture park as an economic development engine as well.

Looking at the art center's impact in the community, we had an opening reception for the sculpture park, and we had people show up for the opening who were in their eighties and nineties. People would come and walk through the park because they wanted to see what it was about.

It was exciting to have kids growing up in New York Mills having had artists come from Poland, Russia, England, and New York and having these arts experiences. The part that I think was most surprising was that people in New York Mills thought, "Well, this is just standard for a small town"—just like you would think it's standard for a big city. You can go see the opera or you can go hear music. It's now the standard. So the arts have become acclimated into the community where people think, "Oh yeah, we have another visiting artist coming," or, "There's another musical performance." It's just part of everyday life. So I think that's been the impact—that it's been accepted. In fact, the bank president's daughter, who as a child grew up with visiting artists from around the world, decided to quit her job in corporate America and move back to her hometown of New York Mills to raise her children surrounded by the arts. She was to become the executive director of the cultural center.

I've found over the years that when people talk about the arts and community development, they often talk about it in theory, but they have rarely worked and lived in a small town in practice. It is a challenge to work and live in a small town long term and overcome negativity and obstacles to achieve positive results in the arts. But it can also be very rewarding to see a community become stronger by embracing the arts, creativity, and new ideas.

Even though I've worked in the arts here for a long time now in Lanesboro—I served on the arts planning commission that helped to build the new three-million-dollar theater in town, and I'm working on other projects—the most interesting community project wasn't an art project. It was this tire burning plant that was proposed for the next town over, which would have been an environmental disaster. It would have been the largest tire burning plant in the world, and it would have been built next to this scenic picturesque trout stream in this community that I live in now.

I couldn't figure out how in the world this huge, massive tire burning plant was coming about. So I looked into it and talked to one of the people who was actively opposed to it. I just found out that the whole idea was to build this multi-million-dollar facility and bring in tires from Chicago, Minneapolis, and all over the country and burn them in this little town because they didn't have a political structure there that the promoters thought would be able to oppose it.

So I quietly worked as a volunteer for a year and a half with the mayor and leaders of two different environmental groups to come up with a strategy and a campaign to defeat this plant. The tire burning plant had serious financial and political backing. They had an ample supply of money to promote this, and it was called Heartland Energy Recycling—it had this very benign name.

Reflecting upon a lot of that community work that I used for the arts to make something positive happen, I thought, "I wonder if I can use that same strategy to prevent something from happening that's negative?" And I just applied all those same principles of politics, strategy, fundraising, and publicity.

Publicity and shaping public opinion was a big factor. The project ended up with a story in *USA Today* and a fifteen-page spread in a Minneapolis paper that talked about the story in detail. A new website was created, as well as a thirty-second TV commercial opposing the plant. The lead environmental organization worked with their own legal team—and politicians from three different states—to apply enough pressure so that the project eventually didn't happen at all. That was quite an education. But those same principles can be used with other projects as well.

With community development work, it's sometimes about trial and error. All communities are unique but share common characteristics, too. I think there's a lot of intuition involved and just a lot of common sense. I think it's crucial to have not just a clear vision, but to collaboratively develop a shared vision to go along with good strategy and process to achieve positive results for a community. We might be able to accomplish more if more time was spent on those parts of it you could actually do—more positive community work with a little more strategy and a sharp focus on the process.

I think that in Lanesboro, because it is a tourist town and people come to it because of its natural beauty—it is surrounded by limestone bluffs and has a pristine trout stream running through it—I've learned to see how a community like that approached the arts as opposed to a community like New York Mills, which is more of a prairie community and not a designated tourist destination. In New York Mills, it was more about, "Here's this small town. Reimagine the possibilities. Go do it." Now, both Lanesboro and New York Mills are looked at as among the top one hundred arts towns in America by author John Villani. So I've had a chance to live in two different places, and to gain a unique perspective on the impact of arts and culture in small-town America.

Conclusion

Collaboration, Difference, and Imagination in Processes of Place Making

The very diversity of these place makers' work may resist easy summary, but that diversity provides good news, with important lessons and fresh directions for future practice and research. The beginning of the encouraging news is that there's no gimmick to place making, no technical fix, no one best way that will encourage vital place making in widely different locales, contexts, and cultural and historical circumstances. There's more hopeful news when we realize that those unique and distinctive contexts provide the materials, the particular histories and memories, the attachments and commitments, the special and significant attributes that enable place makers to do their creative work (Cannavo 2007; Manzo and Perkins 2006; Reardon and Forester 2016). In a diversity of contexts, we can learn from correspondingly diverse practices, sensitive responses, creative experiments, political pressures, and past mistakes (Campbell, Forester, and Sanyal 2018).

The place makers in this book have presented us with stories that are inevitably partial histories of their attempts to create new futures. These are not stories about doing more of the same. These are not stories of lone heroes, isolated geniuses, or solitary explorers of new territories. For every character believing that a city or neighborhood's history can take a turn for the better, we might see a dozen who are more skeptical of change, more discouraged by histories of racism, poverty, the dominance of downtown business interests, or the rigorous but perhaps blindered advice of cloistered transportation engineers or old-school landscape architects. So *these* place makers, as ordinary as many of them might seem to be, have actually been, for all practical purposes, somewhat like working detectives of the future; they have shared their accounts with us of working to figure out what was possible to do now and in the future in each of their particular places.

They had supporters; they had opponents. They had to figure out what resources they had at hand, what resources they might access or draw upon. They had before them yesterday's habits and conventions and today's rules and regulations far more clearly than the emerging possibilities of what they might create—in neighborhood centers, on the banks of this river, in these empty lots, by encouraging the arts and public performances. Against the grain of denial and distrust, power and privilege, these place-making histories revealed political dramas of creating new places. The mystery in each chapter has not been "Who did it? Who was the murderer or thief or culprit?" but instead, "In each place—with its own history of its elites and last wide-eyed do-gooders, its patterns of poverty and racial inequality, its patterns of 'it's always been this way'—how was creating a more vibrant, beautiful, productive, just, and flourishing place really possible?"[1]

So the place-making "stories" in this book present us with far more than mere reportage or a chronicling of events. They give more than just a sense of their meaning and others' interpretations in the actual contexts of their time and place; certainly they are examples of possibilities, examples of challenges and responses, examples of obstacles encountered and strategies of addressing those obstructions creatively, equitably, innovatively. If we read these accounts as mere chronologies of events, we might keep a measure of their complexity, but we would lose and hardly learn from the ongoing possibilities of these unfolding stories. None of our chapters has been scripted; none of the protagonists knew just where their work would take them; none of them could have done the work alone, without supporters whose trust they had earned, without critics who forced them to improve and adjust their work, without codesigners who re-created these places with them.

None of these chapters is without conflicts of interests, without conflicts over resources that could go here or there, to this group or to that one, and so the stories of these place makers exemplify work to thread difficult needles. They sketch possibilities for better future work, possibilities to build support for what no one has done here before, to prevail politically in the face of naysayers with other priorities: budget cutting, faster traffic flows, less change of open space, letting the old boys have their way.

Far beyond chronology or mere storytelling, these chapters present us with the compelling, animated quality of these place makers' voices. As we read and listen to these accounts, we don't sense the distance of a journalist's description of the Detroit Black Community Food Security Network from the outside or navigate the distance of a reporter's chronicle of the evolution of Paris's community gardens. We get instead an insider's view, a more intimate portrayal of the place making in these settings, the felt struggles of their work with others, friends and foes, that have transformed these spaces into surprising and newly flourishing places. We see not only a sequence of *what* happened but also *how* at the Minnesota-Wisconsin border, two bridges became one, *how* speeding traffic in Rochester gave way to an ART Walk, *how* skepticism about fancy outsiders with urban-design jargons gave way to involvement, ownership, and collaborative urban design on the Oregon coast.

But there are still other contributions of these place makers' efforts, their detective work to find future possibilities and create better places:

On the partiality or inadequacy of plans: These place makers use many tools that include but reach far beyond plan making. In every case, their work has produced action on the ground, not only an attractively bound report on the shelf, but festivals performed, community building meals shared and relationships built, streets and intersections reclaimed for new purposes, gardens grown (De Leo and Forester 2018). In Zelinka's and Pyatok's cases, the evolving plans were devices to co-generate suggestions, revisions, and adaptations every bit as much as they promised outcomes (Hoch 2012, 2016; Hopkins 2001).

On the necessity of improvisation: These place makers had no simple scripts to follow. They acted in distinct and unique contexts, acting responsively and creatively, leveraging expertise and using coalition-building skills. Acting creatively, they hoped for both innovative and attractive outcomes, not only for the sake of the aesthetics of gardens or intersections but for community building goals as well (Barrett 2012; Forester 2018). Leveraging expertise, they sought innovations that would work. Coalition building, they built relationships with those in other faith communities, they brought together those interested in economic development, community development, and open-space protection.

Contending with multiple goals, diverse stakeholders, government authorities, complex spaces, these place makers improvised, acting creatively for public benefit in real time, responding to their particular contexts as they worked (Hester 2010; Laws and Forester 2015). This work wove together three ongoing concerns that kept their work grounded: they always worked with others who could affirm that the projects at hand could contribute value; they began with a clear humility to convey that they knew that they needed to learn, that they needed to consult many kinds of expertise, local and more conventionally scientific; and not least of all, they knew that their work required not only writing reports but also acting materially, negotiating with others, to build new community centers and programs, to reclaim public parks, sidewalks, and intersections, to build affordable housing and create new community gardens, even to design a new bridge. Their improvising was as creative and sophisticated place making as any jazz musician's improvising has created fresh, vital, beautiful performances.

On refuting the fallacy of anything goes: Nevertheless, as they improvised practically, these place makers all worked within constraints, so they were not led, driven, or called by visions and ideals alone but by the actual spaces and materials and, indeed, histories of challenging relationships that they inherited and found at hand to work with and to engage. Their contexts were both sources of resources with which to work—as James Brodick worked with AmeriCorps staff drawn from the Red Hook neighborhood—and sources of constraint, including, in Brodick's case, the inherited distrust of residents who had every reason to be dubious about new promises of local community development efforts.

On integrating value, expertise, and negotiation: These place makers all leveraged and drew upon resources of expertise, expert advice from many quarters, expertise not only drawing upon vision and passion and commitment to beauty or social justice, but expertise rooted in technical training. Whether trying to produce safe streets, affordable housing, viable urban agriculture, effective rituals of community building, these place makers integrated into their visions of beauty and justice another passion for objectivity, not for fantasy—not to dictate their goals or objectives but to help them accomplish their practical and technical goals (Innes and Booher 2010; Murdoch 1970).

On keeping expertise accountable, not autonomous: These place makers saw themselves as partners with diverse community members, not as professional royalty handing down decisions for the masses. They knew that non-professional community members could speak powerfully and movingly to the significance of place, home, celebration, and neighborhood in powerful ordinary language, over meals more easily than in public meetings. So these designers knew to listen, knew to protect spaces for ordinary conversation free from the intimidation or subtle agenda setting of professional jargons. They knew to make technical expertise accountable to the goals and qualities they hoped to achieve with community members. They knew that if community members were to help define problems and goals and qualities and character, the technical experts would need to be on tap, not on top: on call, responsive and not controlling, accountable and not autonomous (Matsuura and Schenk 2017).

On the wisdom of two thousand cups of tea: These place makers knew that they had to learn before acting, to listen before deciding. They knew that they had to create informal spaces and places for community members to meet and discuss and invent and create, so that coalition building and developing networks and meeting one another had to happen at least as much over meals and tea and coffee and drinks as in formal public hearings (Adler 2013; Forester 2009). These designers knew that there were aesthetic aspects of even informal meetings, as these needed to be safe rather than threatening, attractive rather than uncomfortable, respectful rather than humiliating, as practitioners as diverse as Lakeman, Sarkissian, and Davis have shown (Forester 2018).

On taking part vs. participation: These place makers all transformed vague and ambiguous ideas of public participation into far more specific, subtle, and effective forms. They did not simply call public meetings or hold public hearings. The very *absence* of big, diffuse public meetings in the accounts in this book provides a damning indictment of the "Call a meeting!" strategy of fostering public voice or participation, user input or accountability. But in none of these cases do we find the place maker as lone wolf, as an isolated, lonely if brilliant solo artist delivering his or her vision to the people at the foot of the mountain.

On making places and making music together: All our chapters have revealed possibilities of cultivating cooperation and coalitions, trust and emergent social groups. And they all have revealed more, too. What these place makers have done in situations of complexity and change echoes the creative work, curiously enough, of other creative collaborators. In a lucid, aptly titled study—*Yes to the Mess*—that explores innovative leadership and creative improvisation, pianist and sociologist Frank Barrett draws lessons from the experiences of jazz ensembles (Barrett 2012). Barrett's concerns are both practical and innovative. He shows us how cooperation among working musicians calls for four qualities that we can cultivate when we work with others: appreciation, the thoughtful evaluation of what's at hand to work with; willingness to follow, to give up the lead, at times, to the initiatives and ideas of others; forgiveness of imperfection, if not also graciousness and humility, when others are less than perfect as we try to break new ground together; and, not least of all, a quality of attention to possibilities that we might call wonder and imagination. In neighborhoods and cities, more rural or more urban spaces, it's easy to see that place making with others makes these same demands and others. If Barrett has made the case for what's possible, our chapters have shown how place makers actually do it, making places together as a first cousin of making music together—even in the face of power and privilege (Forester 2020; Forester, Verloo, and Laws 2021; see afterword).

We see community building here along with place making, conversations and careful organizing, listening and talking through differences of opinion and interest. We can do all this, these practitioners suggest, instead of attending still more horrendous public meetings of three minute testimonies followed by backroom decision-making.

In all these ways, these place makers model real possibilities—real possibilities of what we can do to reclaim spaces and make them vibrant human places. As a result, these chapters might seem deceptively simple—too simple. We don't see the process that created the spectacular New York City High Line that's inspired others around the world. But there are moves here, actions and strategies, approaches and social processes that many place makers in many other kinds of places might find instructive and hopeful, providing ideas and directions to develop in new ways. This is more artistry than science, more practical than narrowly technical, more actually possible in many of our cities and neighborhoods than wishful thinking (Stegner 1953).

Cooperative practices also teach us about the risks of deliberative malpractices (Forester 2019). These practitioners' stories have shown that not only do place makers not work as heroes, not work as solo genius-designers, but that they have to work skillfully with many others. Because they recognize the complexity of physical and socio-legal systems, they have to integrate other expertise into design and planning teams (Bishop 2015; Steinitz 2012). Because they recognize that places are lived through people's lives—that the vibrancy of actual, not fantasized places depends on and must always be accountable to actual residents and neighbors and passersby—these place makers have worked closely and sensitively both with experts and with partners on the ground: local gardeners in Detroit and Paris, low-income families in Oakland and Brooklyn, neighbors and drivers and pedestrians in Rochester and Portland and elsewhere.

In all these ways, place makers show us, too, that they must be more than solo reflective practitioners, learning by themselves from the talkback of their moves, as Schön so well put their individual work (1983). These place makers must also be deliberative practitioners, working sensitively and respectfully, inclusively and collaboratively with others—or they will find themselves rejected and dismissed as the mixed-use propagandists were, as Zelinka discovered on the Oregon coast (Forester 1999).

But working deliberatively with others has not just process implications but also consequences for learning about space and place, coming to see places anew because of the very richness of what community members bring up and bring out, in any given location. So in New York Mills, John Davis brings not a wholly independent artistic vision to the community, but in conversations with farmers, he floats ideas, gains interest and welcome, and by putting visiting artists together with the agricultural and industrial resources at hand—in this case, the stunning grain elevators—he and they change both place and their ordinary world. In Portland, Oregon, Mark Lakeman now asks us to think about public spaces as always potentially being remade, as places of play and imagination, not simply places that reflect a designer's strategically imported solution to a problem.

We have seen Zelinka and Pyatok, Lakeman and Brodick, Hughes and Sarkissian, and others practice design as learning, design as inquiry, design as responsiveness both to the raw potentials of actual sites and to the wishes and hopes of the communities with whom they have been working. We see our place makers as continually working things out with others who are different. This "working things out" spatially may not often be called negotiation, or improvisation, or cooperation, or even collective creativity, but on the ground, in real places, devised through experiments and charettes and brainstorming sessions and community meeting upon community meeting, place making seems to involve all of those qualities of not just being in a place but of more profoundly and deeply designing in virtuous circles, interacting with others in shared spaces to make them lived places.

So our place makers have been as perceptive about community as they have been keenly aware of space. They have not just transformed spaces into places, but they have also wrestled with daunting histories as they have worked to cultivate new community relationships, whether in gardens in Detroit or Paris or on the streets of Oldham or Los Angeles. They all moved beyond the language of neighborhood deficits and assets. They inherited histories of distrust and cynicism and went door to door to build trust—in New York no less than in Oregon. They inherited histories of racial inequality and animosity and they created organizations and places of new coalitions and local autonomy—in Brooklyn no less than in Oakland. They faced officials' distrust of ordinary citizens and the citizens' distrust of bureaucrats, and they convened meetings, built mutual respect, and educated each other—in Rochester no less than on the Wisconsin-Minnesota border. They faced suspicions from community members who felt they'd be left out or dismissed or not taken seriously yet again, and these place makers used charettes and storefronts and surveys and newspapers and accountability sessions to foster inclusion and engagement, not exclusion as usual.

These place-making practitioners—some professionals, some lay residents—had inherited, in case after case and in place after place, what we might call a history of governance malpractices, more precisely "deliberative malpractices" (Forester, Kuitenbrouwer, and Laws 2019). None of these cases began from blank slates. Instead, we saw that earlier planning and design efforts had disrespected and humiliated communities by designing for but not with them; they had dismissed and excluded community members by treating them as know-nothings or not-in-mybackyard-ists; they had perplexed, confused, and alienated community members by using unintelligible language and jargon. Perhaps above all, their presumptions of control and good intentions had threatened community members with unknown consequences, so creating not public trust and consent but rather fear and all too reasonable resistance.

These past consequences of planning and design efforts—disrespect, humiliation, dismissal, exclusion, confusion, alienation, fear, and resistance—formed the practical backdrop, the very real inheritance or initial status quo antes that the place makers in this book all worked and struggled to overcome (Roberts 2020). In case after case, we have seen how these place makers worked with community members immersively and continuously, inclusively and respectfully, transparently and collaboratively. In transforming spaces into the places they have helped to create, they have taught us about the natural and physical environment, about transportation and gardens and housing and economic development, to be sure. But they also taught us something more, something fundamental, about the essential community building aspects of place making: creating environments of respect and safety, of inclusion and recognition, of ownership and imagination.

Afterword

The Relevance of These Place Makers' Stories in the Time of the COVID-19 Pandemic and the Black Lives Matter Movement

The world changed in the first half of 2020. Place making will never be the same. Two widespread but intangible killers, COVID-19 and white supremacy, threatened schools and workplaces, communities and neighborhoods, past and future alike. These killers were both systemic, differently visible and invisible, the first a biological pandemic, the second a socioculturally and institutionally transmitted racism. But these pathologies were not genetic; both spread through human agency and contact (Gates 2019). Both make the lessons of these place makers' stories more important than ever.

Just as shared social practices of mask wearing and social distancing could reduce the contagion of the pandemic, so too the shared political work of unmasking privilege and forging partnerships could begin to counteract unquestioned systemic racism. These killers were not inevitable; instead, they were fully historical, socially and politically malleable, changeable. Nevertheless, with their threats more and less apparent to different populations, we witnessed resistance to efforts to save lives, resistance to recognizing problems, resistance to changing our institutions. All this, we shall see, has implications for place making and place makers.

Fall 2020

Legacies of Denial and Resistance, Possibilities of Health and Justice

If the pandemic and police violence seemed now and then out of control, flawed leadership, deliberate misinformation, and willful denial all played substantial roles (Forester and McKibbon 2020). Police chiefs and school principals were quick to point to individual bad apples on their staffs. They were far slower to acknowledge the stacked decks of institutional racism in our educational and law enforcement systems (German 2020). President Trump, a self-proclaimed world leader, did lead the world's efforts to call the pandemic a hoax, a matter of "fake news" that would soon just go away, a deadly situation that, as he put it in mind-numbing fashion, "is what it is."

The behavior of these face-saving, self-absorbed, but unresponsive leaders matters less than does their spreading of false hope and reassurance in their doing nothing to counteract these biological and political-economic pathologies. Their nonchalance was practiced as they normalized inaction, doing nothing, in response to increasing body counts. They covered up and papered over, dismissed and distracted attention from the passive injustices (Shklar 1990) of the chips falling as they might on the most vulnerable, and so they all encouraged business as usual to proceed on its death march.

But as still more Black and brown people of color die from the bullets and the knees of police officers, and as disproportionately elderly and Black and brown and indigenous people die from COVID-19, two very different responses have taken place in the US. For months following George Floyd's killing, young and old and Blacks and whites and Latinx and Asians and Native Americans marched and protested in city streets to demand institutional change for racial justice. More people than ever before came to recognize that police killings of people of color were systemically influenced, not just the disassociated acts of individuals; systemic racism remains a deeply entrenched uneven playing field, a stacked deck systemically skewing the life chances of people of color from the maternity wards through schools and workplaces and neighborhoods.

At the same time, as if in a natural experiment, New York State "flattened the curve" of COVID-19 contagion and death, showing what could be accomplished, in public health terms, though social cooperation, even as many other states did not respond as proactively. More and more New Yorkers, for example, willingly chose to wear masks, to socially distance, and to engage in compassionate mutual aid to support their communal public health and save lives. Amid threats of contagion and with striking leadership and public education, the pandemic foregrounded both compassion and collective action, simultaneously recognizing interdependence and shared vulnerability and acknowledging the value of acting together and of shared responsible leadership (Forester and MacKibbon 2020). But the pandemic also revealed the costs of failed leadership, failed cooperation, failed protection of our lives together. Our chapters have shown again and again the common good that can be created, produced, and achieved through cooperation—from arts centers to intersections and streets, from interethnic community building to reclaimed parks to newly designed bridges—and these created not just public goods but shared public benefits for diverse communities.

Individualism and Privilege

At the same time, though, in part as a result of the grimaced vanity, if not the narcissism, of American presidential leadership, tens of thousands of people died needlessly because stringent mask-wearing practices were not put in place nationally in the United States. But this was not a matter of one man's folly. The aversion to wearing face masks sometimes took the form of popular claims to individual rights and liberties—however nonsensical, in the face of a pandemic, these claims were. Like obeying speed limits in traffic, wearing masks would, could, and did save lives; neither infringed upon public rights and liberties. But rights claims, along with suspicions of political authority, run deep in the inherited premises of an individualistic liberal political culture.

The aversion to recognizing the stacked decks of systemic racism runs no less deep. The denial of white supremacy and institutional racism continues to be no less muscularly engrained, for it represents the workings of what vast publics have come to recognize as white privilege. White privilege is not only a formal but an informal entitlement (Agyeman 2020). For whites, it can be as invisible as water may be to fish. White privilege depends on a kind of complicity, a taken-for-granted silence, a doing nothing, a not making trouble, a letting things be, all to continue to avoid calling into question or challenging the regular, systemic, quiet biasing of life chances, possibilities indeed skewed down to the level of zip code, of people of color relative to whites. Allan Johnson discusses white privilege as the liberty of not having always to think about systemic racial injustice. But no one has put the subtle perniciousness of white privilege better than James Baldwin, whom Johnson quotes: "To be white in America means not having to think about it" (Johnson 2006, 22; also see Forester 2019; McIntosh 1989).

The COVID-19 pandemic and the police killings of Black men that climaxed with George Floyd's death produced complex and contradictory results. Both revealed real possibilities of change but deep resistance to it as well. Local organizing and public health leadership showed that we could stop unnecessary loss of life and injustice, even as we saw anew that change makers and place makers have serious, structurally rooted obstacles to anticipate and overcome. Neither these obstacles to change nor these capacities and resources for restructuring are new.

Legacies of structural racism—from the fears of people of color racially profiled, to street-level hate crimes, to red-lining by banks or block-busting by real estate agents (Sugrue 1996)—are nothing new. Possibilities of organizing for restructuring—from mutual aid to community organizing to social movement coalitions—have precedents, too (Corburn 2009; Gates 2019; Reardon 2019; Wallerstein and Duran 2010). Furthermore, the place makers who have contributed here have all worked in these subtly and not so subtly biased contexts. So we should ask what lessons these place-making stories teach us. What can we learn from these chapters about entrenched power and privilege, about public suspicion of authority, about overcoming fears of Others?

Place Makers' Lessons

These chapters teach us that places are as complex as the dramas and conflicts that unfold in them. Apparently simple community gardens can present challenges to white supremacy in Detroit no less than to long-standing professional power in Paris, France, as Malik Yakini and Laurence Baudelet have shown. In Oregon or in Queensland, design conversations, exercises, and simulations and variants of focus groups can allow communities to surface fears of dangerous streets or Others and to work together to design housing, to protect parks, to enhance cultural resources, as in Wendy Sarkissian's and Al Zelinka's cases. Working together, community members can bridge religious differences after local riots and violence, as in James Brodick's and Father Phil Sumner's cases. They can design bridges when transportation engineers find such a thing simply unheard of, as Michael Hughes has shown. They can recognize, face, and then carry out practices to address local and structural racism, as in Michael Pyatok's and Karen Umemoto's cases—even as these cases altered discrete relationships, not systems or policies. They can collaborate to diagnose problems and to produce shared programs or projects to enrich the public welfare, as in the accounts of Mark Lakeman, John Davis, Doug Rice, and Barnaby Evans.

All these place makers have wrestled with transforming spaces into places by shaping streets and bridges and churches and community courts. But too, they present accounts of transforming institutions, resisting the conservative power of the professions, the racial and class politics shaping city governance, the cultural and even emotional biases threatening to undermine the design professions. This dual focus on place and institution, on design objects at hand and on prevailing presumptions of power and voice, might well characterize the politics of design and place making in the time of COVID-19 and Black Lives Matter. But how does this work?

The Black Lives Matter resurgence and the COVID-19 pandemic bring into focus the challenges facing place makers as never before. Malik Yakini makes painfully clear that there will be little understanding of space and place in Detroit separate from the recognition of Detroit's racial struggles. Karen Umemoto makes clear that no one will be walking the streets of Azusa without fear of violence in the absence of residents' concerted attempts to address racial violence there. Michael Pyatok and Michael Hughes show us not just that differing, even conflicting, stakeholders *can* fuel creative designs, but they show us *how* that can happen practically as well. They show us a dialectics of design, as object and context, place and power co-define each other.

But notice that even in our cases where racial difference did not play a central role, differences in institutional power and privilege still mattered. When John Davis went to the state council for the arts with his ideas about developing a distinct type of artist residence in a small rural community, he heard, essentially, "Well, that's *not* how you do it." When Laurence Baudelet served on a design jury for a graduating landscape architecture student whose design would enable community residents to shape the built form, a senior designer on the jury was appalled. He warned, "This will be the death of our profession"—implying, of course, the death of just those privileges of voice and deference that the profession has long enjoyed. When Doug Rice proposed to slow traffic and create ARTWalk in Rochester, New York, he found the transportation staff even less prepared to work with neighborhood residents than the residents were prepared to deal with city officials. In all these cases, design advocates sought innovations to improve neighborhoods, to promote the arts, and to support communities. In every case, they inherited not only the histories of these places, but also the prevailing structures of power, expertise, and authority that threatened to replace or displace their efforts.

This interrelationship of place and political context—as these co-define and constitute each other—could hardly have been more striking and more instructive than in Michael Hughes's case of the two bridges spanning the St. Croix River. However extraordinary the case seems as he mediated the conflicts between twenty-eight stakeholders, very little seems extraordinary about the tensions between the designers, the engineers, the historic preservationists, and the environmentalists. Of course, in this case, the engineers fancied themselves as the designers, so we can imagine their surprise and consternation when told by Hughes, in effect, that the stakeholders just didn't trust them to design an attractive bridge and that without having their willing support, the engineers were never going to be able to build any new bridge at all. This case is not a hero's story, but a warning: infrastructure design and place making are all about inherited and encompassing structures of power, negotiations between proponents and opponents, delicate processes of invention and creative search across alternatives, and the skillful mediation of differences. None of these chapters present cookie-cutter models or frozen ideals of best practices, but all characterize place-making complexity and reveal the practically responsive improvising that is still possible in processes of search and listening, inventing and proposing, negotiating and deciding and following up (Forester 2018).

The cataclysms of the COVID-19 pandemic and the Black Lives Matter resurgence can help us to learn about place making in striking ways. They urge us all to focus more expansively on how spaces become places. If we examine the stories of this volume's place makers, we can learn about both mutual aid and social justice. We can learn about the challenges of responding both to the threats of the pandemic—dealing with interdependence, vulnerability, denial, and precarious cooperation—and to the demands of social justice and recognition—dealing with relationships of power and privilege, encouraging not just inclusion but belonging, encouraging organizing, and community building.

Place-Making Practices in the Shadow of the Pandemic and the Black Lives Matter Resurgence

The lessons of the COVID-19 pandemic reach far beyond wearing masks and social distancing. As a pervasive threat to ongoing community life and public welfare, the pandemic forces our attention to our global interdependence, the vulnerability that connectedness implies, and the roles that public denial or acknowledgment of effective strategies can play. The significance of public leadership—for example, encouraging widespread practices of mask wearing or failing to do so—could hardly have become more clear, as such leadership arguably might prevent tens of thousands of needless deaths. Similarly, we have witnessed a small cultural revolution, a transformation of ordinary daily life practices, as practices of respect, recognition, and compassion spread in the shared acknowledgment of one another through mask wearing and in broad public acceptance of social norms of social distancing. So as the pandemic confronted us with shifting landscapes of public information and wildly inconsistent political leadership, and as COVID-19 testing advanced in fits and starts, diverse publics struggled to come to terms with problems and to find ways to respond to threats of contagion. What does this mean for place making?

Trained Blindness

The challenges posed by the Black Lives Matter resurgence were every bit as graphic as the pandemic's scenes of patients on ventilators—unforgettably witnessed in the imagery seen round the world of nearly nine minutes of the Minneapolis policeman's knee suffocating and killing George Floyd. But the BLM challenges always were and remain far more pervasive, even insidious. While public health data and testing and the inferred threats might have been contested, manipulated, and politicized for President Trump's benefit (Forester and McKibbon 2020), the systemic character of white supremacy endures as a phenomenon that the majority of the white population has learned and even trained and acculturated itself *not* to see. White privilege does not explain this blindness; it exemplifies it and puts it into practice. As Ta-Nehisi Coates wrote, "Race is the child of racism, not the father" (Coates 2015, 7).

If Black men might well fear for their lives when pulled over for a suspected traffic violation—knowing that their reach for their driver's license or their registration papers might be read by police as reaching for a weapon, that their nervous slip of speech or exasperation might be read by police as resistance or intransigence or interference—white drivers presume they do not begin with a strike against them, with a heavy foot on the scales of just treatment. What seems a normal annoyance of being pulled over for the white driver can be a source of learned fear or terror for the Black driver.

But learned privilege involves not just the police but our schools, our health care systems, our city bureaucracies. As a Black student confided to me once that he had often wondered about being served smaller portions in a college cafeteria line, so might Black and brown residents wonder if they will receive the same services and attention when they wait in lines at city hall. So place makers need to expect that their very same questions regarding concerns, or announcements regarding events, or promises of future programs, or invitations to meetings may well be interpreted very differently by more or less privileged, whiter or less white, higher- or lower-income populations.

So even when Karen Umemoto had organized a workshop in the face of hate crimes and racialized violence in Azusa, California, she found politically appointed representatives of the human relations commission who actually doubted the very premise of their workshop. They doubted that racism was actually a problem in Azusa. If the doubters came to the workshop with skepticism, feeling little at stake for themselves, Latinx and Black participants came with feelings of loss and raw vulnerability, slender hopes mixed with real fears.

When Wendy Sarkissian worked with Eagleby residents to learn of their concerns about the safety of the public realm, she found, along with issues of poverty, the class dimensions of privilege, the felt humiliation and stigma suffered by residents, the sense that they were not respected and listened to by government bureaucrats and their more affluent neighbors. They sensed that they did not count, feeling that they had little chance of being taken seriously by those in positions of influence.

When James Brodick began his work in Red Hook, Brooklyn, community members' confidence in the criminal justice system and local courts could hardly have been much lower. Brodick could not expect a community welcome of trust and good will; he had to earn that, step by step, as he did.

In Oldham, England, Father Phil Sumner found that despite histories of racialized, religiously rationalized, and anti-immigrant violence, clergy of Christian and Muslim communities—and lay leadership of those communities—were not talking to each other. Not talking, of course, produced not just silence but further ignorance and suspicions of one another.

Recognizing Difference: On Identity and Belonging

These stories of engaged place makers can teach us not only about increasing inclusion but about encouraging belonging, too, about practices not just of recognizing but also of embracing diverse identities. These accounts urge us to pay attention to more than merely formal interactions, to more even than formal or polite respect. Father Phil Sumner did not just argue that all faiths mattered; he demonstrated it, enacted it. He brought members of different faith communities together in celebrating traditional festivals, in breaking bread, in sharing music and song, and in dialogue, all as priest and imams visibly, publicly, worked together.

Just as the name Black Lives Matter resists the long-standing dismissal of the distinctiveness and particulars of Black identity and experience under the much broader banner of All Lives Matter, so these chapters suggest similarly that really recognizing distinct community residents matters. People who have been left out matter—youth in Brodick's Red Hook, Latinos in Pyatok's Oakland, poor whites in Sarkissian's Eagleby, African Americans and Latinos in Umemoto's Azusa, Blacks in Yakini's Detroit. Each of these groups, our chapters have shown, were not just invited to participate; they were asked, tasked, empowered, and encouraged to play visible roles—to be advocates and jury members/ judges in the youth courts, designers with the design kits, guides and facilitators and marchers in Eagleby, speakers in the Azusa workshop, decision-makers in Detroit's Black Community Food Security Network.

Speaking of a "multicultural collaborative," for example, Umemoto tells us that she "found those types of models hopeful—especially the grassroots work that really engaged people in positive, forward-looking activities where people were able to build an identity inclusive of racial difference, an identity built upon making a change in a place that everybody will benefit from—so that people can have multiple identities." Here, she might as well have been writing about work like that of Brodick's in Red Hook, Sumner's in Oldham, Baudelet's in Paris.

Umemoto deepened her point as she noted that yet another so-called community coalition "*added* to racial identities that were salient at the time, so there was something in that process of identity building that was inclusive. We weren't just African Americans, or Latinos, or Koreans. So knowing that there were going to be racial divides and differences and all of that, we could work through them, and we could build upon the unique contributions that people might bring with them because of their differences in experience."

So, too, Laurence Baudelet-Stelmacher noted (in a draft of this chapter), "Community gardens aim to include all kinds of people, no matter what age, sex/gender, color of skin, social class, religion, or cultural background. It's often explicitly mentioned in their charters that no discrimination is accepted. We believe that to prevent racism and racial prejudices, we need to bring people together and offer them the opportunity to build social ties. When people go through a process of participative design in their neighborhood to create a community garden, they open up and socialize. It can't solve all problems, of course, but the community gardens are small laboratories for our democracies where we can shape new social experiences." Small laboratories for democracy, indeed, and in deeds.

Father Phil emphasizes these points as well: "I would argue that interaction, in itself, without also addressing a person's (or a community's) self-concept, could simply result in superficial relationships that can be full of insecurity and prone to outbursts of violence. I also work as a judge in an ecclesiastical marriage tribunal and, again and again, insecurity that has not been dealt with and that is brought with someone into a relationship is devastating for the relationship and often results in jealousy and violence. It's the same with community relationships. People need to have a sense of belonging. They need to see people like themselves as decision-makers and leading citizens."

But Father Phil adds a warning. He writes, "The Greater Manchester Police used to have a stated philosophy of 'treating everyone equally, irrespective of race, culture,' etc. I used to ask them to change this from 'irrespective' to 'respecting.' Far from aspiring to be color blind, we need to be able to see difference/color so that we can respond to the particular needs of particular communities. . . . When people speak of 'all lives matter,' they often miss the importance of seeing the particular needs of communities, and especially stigmatized ones. . . . So to treat people equally, this will involve treating people differently, according to their particular needs. And to understand those needs, you can't presume to know, that is, to stereotype—you have to do a lot of listening."

Anticipating Suspicion and Denial, Listening and Building Trust

In case after case, we have seen, these place makers met with skeptical reactions; if we want to slow traffic or transform an intersection into a piazza or to cultivate community gardens, will the powers that be even listen to us and take action on our proposals? Will our efforts make any difference? If community members felt they were going to waste their time trying, wouldn't their reluctance and resistance to organize for change make more sense? All these cases predated the Black Lives Matter resurgence of 2020, but they all anticipated and skillfully engaged the deep problems of denial, privilege, disenfranchisement, fear, and doubt that the Black Lives Matter movement has once again brought to national consciousness (Roberts 2020).

In all these cases, these place makers reveal lines of response and strategies of community building that might transform local spaces into vibrant places—incorporating the arts, encouraging community control and ownership, even developing virtuous circles of engagement, as we shall see below. These place-making moves and processes are not rocket science, not one-time wonders, for even as they demand improvised responses to local settings, they may be complementary, at times even combined (Forester 2017).

So Mark Lakeman and Mike Pyatok and Mike Hughes, for example, among others here, all convened various kinds of meetings of concerned citizens or stakeholders who were willing to learn about the places in which they lived and the possibilities that they might come together to influence. Each of them knew, as did James Brodick and Laurence Baudelet and John Davis and others, that commitment to these places they lived in could motivate residents to speak up about their fears and their hopes, the qualities of place they loved and dreaded. All these place makers had strategies of listening carefully not for the first thing that came to mind but for the deeper concerns and observations that might surface, too.

So along with meetings, we have read about Sarkissian's SpeakOuts and Yakini's public listening sessions. We have read about the depth and power of Umemoto's storytelling exercise that taught Azusa participants so much about one another and their experiences. We have read about Mike Hughes's revelation that when he tried to be accountable, the lack of objection did not really mean "OK"; and we have read, too, about his tip, the importance of exploring *how* we might do something before asking *whether* it should be done. We have read about James Brodick's realizing that despite his early presumption that Red Hook needed a drug treatment court, his listening via the community surveys suggested that providing job counseling might be just as vital. We have read, too, of Mike Pyatok's subtle but catalytic design kits, which provided materials that enabled diverse users to probe, experiment, test, and evaluate differing housing designs iteratively, creating a shared history of place making together with experts accountable to residents (Balducci and Mantysalo 2013).

In all these cases and others, the transformation of space into place only comes through careful processes of engaging with others socially and with spaces materially and visually—after the preparatory work of listening in many ways for what matters, of building trust and relationships together, of gathering new information and leveraging expertise as new problems come into focus, along the way building support for future actions, whether these are, for example, in the form of city council resolutions (Lakeman, Yakini, and Zelinka), mayoral support (Baudelet), or congressional action (Hughes).

We have seen, then, that as the Black Lives Matter resurgence demands that we anticipate relationships of power and privilege, relations of dominance and deference that can fuel resistance to change, so too can place makers devise strategies of listening, convening, organizing, experimenting, negotiating, and advocating for change that allow conventional spaces to become special places: streets, parks, gardens, downtowns, even bridges (Forester 2020; Moulden 2019). We have provided here not recipes for place making, but repertoires of critical moves and methods, techniques and processes, none rocket science, all pragmatic, none heroic, all demanding an eye on conventional spaces—and an eye on the relationships of power, trust, and support that might reanimate these spaces into vibrant places.

Leveraging Place Attachment into Virtuous Circles

If we consider how these place makers' practices—their overtures and responsive efforts—resonate with each other, we can begin to see an emergent virtuous circle of place making. We see this in one of the deeply shared themes that link these chapters, a red thread expressed in Father Phil Sumner's story. Coming to Oldham to address racial and religious differences, Father Phil quotes his parish members saying early on, speaking of Oldham's Muslims, "We don't talk to them, do we?" His story, resonating with Umemoto's work in Azusa, with Brodick's work in Red Hook, and with Sarkissian's in Queensland, then showed how community members moved beyond such self-segregation, beyond such mutual isolation, to take real steps together, in concert, to improve their communities, to transform dangerous spaces into safe, convivial places. In doing so, they took initial steps into the virtuous circles that all these designers encouraged, all beginning with a shared commitment to place and then asking about possibilities, listening to options, then responding together.

Whether trained as architects or public administrators, planners or educators, mediators or clergy, all have described—have accomplished!—iterative, interactive, community-based, expert-informed problem-solving processes fueled by place attachment, at times catalyzed by the arts and cultural traditions. Their design and problem solving, their place-making practices, began with problematic spaces. Working with residents, they responded iteratively to commitments, hopes and fears, and by crafting together new ways of meeting, using, and living together in those spaces, community residents were able to articulate and address their own concerns, needs, and interests while developing external political support along the way. Doing that together, they created public value, in part as they created new trusted and respecting, virtuous relationships, in part, too, as they re-created streets and parks and gardens and bridges as newly vibrant places, providing tangible benefits of their cooperation. Working together, with expertise accountable and responsive rather than autonomous, these practitioners brought virtuous circles, virtuous spirals, of place making to life. Mike Hughes captured these place makers' senses of commitment and responsibility: "It's not done *to* you; it's done *with* you and *for* you, and if you ever think it's not being done for you, then it has to be done with you, and you should stop me if you don't like it."

The emergent power and subtly interactive politics of Mike Pyatok's use of design kits provides an instructive example. Beginning with suspicion and uncertainty, racism and fear, resistance and privilege on the neighbors' parts, the design kits engaged community members in a ritualized—safe, stepwise, iterative, dialogic—design process of inquiry and invention, experimentation and visualization, reciprocity in asking and answering, "What if we did *this*?," exploring together what might become real, what they might realize together. Along the way, community members' relationships of trust, respect, confidence, and hope changed with Pyatok's staff, and both came to imagine their own futures differently than they did before, along with the imagined relationships to the new residents who would come in later. But not only would community members and place makers come to feel differently, some of them would turn out in public meetings of the city council to formalize and perform all this. We have seen iterative and interactive virtuous circles like this in the work of Zelinka in Oregon and Yakini in Detroit and in the practices of Brodick in Red Hook and Father Phil in Oldham, as in related work of Lakeman in Portland and Baudelet in Paris and Hughes at the St. Croix River.

Inheriting Painful Histories, Place Makers' Struggles Continue

None of this suffices to overthrow white supremacy, and none of this guarantees the widespread social coordination that New York's crisis response to the novel coronavirus exemplified. But that hardly diminishes the value of these lessons; it calls for further work, for further institutional analysis, for further organizing. Listening that allows surprise and recognition can interrupt and erode the presumptions of white supremacy as Brodick, Umemoto, Father Phil, and others suggest. Listening, though, is not a gimmick but a social and political practice; done decently, it might prevent solving the wrong problems, focusing better, respecting others more, and humiliating and dismissing others less. Recognizing others more allows experts, place makers, and those with whom they might work to be less presumptuously autonomous and more responsively accountable. We glimpse this in Baudelet's recollection of the parks and gardens engineer, wholly new to community engagement, who exclaimed that his interaction with community members was exciting, not heretical, not dumbing anyone down, but obviously invigorating, promising. Engaging stakeholders and other local people, these place makers have shown, can resist standing orders of privilege and power, and it can recognize difference, create public value, improve urban design, and empower citizens and residents alike.

When sociologist Ash Amin wrote of living with diversity in the multicultural city, he captured what we can call the "critical pragmatism" of the place making we have explored here:

> Problems of interaction and therefore also their resolution are fundamentally related to the political culture of the public domain, more specifically, to the scope there is for vigorous but democratic disagreement between citizens constituted as equals. This shift in register from the language of policy fixes to that of democratic politics is important, first because it highlights the significance of questions of empowerment, rights, citizenship, and belonging in shaping interethnic relations; second, because it shows that an open public realm helps to disrupt fixed cultural assumptions and to shift identities through cultural exchange; and, third, because it reveals that living with diversity is a matter of constant negotiation, trial and error, and sustained effort, with possibilities

crucially shaped by the many strands that feed into the political culture of the public realm from the entanglements of local institutional conflict, civic mobilization, and interpersonal engagement, to national debates on who counts as a citizen, what constitutes the good society, and who can claim the nation. (Amin 2002, 976; emphasis mine)

In a time of the need for concerted collective action in the face of pandemic-like threats to public health and the abiding quest for racial justice, the range of strategies employed by the place makers whose stories we have read are more vital and pressing, more significant than ever, incomplete as they—and any of our existing theories—may be.

APPENDIX 1

Overview of Community Development and Crime Prevention,
New York Center for Court Innovation

JAMES BRODICK

The Center for Court Innovation seeks to increase public safety in neighborhoods throughout New York City by investing in residents, transforming public spaces, and reengineering the criminal justice process. The center envisions neighborhoods in which crime and incarceration are reduced, local faith in the justice system is restored, and civic life is vibrant.

The center aims to help change the narrative of disadvantaged neighborhoods throughout New York City. It advances solutions to crime that focus on making positive investments in specific people and places. The center recognizes that safe and healthy neighborhoods have strong local institutions, dynamic connections among residents, and meaningful relationships with government agencies. The center endeavors to create these preconditions for safety by a strengthening neighborhood's social infrastructure, activating its public spaces, and expanding the opportunities available to young people. When crime does occur, the center works to ensure that the justice system responds in ways that are proportionate, constructive, and restorative.

PRINCIPLES

Our work at the center is guided by the following principles:

ENGAGE THE COMMUNITY: The center's approach to public safety is simple: ask residents where and why they feel unsafe and involve them in helping to address these issues. In particular, we think it is important to engage, as part of the solution, young people who are most likely to commit crimes.

A commitment to participatory problem-solving pervades all aspects of the center's work. Each of the center's projects follows the same development process. Residents, often youth, identify an issue and then study, design, and implement a solution. The center's staff help guide this process—gathering data to inform decisions, identifying partners, and coordinating the intervention. In short, the center helps residents think through new approaches to safety and then works with them to make these ideas happen.

This approach ensures that all residents, especially those most affected by crime and the justice system, can play an active role in their community's response to public-safety concerns.

CREATE SAFETY: The center seeks to move the justice system from a reactive posture—responding after crime has occurred—to a mindset that recognizes the value of crime prevention. Safe and healthy neighborhoods have vibrant public life and strong social connections. As Jane Jacobs observed in *The Death and Life of Great American Cities*, "eyes on the street" can increase a neighborhood's capacity to confront disorder (1992). Similarly, Robert Sampson of Harvard University has demonstrated how trust and solidarity among local residents can improve a neighborhood's ability to regulate behavior.

The conventional tools of the criminal justice system, particularly heightened police enforcement and over incarceration, can have significant unintended consequences, including undermining neighborhood trust and social infrastructure.

In contrast, the center focuses on increasing the neighborhood's capacity to create safety for itself. Our place-making work activates neglected public spaces, drawing in people and businesses to underused areas. Our youth programming and community events promote social connections. Together, these interventions form a virtuous feedback loop. Inclusive public spaces and appealing businesses bring people out onto the street. Vibrant public life and strong social ties reduce crime. And declines in crime drive the cycle onward by further increasing trust and solidarity and encouraging more people to use public spaces.

FOCUS ON THE PEOPLE AND PLACES AT GREATEST RISK: The center focuses its resources where needs are most acute: young people at high risk of future involvement with the justice system, and places where crime and social disorder are prevalent. Investments in people and places are essential to effective crime prevention. The center invests in young people and their capacity to instigate local change. Our youth programming challenges preconceived notions regarding who young people are and what they are capable of. Our investments in places transform local hot spots into safe and welcoming environments.

HEAL INDIVIDUAL AND COMMUNITY TRAUMA: Trauma is a common experience, at both the individual and community level. The center seeks to repair harms and restore relationships. To heal people, the center offers counseling, promotes wellness, and supports individuals in the pursuit of their passions. To heal the community, we engage residents in transforming streets and empty lots once characterized by fear and neglect. In these ways, we are helping build a safer and more resilient community.

BUILD PARTNERSHIPS: Sociologist Patrick Sharkey has documented that nonprofit organizations have an essential role to play in reducing crime and helping bring together residents, businesses, and local government to address problems and coordinate resources. The center plays this role in neighborhoods.

The center works particularly closely with justice agencies (e.g., police, probation, and courts) in an effort to improve the ways that they serve the community. Strong ties with area businesses and nonprofits support the continued vitality of public spaces and provide opportunities for local youth. These collaborations help to strengthen the social infrastructure of neighborhoods and increase residents' faith in their community's capacity to address local issues.

PROGRAMMING

The center seeks to prevent crime and improve safety by working in three principal areas:

1. Investing in local residents—offering services, such as counseling, entrepreneurship training, and professional internships that provide participants, particularly young people, with meaningful opportunities;
2. Transforming public spaces—turning hot spots and eye sores into valued community assets and encouraging local residents to take ownership of these spaces;

3. Reengineering the criminal justice process—working with justice agencies to create off-ramps that lead away from incarceration and toward more proportionate, meaningful, and restorative outcomes.

INVESTING IN LOCAL RESIDENTS

The center offers services to local residents that are designed to build on their strengths, address their trauma, and provide them with opportunities to become community leaders.

Young people are a particular area of focus. The center does not make hard-and-fast distinctions among the young people it serves. Some have been mandated by the justice system. Others are walk-ins from the community.

The center offers all young people who come to us—regardless of how they come—opportunities to pursue their passions and learn marketable skills. This includes an eight-month paid internship program that offers training in entrepreneurship, technology, and the arts, as well as pipelines to employment in these fields. The center has helped launch several youth-led social enterprises, such as a music collective that teaches recording, production, and performance, and the Lab, a virtual- and augmented-reality incubator space that offers training in cutting-edge technologies.

The center encourages participants to use their skills to make a positive difference in their neighborhoods. Among other things, young people from the center have organized music festivals attended by hundreds of residents and have created online platforms that attempt to break down the barriers between sets, crews, and gangs.

Transforming Public Spaces

Decades of disinvestment have left many communities with distressed business corridors, vacant lots, and underutilized public spaces that encourage crime. The center works to revitalize these neglected places. By investing in a neighborhood's physical infrastructure, we seek to strengthen the community's social infrastructure and thus its ability to regulate behavior without requiring conventional law enforcement responses (arrest, prosecution, incarceration).

The center's place-making work transforms high-crime areas into safe and inclusive public spaces in which social and commercial activity can flourish. In Brownsville, Brooklyn, for example, the center has made a significant commitment to improving Belmont Avenue, a struggling shopping corridor that has been the scene of a great deal of criminal activity in recent years. Working with a range of local partners—and hundreds of young people—the center has removed trash and graffiti, installed public art and plantings, improved lighting, created a pedestrian plaza, and attracted new, resident-owned businesses. Elsewhere in Brownsville, young people from the center worked with a local housing developer to spearhead the creation of a neighborhood clubhouse in an empty lot. The center's commitment to community participation in the planning process has engendered local pride in, and regular use of, these spaces.

The revitalization of Belmont and the neighborhood clubhouse are two examples of how the center is reactivating the public square and encouraging local residents to come out of their apartments and take advantage of all that their neighborhood has to offer. In doing so, we are deterring crime and encouraging a more active civic life.

Reengineering the Criminal Justice Process

Too often, the justice system feels like a conveyor belt, transporting people from arrest to prosecution to incarceration like so many widgets in a factory. Experience suggests that criminal justice practitioners will embrace alternatives to this process if they have confidence that they are meaningful. Accordingly, the center provides an array of diversion and alternative-to-incarceration opportunities that work with individuals with justice involvement ranging from low-level misdemeanors to serious felonies. The center seeks to help them resolve their cases without jail time, fines, and other traditional sanctions. Instead, the center engages participants in restorative and constructive programming, including community service, psycho-educational groups, and intensive individual support.

The center approaches a criminal case as a window of opportunity in which to heal justice-involved individuals and the community as a whole. Our programming encourages participants to hold themselves accountable for their actions and to repair any harm they have caused.

The center also seeks to bridge the gap that has emerged between local residents and the justice system. This includes helping educate police, prosecutors, probation officers, and others about the neighbor-hood and creating opportunities for frontline practitioners to interact with local young people in positive settings. For example, the center co-ordinates a youth-led precinct community council to facilitate discus-sions about public safety issues with police and to engage officers in its community service projects.

APPENDIX 2

On Optimism

MICHAEL HUGHES

On August 2, 2017, I was given a gift, a small piece of red ribbon. It is a tiny part of the ribbon that the St. Croix River Crossing stakeholders cut to open the new bridge connecting Wisconsin and Minnesota, a bridge that is virtually identical to the one they worked together to imagine.

Before the ribbon cutting, there were, of course, a series of speeches. Elected officials recounted for those who did not know the particulars the hard work, the countless meetings between Republicans and Democrats, the intricate legislative sequence, and the sense of shared purpose and commitment, all painting a picture of the extraordinary bipartisan effort to move the project through to completion.

It looks just like other red ribbons I have, those calling us to a unified effort to fight a pandemic. On that front, I have also seen the results of bipartisanship and shared purpose. Today, I am a member of the board of directors of Vivent Health. We have created a fully integrated medical home for people living with HIV, ensuring that they have medical care, dental care, a pharmacy, a food bank, substance use counseling, behavioral and mental health care, legal services, HIV prevention services, and housing support, all connected by case management. This is possible because of a carefully constructed arrangement of public policy, private philanthropy, corporate responsibility, and not-for-profit management.

By contrast to the ribbon cutting in August, on Monday, December 11, 2017, I facilitated a conference call that confirmed the end of the State and Federal Joint Task Force for Endangered Species Act Implementation at the direction of the federal officials. I helped the task force from 2013 through the end in 2017 as they discussed best practices in state and federal cooperation to protect threatened and endangered species and examined ways to improve the act itself and the implementing rules and regulations under NOAA Fisheries and the US Fish and Wildlife Service.

From the vantage point of 2020—in an age of both pandemic and protest—the ribbon-cutting ceremony seems quaint and naïve, rooted in another time and country. No one is convening a task force for state and federal cooperation today. The timeline—from 2012, when Congress and the president authorized construction of the bridge, through 2017 to 2020—is evidence of the decay of national unity and the loss of shared national purpose.

And yet I know that we ebb and flow, that there is action and reaction, growth and evolution. I know that everything will change. The optimism that it took for me to help a small group of community leaders end three decades of conflict and stalemate to get the bridge built remains. The optimism I have as I watch Vivent Health drive HIV viral loads to undetectable levels for people of color, as I see that shared purpose will end the pandemic of HIV in America in my lifetime, remains.

Why do I choose optimism? The choice that government officials made to convene the St. Croix River Crossing stakeholders and to honor their work, the choice to work across party lines to see that their agreement would translate into two exceptional bridges, the choice by federal and state leaders to create a joint task force to save endangered species, and the choice to commit ourselves to the end of the HIV pandemic are just that—choices. Cooperation and conflict are not fated, not inevitable. We can choose. I choose optimism.

I am also optimistic because the definition of national unity is expanding. Yes, there are growing pains, but the pain is evidence of growth. Today, we must understand national unity in a much deeper way, and the very fact of that gives me even more optimism. Today, those who have a place at the table are seeing, as if for the first time, those whose place at the table has been denied. We are beginning to understand national unity, not in a superficial way, but as a call to action.

National unity is possible if we decide we want it. I have a piece of red ribbon to prove it.

APPENDIX 3

Interviewees, Interviewers, and Dates and Approvals of Interviews

The following record of interviewees and interviewers is organized according to the order of practitioners' stories as presented in this volume. In all cases, I have done extensive editing; practitioners have reviewed and approved both the initial edits for classroom use and subsequent edits for publication in 2021.

Part 1: Joanna Winter interviewed Michael Pyatok in November 2006; initial editing was approved in 2011. Sara Pressprich interviewed Al Zelinka in November 2007; initial editing was approved in 2011. Jessica Yoon interviewed Mark Lakeman in March 2008; initial editing was approved in 2011. John Forester interviewed Michael Hughes in October 2013; initial editing was approved in 2014.

Part 2: Jeremy Siegfried interviewed James Brodick in March 2008; initial editing was approved in 2011. John Forester interviewed Karen Umemoto in March 2002; initial editing was approved in 2004. Khairul Anwar interviewed Father Phil Sumner in March 2007; initial editing was approved in 2011. Eleanor Bomstein interviewed Malik Yakini in October 2011; initial editing was approved in 2012.

Part 3: Stephen Miller interviewed Barnaby Evans in March 2006; initial editing was approved in 2011. John Forester interviewed Wendy Sarkissian in September 2002; initial editing was approved in 2004. Kerry Quinn interviewed Doug Rice in March 2008; initial editing was approved in 2011. Agnes Ladjevardi interviewed Laurence Baudelet in March 2008; initial editing was approved in 2011. Christopher Donohoe interviewed John Davis in April 2008; initial editing was approved in 2011.

NOTES

INTRODUCTION. PLACE MAKING, NOT PLAN MAKING

1 On the method of interviewing, editing, reediting, checking, and rechecking before gaining approval for publication, see Forester 2006, 2012.

2 We realize that narrative accounts like these do not present facts only, as if any set of facts or observations or recollections were not already framed in some selective way. We have evoked place makers' insights not by asking them for their working theories but by asking them what they had learned from their cases, how they might have focused their efforts differently, how new staff they might hire could best continue their work, and so on.

3 These and other stories of place making will teach us that geographic spaces without materiality and morality will never be memorable and significant historic places. These stories challenge planning and place making alike. They are not merely stories. They work against the grain of professional fix-it techniques; they are surprising, hopeful, entangled, and detailed, not reductive. Compare the efforts of the Kresge Foundation regarding issues of community engagement and racial equity (Kresge Foundation 2019).

4 See appendix 1.

5 If we remember the actions that characterize a place, we might also re-member— that is, become parts of greater wholes, as when we walk through a church or temple in another city. As we move in and to different places, so we re-member and recall different times and worlds. Disciplinary boundaries separate us more than join us here, for what is spatiality to the geographer is moral entanglement to the ethicist, moral phenomenology to the sociologist, membership to the political scientist. Consider the ordinary sense of being "in trouble" as opposed to being "in the room"; so "being in a place" involves both the relationality of the former (being) and the spatiality of the latter (space). As a result, if you don't know how to use the tools around you, you are likely to feel more in the *space* of the kitchen than in the *place*. Similarly, when watching a game, our sense of space and place will differ depending on whether we do or don't know the rules. So legibility matters!

6 Notice how a place can capture those qualities of being dramatic, beautiful, warm, and historic. In the space of a baseball field, no longer an expanse of dirt and grass, we need not only markers and props, devices and signs and symbols, a home plate and drawn foul lines, but players to enact the game, here baseball.

So we see the game-like equivalents of table and chairs in a garden, materials in space symbiotically attached to users whose deeds transform an empty space with objects into a more or less welcoming or carelessly arranged garden. In his political critique of autonomous technology, Langdon Winner wrote wonderfully about technologies not simply as instrumental means and materials but as infrastructures for moral relationships, for socially normative uses, forms of life, and institutions of actually performed and not simply promised or merely intended relationships (Winner 1977).

7 But in all our cases, no necessarily ambiguous labels—"negotiating," "mediating," "communicating," or "improvising"—can convey the richness of the practice stories that provide such a fine-grained sense of what these place makers have really done (Forester 2009, 2013).

8 The fact that in practice, we rarely call questions of choice "questions of ethics" does not, of course, make them any less ethical. If I break a promise or betray a confidence or lie without justification, I might not want to think about this as ethically problematic, but my thoughtlessness no more justifies my actions than does my thinking that I am LeBron James make me LeBron James. To say that the silence about ethics in the place-making literature is deafening seems to be an understatement, but it makes place making no less ethically rich, interesting, and problematic.

9 Recognizing this triple helix also signals the moral, political, and scientific complexity of the skill that place making actually involves. If place makers share these problems with other planners, worrying about solving the wrong problems, acting without adequate knowledge, and acting ineffectually, then we should not be surprised that doing justice to the work of place making will inevitably involve correspondingly essential questions of values and ethics, knowledge and science, and politics and negotiation, as these chapters will demonstrate (Forester 1999, 2019).

10 Over the last fifteen years or so, as my students and I studied practices of place making, we identified and interviewed practitioners from coast to coast and sometimes from abroad. On the development of the method of producing profiles of practitioners trying to account not for their theories but for challenging and difficult but worthwhile projects they have worked on, see Forester (2009, 2013). Students have contributed remarkable interviews in both undergraduate and graduate courses devoted to studies of innovative and boundary-pushing planning practices.

11 Similarly practice-focused profiles of urban planners and designers in the US, Holland, Israel, and Italy have provided the basis for seven books—Forester 1999, 2001, 2009, 2013, 2015 (with David Laws), 2016 (with Ken Reardon), and 2018 (with Daniela De Leo)—along with the substantial work of Scott Peters and colleagues in related fields (Peters 2010; Peters, Alter, and Shaffer 2018). For recent related profiles of street-level democrats in Holland, see Laws and Forester (2015). On the ways Italian planners have moved well beyond plan making, see De Leo and Forester (2017, 2018).

4. BRIDGING MINNESOTA AND WISCONSIN WITH TWENTY-EIGHT STAKEHOLDERS

1 For an earlier account involving public health, governance, race, and deep value differences, see Hughes's account in Susskind et al. (1999) and Forester (2013).

6. DEVELOPING THE RED HOOK COMMUNITY JUSTICE CENTER

1 For a striking overview of the principles and crime-prevention and community-development practices of New York's Center for Court Innovation, see appendix 1.

9. PUBLIC ART, ECONOMIC DEVELOPMENT, AND THE ORIGINS OF WATERFIRE

1 "We've now done it for New Year's Eve four or five times. We did it for this past New Year's Eve [2006], the one before that, the millennium, and a couple of others. It snowed on the most recent one—not quite enough to be beautiful. The first time we did it was one of those super, super cold New Year's. In fact, the river was frozen. We had to break all the ice off with sledgehammers. It wasn't thick, but there was ice. I fell in. Got totally frozen."

2 "We have to get permits from everybody. DEM, Coast Guard, the freshwater council, coastal resources management council [CRMC], parks department, fire department, fire marshal (both state and city), the health department for food vending, the police department for public gatherings, the license bureau for entertainment permits, the sales division of the state of Rhode Island for selling T-shirts and for having a permit to allow food vendors on the street. We need permits for every tent from the state and city fire marshal, and we need permits from the design review committee of the city of Providence and the capital center commission. We went to DRC and CCC as more of a courtesy. Now, in almost all of those cases, we have permits that have now been extended on a long-term basis. For our CRMC permit, after two or three years, they gave us a ninety-nine-year permit. But for the marine safety permit, we send the application off as soon as we establish the dates, because that closes the river to boat traffic. It's closed from sunset to midnight on these dates, and that's between the Coast Guard and the marine safety office of DEM."

3 "Our music choice was very deliberately international. Probably the most represented continent would be Africa, followed by Europe, South America, North America, and then Asia. The diversity of the music is quite intentionally eclectic, both ethnically and chronologically, so that we play music ranging from new works that we've commissioned to historical reconstructions from ancient Greek, Persian, and Egyptian cultures. We prefer to present recorded music."

4 Buff Chase was the founder of Cornish Associates, a Providence real-estate development firm known for its commitment to New Urbanist principles. Among its marquee projects are Mashpee Commons on Cape Cod and the conversion of historic buildings in downtown Providence into high-end residential lofts.

5   Vincent A. "Buddy" Cianci was the long-serving mayor of Providence with a color-ful history. Often the city's biggest booster, he served as mayor from 1974–84 and again from 1991–2002. After an FBI investigation of city hall corruption, Cianci was indicted on charges of racketeering, conspiracy, extortion, witness tampering, and mail fraud. At the time of this interview, he was incarcerated at a federal corrections facility in Fort Dix, New Jersey. For more information, refer to Mike Stanton's book, *The Prince of Providence: The Rise and Fall of Buddy Cianci America's Most Notori-ous Mayor* (Random House, 2003), or Cherry Arnold's 2005 film, *Buddy*.

6   "[The sandbar emerging in Waterplace Basin has been] an ongoing problem; it needs dredging very badly. They dredged it for us in 1998, and it should've been dredged again in 2004, but they didn't do it. In theory, the river should be deep enough that even at low tide, it should be passable for boats. But because they haven't dredged, we have to pay attention to the tide schedule. There are many times when we cannot light WaterFire because the river is too shallow. It's two to three million dollars for dredging, and no one is interested in it except for WaterFire. One of the approaches we're looking at is spending two million dollars to put in a tide gate, so you can maintain the water level at high tide. You'd still have to dredge. The silt will still come down the river; a tide gate just keeps you at high tide. So now you could dredge less frequently. But the tide gate causes all sorts of problems with marine life in the river with the migration of fish. We just got notice that we will be awarded a grant to do the environmental assessment, which will decide how often the tide gate could be closed and what effect that will have with increasing the rate of siltation."

7   "The study's big interest was in out-of-state visitors who choose to come to Provi-dence because of WaterFire and stay in a hotel or eat at a restaurant. They did two things that I would've preferred that they did differently. One was that they looked at only the economic impact of visitors that evening in Providence. So if you were staying in a hotel in Newport and came up to see WaterFire and were here for four days in Rhode Island, they didn't count any of your expenditures for your hotel or any of your expenditures on the trip. They only looked at what you spent in Providence that night. So it was a very narrow question. And they came up with 40.5 million dollars. The state economic development staff say that the number is probably a great deal larger."

8   "Something like ninety percent of WaterFire visitors come from outside Provi-dence, and fifty-seven percent come from outside Rhode Island. That's very unusual for an arts event, but also, Rhode Island is a small state, so it's hard to figure this out. Sixty-nine percent of the Rhode Island visitors said they would not have been in Providence that night if there had been no WaterFire; seventy-nine percent of the out-of-state visitors said that the only reason why they were in Providence was to see WaterFire. They got these numbers by interviewing [*reads from report*] '4,248 attendees randomly selected on four WaterFire evenings.' And that was only on the river. They did not count visitors outside the immediate area or dining in restaurants."

9 "Now, Providence rented some equipment to Columbus. It was not equipment that I owned; it was owned by WaterFire Providence, the nonprofit. So they paid WaterFire Providence for that rental. So WaterFire Providence made some money off that; I think they made eight thousand dollars off Columbus last year. But it isn't necessarily designed that way. WaterFire Providence cannot spend its funds outside of Providence. It would be illegal for us to take a contribution in Providence and spend one penny to do it in Houston or Columbus, because the contribution was given to us to support WaterFire in Providence. We're so strict about that that the computer I use to do email to Columbus is a computer that *I've* paid for; it's not a computer that WaterFire's paid for. You've got to have absolute separation, because there's no formal relationship."

11. GIVING PARIS A GREEN HAND

1 In memory of Claudine Raillard Clément, cofounder of Jardin Nomade (Paris).
2 Today called Réseau national des Jardins Partagés, National Network of Community Gardens
3 http://www.qsb11.org/.
4 The city has abandoned the project, and the garden has stayed on this vacant lot.
5 As a consequence of the loss of public funding, this regional network has stopped its work in 2012.
6 Graine de Jardins now has a team of consultants and no more employees, because the subsides are decreasing.
7 https://www.jtp.co.uk/.

CONCLUSION. COLLABORATION, DIFFERENCE, AND IMAGINATION IN PROCESSES OF PLACE MAKING

1 C. Vann Woodward (1986, 51) put this beautifully as he reflected on his struggles to explain the North-South negotiations marking the end of Reconstruction: "[Writing Reunion and Reaction] proved to be more fascinating than any other. . . . The main reason, I think, was the shift from the customary role of historian as recorder-reporter to the more active role of historian as detective. There is some of that in us all, and in much of our work. . . . But here all those latent impulses were called forth by a subject crowded with intrigue, concealment, connivance, dissembling, plot and counter plot, hidden motives, bribery, betrayal, and cover-up. In sum it added up to a mystery to be solved. . . . With the historian in a detective role, there are thrills along the way with discovery of clues, of course; but the denouement . . . does not arrive until the pieces are put together in the book. So the main excitement of the adventure comes in the writing."

BIBLIOGRAPHY

Adler, Peter. 2008. *Eye of the Storm Leadership*. Eugene, OR: Resourceful Internet Solutions.

———. 2013. "Dispute Resolution Meets Policy Analysis: Native Gathering Rights on Private Lands." In *Planning in the Face of Conflict*, edited by John Forester, 41–58. Chicago: American Planning Association Press.

Agyeman, Julian. 2020. "Urban Planning as a Tool of White Supremacy—The Other Lesson from Minneapolis." *US News and World Report*, July 27.

Amin, Ash. 2002. "Ethnicity and the Multicultural City: Living with Diversity." *Environment and Planning A* 34, no. 6: 959–80.

Anguelovski, Isabelle. 2014. *Neighborhood as Refuge: Community Reconstruction, Place Remaking, and Environmental Justice in the City*. Cambridge, MA: MIT Press.

Balducci, Alessandro, and Raine Mantysalo, eds. 2013. *Urban Planning as a Trading Zone*. New York: Springer.

Barrett, Frank. 2012. *Yes to the Mess: Surprising Leadership Lesson from Jazz*. Cambridge, MA: Harvard Business School Press.

Beauregard, Robert, and Laura Lieto, eds. 2016. *Planning for a Material World*. New York: Routledge.

Bishop, Jeff. 2015. *The Craft of Collaborative Planning*. New York: Routledge.

Blight, David W. 2018. *Frederick Douglass: Prophet of Freedom*. New York: Simon and Schuster.

Bose, Mallika, Paula Horrigan, Cheryl Doble, and Sigmund C. Shipp, eds. 2014. *Community Matters: Service-Learning in Engaged Design and Planning*. New York: Routledge.

Campbell, Heather, John Forester, and Bishwapriya Sanyal. 2018. "Can We Learn from Our Mistakes?" *Planning Theory and Practice* 19, no. 3: 426–46.

Cannavo, Peter. 2007. *The Working Landscape: Founding, Preservation and the Politics of Place*. Cambridge, MA: MIT Press.

Coates, Ta-Nehisi. 2015. *Between the World and Me*. New York: Siegel and Grau.

Coons, Samuel. 2020. "It's Always for Our City: Stories of Art and Identity in Detroit, Michigan." John W. and Constance P. Reps Summer Research Award Presentation, Department of City and Regional Planning, Cornell University, September 21.

Corburn, Jason. 2009. *Toward the Healthy City*. Cambridge, MA: MIT Press.

De Leo, Daniela, and John Forester. 2017. "Reimagining Planning: Moving from Reflective Practice to Deliberative Practice—A First Exploration in the Italian Context." *Planning Theory and Practice* 18, no. 2: 202–16.

———. 2018. *Reimagining Planning: How Italian Urban Planners Are Changing Planning Practices*. Rome: INU Edizioni.

Forester, John. 1999. *The Deliberative Practitioner: Encouraging Participatory Planning Processes*. Cambridge, MA: MIT Press.

———. 2006. "Exploring Urban Practice in a Democratizing Society: Opportunities, Techniques, and Challenges." *Development South Africa* 23, no. 5: 569–86.

———. 2009. *Dealing with Differences: Dramas of Mediating Public Disputes*. New York: Oxford University Press.

———. 2012. "Learning to Improve Practice: Lessons from Practice Stories and Practitioners' Own Discourse Analyses (Or Why Only the Loons Show Up)." *Planning Theory and Practice* 13, no. 1: 11–26.

———. 2013. *Planning in the Face of Conflict*. Chicago: American Planning Association Press.

———. 2017. "Deliberative Democracy, Not Smothering Invention." In *Oxford Handbook on Deliberative Democracy*, edited by André Bächtiger, John F. Dryzek, Jane Mansbridge, and Mark Warren, 595–610. New York: Oxford University Press.

———. 2018. "Ecological Wisdom through Deliberative Improvisation." *Journal of Urban Management* 8: 12–19.

———. 2019. "Five Generations of Theory-Practice Tensions: Enriching Socio-ecological Practice Research." *Socio-Ecological Practice Research* 2 (July): 111–19. doi.org/10.1007/s42532-019-00033-3.

———. 2020. "Our Curious Silence about Kindness in Planning: Challenges of Addressing Vulnerability and Suffering." *Planning Theory 20, no. 1* (June): 63–83. doi.org/10.1177/1473095220930766.

Forester, John, Raphaël Fischler, and Deborah Shmueli, eds. 2001. *Israeli Planners and Designers: Profiles of Community Builders:* Albany: State University of New York Press.

Forester, John, Martin Kuitenbrouwer, and David Laws. 2019. "Enacting Reflective and Deliberative Practices in Action Research." *Policy Studies* 40, no. 5: 456–75.

Forester, John, and George McKibbon. 2020. "Beyond Blame: Leadership, Collaboration and Compassion in the Time of COVID-19." *Socio-Ecological Practice Research* (August 17): 1–12. doi.org/10.1007/s42532-020-00057-0.

Forester, John, Nanke Verloo, and David Laws. 2021. "Creative Discretion and the Structure of Context-Responsive Improvising." *Journal of Urban Affairs*. DOI: 10.1080/07352166.2021.1901589.

Gates, Henry Louis, Jr. 2019. *Stoney the Road: Reconstruction, White Supremacy, and the Rise of Jim Crow*. New York: Penguin.

Gavin, Alexander. 2016. *What Makes a Great City*. Washington, DC: Island Press.

Gehl, Jan. 2010. *Cities for People*. Washington, DC: Island Press.

German, Michael. 2020. "Hidden in Plain Sight: Racism, White Supremacy, and Far-Right Militancy in Law Enforcement." Brennan Center for Justice, August 27.

Grose, Margaret. 2017. *Constructed Ecologies: Critical Reflections on Ecology with Design*. New York: Routledge.

Healey, Patsy. 2010. *Making Better Places: The Planning Project in the Twenty-First Century*. New York: Macmillan.

Hester, Randolph. 2010. *Design for Ecological Democracy*. Cambridge, MA: MIT Press.

Hoch, Charles. 2012. "Making Plans." In *Oxford Handbook of Urban Planning*, edited by Rachel Weber and Randy Crane, 241–58. New York: Oxford University Press.

———. 2016. "Utopia, Scenario and Plan." *Planning Theory* 15, no. 1: 6–22.

Hoch, Charles, Marcus Nollert, and Anita Grams. 2018. "Puzzling: Making Plans Together Works." In *How Plans Matter: Inspiring Stories and Fundamental Topics*, edited by Bernd Scholl, Anna Perić, and Rolf Singer, 179–82. Zürich: vdf Hochschulverlag AD an der ETH Zürich.

Hopkins, Lewis. 2001. *Urban Development: The Logic of Making Plans*. Washington, DC: Island Press.

Hou, Jeffrey, ed. 2010. *Insurgent Public Space: Guerrilla Urbanism and the Remaking of Contemporary Cities*. New York: Routledge.

———. 2013. *Transcultural Cities: Border-Crossing and Placemaking*. New York: Routledge.

Innes, Judith E., and David E. Booher. 2010. *Planning with Complexity: An Introduction to Collaborative Rationality and Public Policy*. New York: Routledge.

Jackson, Maria Rosario. 2012. "Developing Artist-Driven Spaces in Marginalized Communities: Reflections and Implications for the Field." Washington, DC: Urban Institute, Leveraging Investments in Creativity, October.

Jacobs, Jane. 1992. *The Death and Life of Great American Cities*. New York: Vintage.

Johnson, Allan G. 2006. Privilege, Power, and Difference. 2nd ed. Boston: McGraw Hill.

Kresge Foundation. 2019. *Inside Out & Outside In: 2019 Annual Report*. https://kresge .org.

Latour, Bruno. 1992. "Where Are the Missing Masses? The Sociology of a Few Mundane Artifacts." In *Shaping Technology-Building Society: Studies in Sociotechnical Change*, edited by Wiebe E. Bijker and John Law, 225–58. Cambridge, MA: MIT Press.

Laws, David, and John Forester. 2015. *Conflict, Improvisation, Governance: Street Level Practices for Urban Democracy*. New York: Routledge.

Lefebvre, Henri. 1991. *The Production of Space*. Oxford: Basil Blackwell.

Lydon, Michael, and Anthony Garcia. 2015. *Tactical Urbanism: Short-Term Action for Long-Term Change*. Washington, DC: Island Press.

Manzo, Lynne C., and Douglas D. Perkins. 2006. "Finding Common Ground: The Importance of Place Attachment to Community Participation and Planning." *Journal of Planning Literature* 20, no. 24: 335–50.

Markusen, Ann. 2014. "Creative Cities: A Ten-Year Research Agenda." *Journal of Urban Affairs* 36, no. s2 (August): 567–89.

Markusen, Ann, and Anne Gadwa. 2010. "Creative Placemaking." Washington, DC: Mayors Institute on City Design and the National Endowment for the Arts. www.arts.gov.

Matsuura, Masahiro, and Todd Schenk, eds. 2017. *Joint Fact-Finding in Urban Planning and Environmental Disputes*. New York: Routledge.

McIntosh, Peggy. 1989. "White Privilege: Unpacking the Invisible Knapsack." *Peace and Freedom Magazine*, July/August: 10–12.

Moulden, Dominic T. 2019. "Shared Economy: WeWork or We Work Together." *Planning Theory and Practice* 20, no. 3: 441–46. doi.org/10.1080/14649357.2019.1629197.

Murdoch, Iris. 1970. *The Sovereignty of Good*. London: Routledge.

Nicodemus, Anne Gadwa. 2013. "Fuzzy Vibrancy: Creative Placemaking as Ascendant U.S. Cultural Policy." *Cultural Trends* 22, nos. 3–4: 213–22.

Nowak, Jeremy. 2007. *Creativity and Neighborhood Development: Strategies for Community Investment*. The Reinvestment Fund. www.reinvestment.com.

Parkinson, John R. 2012. *Democracy and Public Space: The Physical Sites of Democratic Performance*. New York: Oxford University Press.

Peters, Scott J. 2010. *Democracy and Higher Education: Traditions and Stories of Civic Engagement*. East Lansing: Michigan State University Press.

Peters, Scott J., Theodore R. Alter, and Timothy J. Shaffer. 2018. *Jumping into Civic Life: Stories of Public Work from Extension Professionals*. Dayton, OH: Kettering Foundation Press.

Purcell, Mark. 2014. "Possible Worlds: Henri Lefebvre and the Right to the City." *Journal of Urban Affairs* 36, no. 1: 141–54.

Reardon, Kenneth. 2019. *Building Bridges: Community and University Partnerships in East St. Louis*. New York: Social Policy Press.

Reardon, Kenneth, and John Forester. 2016. *Rebuilding Community after Katrina*. Philadelphia: Temple University Press.

Roberts, Andrea. 2020. "Haunting as Agency: A Critical Cultural Landscape Approach to Making Black Labor Visible in Sugar Land, Texas." *ACME: An International Journal for Critical Geographies* 19, no. 1: 210–44.

Rydin, Yvonne. 2011. *The Purpose of Planning: Creating Sustainable Towns and Cities*. London: Policy Press.

Schein, Richard H. 2006. *Landscape and Race in the United States*. New York: Routledge.

Schneekloth, Lynda H., and Robert G. Shibley. 1995. *Placemaking: The Art and Practice of Building Communities*. New York: Wiley.

Schön, Donald. 1983. *The Reflective Practitioner*. New York: Basic.

Shklar, Judith. 1990. *The Faces of Injustice*. New Haven, CT: Yale University Press.

Staeheli, Lynne A. 2003. "Place." In *A Companion to Political Geography*, edited by John Agnew, Katherine Mitchell, and Gerard Toal, 159–70. New York: Wiley.

Stegner, Wallace. 1953. *Beyond the Hundredth Meridian*. New York: Penguin.

Steinitz, Carl. 2012. *A Framework for Geodesign*. Redlands, CA: Esri Press.

Sugrue, Thomas. 1996. *The Origins of the Urban Crisis: Race and Inequality in Postwar Detroit*. Princeton, NJ. Princeton University Press.

Susskind, Lawrence, and Jeffrey Cruikshank. 1987. *Breaking the Impasse: Consensual Approaches to Resolving Public Disputes*. New York: Basic.

Susskind, Lawrence, Sarah McKearnan, and Jennifer Thomas-Larmer, eds. 1999. *The Consensus Building Handbook: A Comprehensive Guide to Reaching Agreement.* Thousand Oaks, CA: Sage.

Vazquez, Leo. 2012. "Creative Placemaking: Integrating Community, Cultural and Economic Development." Montclair, NJ: National Consortium for Creative Placemaking.

Wallerstein, Nina, and Bonnie Duran. 2010. "Community-Based Participatory Research Contributions to Intervention Research: The Intersection of Science and Practice to Improve Health Equity." *American Journal of Public Health* 100, supplement 1: S40–S46.

Wideman, John Edgar. 1985. "The Language of Home." *New York Times*, January 13.

Winner, Langdon. 1977. *Autonomous Technology.* Cambridge, MA: MIT Press.

Woodward, C. Vann. 1986. *Thinking Back: The Perils of Writing History.* Baton Rouge: Louisiana State University Press.

Zelinka, Al, and Susan Harden. 2005. *Placemaking on a Budget: Improving Small Towns, Neighborhoods, and Downtowns without Spending a Lot of Money.* American Planning Association: Planning Advisory Service Report 536.

Zitcer, Andrew. 2020. "Making Up Creative Placemaking." *Journal of Planning Education and Research* 40, no. 3: 378–88.

CONTRIBUTORS' INFORMATION

CHAPTER 1

Since the interview, MICHAEL PYATOK, FAIA, retired from more than two decades of teaching at the University of Washington, but he remains very active in his Oakland, California, office, PYATOK, which has grown to forty-five people from six. Of the approximately thirty-five projects in the office, about 75 percent are affordable housing of various types for our nonprofit clients, about 20 percent are market-rate, and 5 percent are student housing. PYATOK has over eight thousand units on the boards, excluding another six thousand or so in master planning and urban design stages. The affordable projects range in size between 40 and 125 units, while the market-rate projects range between 200 and 500 units. This work extends up and down the West Coast from Seattle to San Diego, and staff continue to facilitate many community meetings, helping to ensure community members' participation in what staff are designing. Contact mpyatok@pyatok.com.

CHAPTER 2

AL ZELINKA, FAICP, is City Manager for America's fifty-eighth largest city, Riverside, CA. Within a span of twelve years, Al's career evolved from Principal of RBF Consulting's Urban Design Studio to roles with the cities of Fullerton and Riverside, CA. With Riverside, he has empowered staff and community to establish a second-to-none online and in-person one-stop shop; to implement GrowRiverside, a community-wide effort to develop a sustainable and self-reliant local food system; to inspire over $1 billion in downtown urban development; to improve the city's municipal equality index from a score of 65 to 100 in less than three years; to implement an office of sustainability and drive outcomes toward environmental stewardship, economic prosperity, and social responsibility; and to effectively manage the city's financial stability. He continues to carry out the mission that has guided him throughout his professional journey: to make a difference in the communities he serves. Contact alzelinka@icloud.com.

CHAPTER 3

MARK LAKEMAN serves as Design Director at the architecture, planning, and design firm communitecture, and he continues to propel the ongoing efforts of the City Repair Project through speaking, teaching, and online and physical infrastructure projects. Recent communitecture projects include public-space designs that retrofit urban centers with community gathering places while also solving endemic urban challenges related to neglect, undeveloped infrastructure, violence, and poverty. Other projects include whole-city-scale participatory visioning and master planning for climate resilience in multiple cities; multifamily housing projects, including urban cohousing and ecovillages; neighborhood re-villaging and DIY villages by and for houseless people; and a wide spectrum of regenerative residential and commercial projects that address civic and regional goals. Recent city-repair projects include the development of a permanent headquarters building that exemplifies regenerative design principles and supports ongoing community organizing and project development across the Portland, Oregon, region. Contact moontrout@gmail.com.

CHAPTER 4

MICHAEL HUGHES launched Hughes Collaboration, specializing in conflict resolution, public engagement, and consensus building, in 2012. On public policy issues of transportation, land use, public health, the environment, and arts and culture, he has worked with Colorado's Department of Public Health and Environment and Governor's Alliance for HIV Care, Prevention and Treatment; Nebraska's Department of Roads; the State and Federal Joint Task Force for Endangered Species Act Implementation; Denver's Office of Community Planning and Development and Department of Public Health and Environment; the Federal Advisory Committee for Forest Planning Rule Implementation; and the Denver region's West Corridor Transportation Management Association. With the Robert Woods Johnson Foundation and Johns Hopkins, he engaged the public to assess willingness to receive COVID-19 vaccines. In 2013, Hughes joined the University of Denver's Korbel

School of International Studies faculty to offer master's courses in conflict resolution. Contact mike@hughes-collaboration.com.

CHAPTER 5

KAREN UMEMOTO, PhD, is Professor in the Departments of Urban Planning and Asian American Studies at the University of California, Los Angeles. She is currently the Director and the Helen and Morgan Chu Chair of the UCLA Asian American Studies Center. After receiving her doctorate in Urban Studies from MIT, she worked for twenty-three years as Professor of Urban and Regional Planning at the University of Hawai'i at Manoa before returning to UCLA, where she had received her master's degree in Asian American Studies. She dedicated much of her career to training students and working in and with Native Hawaiian communities to develop their planning capacities to shape their own futures. She also worked on change efforts to reduce the number of youths in the Hawai'i juvenile justice system, to support alternatives to incarceration that are healing, and to get to the root causes of the problems facing youths. Contact kumemoto@ucla.edu.

CHAPTER 6

JAMES BRODICK is the Center for Court Innovation's Director of Community Development and Crime Prevention. James leads the center's work on a range of community-development and crime-prevention initiatives in New York City, including the Brownsville Community Justice Center, Harlem Community Justice Center, Queens Youth Justice Center, Neighbors in Action, Cure Violence (South Bronx, Crown Heights, and Bedford-Stuyvesant), and the Mayor's Office Neighborhood Safety Initiatives. James leads a team of senior staff members to define a vision for the center's involvement in community-based crime prevention. James continues to implement data-driven methods to measure the effectiveness of the center's crime prevention work. Since 1998, his leadership roles have included directing NYC Community Courts, the Red Hook Community Justice Center, and NYC Community Cleanup. James served as lead planner and inaugural director of the Brownsville Community Justice Center. A graduate of Saint John's University, James is a New York State Certified Mediator. Contact JBrodick@nycourts.gov.

CHAPTER 7

FATHER PHILIP SUMNER is Parish Priest of Our Lady and St. Patrick's Parish, Oldham, England, and Rural Dean for Oldham and Ashton. Trustee of both the Catholic Association for Racial Justice (CARJ) and the Oldham Interfaith Forum, he is a presenter for the BBC's longest-running radio program, *The Daily Service*. He has continued to support and expand the Oldham Interfaith Forum, also working to provide interfaith workshops in schools and colleges. Facing COVID-19, forum members worked with others to bring Muslim and Christian charities together to provide food for socially isolated and vulnerable residents. Father Phil's church building now displays stained glass windows that celebrate the presence of different national communities. He also works nationally, within the Roman Catholic Church, to give people tools to address institutional racism and to encourage people from every background to feel they belong in the church. Contact: Philip_sumner @tiscali.co.uk.

CHAPTER 8

MALIK YAKINI serves as Executive Director of the Detroit Black Community Food Security Network. The organization has had multiple challenges in the past five years, including being forced to move its offices in response to a doubling in rent, the untimely death of the D-Town Farm manager, multiple thefts at the farm, and most recently, the operational challenges brought on by the COVID-19 pandemic. The organization has adjusted to all these challenges and is poised to begin construction on its largest project to date, the 34,000-square-foot Detroit Food Commons. Yakini has continued to speak nationally on urban agriculture, Black food sovereignty, and related topics and has continued to organize with other radical Black farmers and food activists in the National Black Food and Justice Alliance. Contact: malik .yakini@gmail.com.

CHAPTER 9

BARNABY EVANS is an artist who works in the medium of creating engaging community places. He received Providence's Renaissance Award in 1997 and MIT's 2003 Kevin Lynch Award (with William Warner), both in recognition for the impact of WaterFire on revitalizing

Providence, Rhode Island. In 2010, he received the Distinguished Service to the Arts Award from the National Governors Association. Evans and WaterFire were honored in 2011 with the first RI Arts and Tourism Award, from Tiffany & Co., for his "Contribution to the Renaissance of Providence," and the RI Council on the Humanities' 2011 Tom Roberts Prize for Creative Achievement in the Humanities. WaterFire remains an ongoing nonprofit art installation dedicated to inspiring Rhode Island and its visitors, fostering community and civic engagement, and creatively transforming the city. Recently, Evans has been involved in designing innovative climate resiliency approaches for Providence and developing the WaterFire Arts Center, a dramatic, award-winning transformation of a historic mill building into a contemporary art space that opened in 2017.

CHAPTER 10

THE EAGLEBY project stimulated many bold and creative projects by Wendy Sarkissian's social planning group, Sarkissian Associates Planners, which continued to be inspired by that project's success. Many of those projects have been featured in books published by Earthscan/Routledge: *Kitchen Table Sustainability* (with Nancy Hoffer, Yolanda Shore, Steph Vajda, and Cathy Wilkinson), *SpeakOut* (with Wiwik Bunjamin-Wau), and *Creative Community Planning* (with Dianna Hurford). Wendy's career came to a dramatic halt in early 2016 when a car crash claimed the life of her husband, Karl Langheinrich. That terrifying experience yielded a new book, *Stay Close: How to Heal from Grief and Keep Connected to One Who Has Died* (2020, https://amzn.to/2CR6q29). Completing her midlife memoir, *Creeksong: What the Forest Taught Me*, scheduled for release in 2022, she now lives in Vancouver, Canada. Contact wendy@sarkissian.com.au.

CHAPTER 11

LAURENCE BAUDELET-STELMACHER serves as consultant for the nonprofit organization Graine de Jardins in Paris. She continues to design public programs through participatory processes—for example, Paris Main Verte and the Arcueil Edible City project—and she has worked on green infrastructure programming, articulating social and environmental issues. She has been part of several applied science

328 CONTRIBUTORS' INFORMATION

projects, and since 2013 has been a member of the National Heritage Commission for parks and gardens at the French Ministry of Culture. Over the years, she has continued to provide organizational assistance to community gardening projects and to advocate for community gardens in France and Europe. She lives in Berlin and Paris. Contact lba. grainedejardins@gmail.com.

CHAPTER 12

Since 2012, ARTWALK OF ROCHESTER as a corporation has gradually dissolved. In 2019, a new city administration tried very hard to make up for the prior administration's bad deeds, but it was too late. Doug Rice recalls, "We were actually told privately that the city would no longer work with us if our organization had a 'Black or gay public face.' We did not believe that could be enforced. But as I have learned, it was." He adds, "Nevertheless many other people inspired by ARTWalk have been privately implementing public art visible to the public. Public art has popped up all over the city, supported by the city—an important legacy of ARTWalk." The theater Doug Rice founded, the Multi-Use Community Cultural Center (MuCCC), has supported many area theater companies and playwrights and helped them to grow. Rice serves as Managing Director of the theater. Contact dougricex@me.com.

CHAPTER 13

JOHN DAVIS's work with the Lanesboro Arts Campus initiative has resulted in the city's selection as one of the top twelve small-town artplaces in America for 2013 and in its being named a 2014 Bush Prize winner for community innovation. In 2018, Davis left his position at Lanesboro Arts after he received a Bush Fellowship to further study and advance the field of rural arts and rural sustainability. He was named Senior Policy Fellow at the Rural Policy Research institute for 2018–20 and is currently Senior Policy Fellow with the Art of the Rural. Appointed to the Americans for the Arts Creative Economy National Advisory Board in 2019, he is currently working on an initiative to establish culture as a cabinet-level position in America. He serves also as a mentor, coach, and national speaker on innovation, rural sustainability, and the arts. Contact airstreaminmotion@gmail.com.

INDEX

City Repair, 48–50

Community, and cherished buildings, 23, 32; and ethnicity 139; and immigration, Bangladeshi 140; Kashmiri 140,144; Pakistani 140, 144; art and community development 39–41, 143, 146, 172, 177; belonging 138, 293; building support 2, 4, 10, 25, 94, 161, 170, 177, 182, 256, 286; building trust 36–38, 115, 160, 259–260, 269; capacity building, strategies 94–95, 191; peace making 113; peace keeping 113; peace building 113; church choirs, by nationality 143; coalitions 2, 12, 101, 282, 288, 294; Block clubs 237; Black and Latino 94, 97, 101; Multi-Cultural collaborative 101; code-switching 97; collaboration, neighborhood 242, 272; accountability 43, 127, 238, 298; deliberative malpractices 281–282; more artistry than science 280; place attachment as fuel 265, 298; community cohesion advisory group 139, 143, 151; community safety and cohesion partnership 139; complaining or stepping up 238; crime prevention 120, 122–123, 130, 313n6.1; design bridging differences; development and crime prevention 130, 301. See also Appendix 1; domestic violence 124; drug-related violence 102, 119, 123; economic diversity 37–38; education 38–39, 121–125, 128, 130; engagement 36, 38, 120–123, 150, 250; faith based organization 138, 293; gangs and violence 102, 103, 104; hate crime task force 105; human relations infrastructure 100; identity and iconic structures 86; insider-outsider relations 161, 166, 198; local leadership 164–165, 293, 304; misconceptions of public housing 20–22; multiple services 117, 122–3; networking, Spider Web 147; organizing 5, 6, 53–56, 238; planning and program supervision, 125; prevention vs treatment 122, 127, 130; recognizing identity 101, 265, 293, 299; religious holidays. 146–147; representation 105; resistance to lower incomes 56; segregation 140, 145; stigmatization 170, 202; and alienating judgments 212; survey for assessment 59, 118–119, 121–122, 265–266, 296; Victim Services 117–119; white flight 140, 154, 162; Women's Interfaith Network 145; workshop on hate crimes 105–116; youth baseball league 5, 130, 134; youth court 294

Community Gardens, and community development, 218–219, 277; opportunities for engagement 220–222, 224–225; timing 220–221; challenging design traditions 216; deliberations and objections 218, 228; democratizing effects 232, 294; discovery of possibilities 222; diverse designs fit contexts 217, 220; educating and organizing, engineers 216, 218, 223; landscape architects 214, 218, 232–233; politicians 217, 225; community members 225; conviviality 221; regaining knowledge 220; community building 227, 232, 283; funding 229; Green Hand Charter 224–225, 230; integration with other agencies 223; Jardin dans Tous Ses Etats 214–215, 229; Jardin Nomade 218, 224–225; co-founder Claudine Raillard Clément; Networks across France 214–215, 228; Graine de Jardins (Garden Seeds) 214, 218, 228–229, 231, 315n11.6; New York model 214, 217; offering options for design 218, 221, 224–227; organizational requirements 223; ornamental vs engaging residents 219; Paris, Parks and Gardens Dept 216–217, 223; engineers' power 216, 218; engineers' learning 218, 223; nay-saying 218, 226; political support